JEWISH THEOLOGY

A COMPARATIVE STUDY

Barry L. Schwartz

BEHRMAN HOUSE, INC.

Dedicated to my wife, Debby,
and to my children, Nadav, Talia, and Noam.

COVER DESIGN: ROBERT J. O'DELL
PROJECT EDITOR: ADAM SIEGAL

© COPYRIGHT 1991 BY BEHRMAN HOUSE, INC.
11 EDISON PLACE, SPRINGFIELD, NEW JERSEY 07081
ISBN: 0-87441-523-3
MANUFACTURED IN THE UNITED STATES OF AMERICA

Contents

INTRODUCTION	4
I. GOD	9
An Orthodox Perspective	10
A Reform Perspective	13
A Conservative Perspective	16
A Reconstructionist Perspective	19
II. TORAH	22
An Orthodox Perspective	23
A Reform Perspective	26
A Conservative Perspective	29
A Reconstructionist Perspective	32
III. HALACHAH	35
An Orthodox Perspective	36
A Reform Perspective	39
A Conservative Perspective	42
A Reconstructionist Perspective	45
IV. ISRAEL	48
An Orthodox Perspective	49
A Reform Perspective	52
A Conservative Perspective	55
A Reconstructionist Perspective	58
CONCLUSION	61
LIST OF SOURCES	63

INTRODUCTION

To understand contemporary American Judaism, one must come to appreciate an exceedingly diverse theological spectrum. Among the major religious movements of American Judaism—Orthodox, Reform, Conservative and Reconstructionist—there are significant disparities in what we believe about God, Torah, and Israel. At the same time, however, there is a common affirmation of the importance of all three and the great wisdom to be found in the exploration of our 3,000-year tradition.

In examining the different movements, three questions immediately present themselves:

What are the basic similarities and differences between the branches of
American Judaism?
What are the practical implications of their theological beliefs?
On what issues can we expect consensus or discord?

To answer these questions, I offer the reader a guided journey through primary sources. This compilation permits the thinkers and shapers of denominational Judaism to speak for themselves. In the best tradition of Jewish learning, this book requires the student to confront the text, to scrutinize with devotion the written word. Such study is often confined solely to ancient or medieval texts. As a result, important documents of contemporary Judaism are often neglected.

The collection of texts gathered here is presented in a comparative, thematic fashion, organized around four central issues: God, Torah, *halachah* (Jewish law), and Israel. Each of the subjects is viewed from the perspective of Judaism's four major movements: Orthodox, Reform, Conservative, and Reconstructionist. When possible, citations are taken from platform statements of a particular movement; presumably, this is as close to an official position or consensus opinion as exists. When such a text is unavailable, a prominent representative of a movement is selected. It should be emphasized that no source is likely to reflect a unanimity of opinion on a given issue. This is particularly true for those movements that permit or even encourage differences of belief and practice.

The rich tapestry of contemporary American Judaism is not confined, of course, to officially incorporated movements. As Mordecai Kaplan taught us, Jewish civilization extends far beyond the contribution of religious denominations. A brief selection of primary sources can not reveal the rich diversity within each movement. Yet the sources that follow do provide the student with a basic familiarity with the ideology of each major religious movement in American Judaism. Study of these sources is the first step in determining where you stand on that spectrum.

ORTHODOX JUDAISM

The Orthodox position is presented first. Orthodox is a term meaning "correct belief." In Judaism it has come to mean that segment of the Jewish community that is most traditional and adheres strictly to *halachah*, traditional Jewish law.

Modern Orthodoxy arose in nineteenth-century Germany. After the French Revolution, the doors of the ghetto (in Western Europe) were opened. Jews were finally given the same rights and privileges as the people among whom they lived. But with this new freedom, many Jews began questioning whether their traditional beliefs and practices would interfere with their ability to integrate into the society around them. Some Jews began to argue that sweeping changes in Jewish tradition needed to take place. Orthodox Judaism rejected this approach, maintaining a strict observance of traditional Jewish law.

Samson Raphael Hirsch (1808—1888), considered by many to be the spiritual father of modern Orthodox Judaism, sought to maintain adherence to *halachah* while still advocating the study of modern, secular disciplines. The Orthodox world to this day is divided between adherents of Hirsch's view and ultra-Orthodox groups that generally eschew secular learning and involvement. On the basic issues of theology, however, there is no major disagreement. All sides espouse a dogma that they view as consistent with that outlined by Maimonides and a succession of philosophers and *halachists*.

As a result of this *halachic* orientation, the Orthodox movement has not accepted many of the changes in ritual and liturgy embraced by the other movements. For example, Orthodox Judaism upholds the prohibition against ordaining women rabbis and cantors and permitting female Torah readers and leaders of prayer; separate seating for men and women in the synagogue is maintained. Prayers are recited only in Hebrew, and Sabbath observance prohibits automotive travel or activities that will require turning on electricity. *Kashrut* (dietary laws) and laws of personal status (concerning marriage, divorce, death, etc.), are upheld according to traditional *halachah*.

The modern Orthodox movement is organized around a congregational body known as the Union of Orthodox Jewish Congregations of America (UOJCA). Rabbis are trained primarily at the Theological Seminary of Yeshiva University in New York and become members of the Rabbinical Council of America (RCA). Yeshiva University also serves as the educational center for Orthodox leaders in many disciplines. The ultra-Orthodox community maintains its own organizational bodies and *yeshivot*. It is estimated that Orthodox Judaism accounts for 15 to 20 percent of America's affiliated Jewish community.

Reform Judaism

To maximize the contrasts often found on the theological spectrum, the Reform position is presented next. Also with roots in nineteenth-century Germany, Reform advocated evolution in Jewish ritual and thought in response to the changes brought about by the emancipation of Western European Jewry. With the new opportunities for citizenship and full participation in society, some Jews felt that certain traditional beliefs and practices were at best no longer relevant, at worst a hindrance to their attempt to lead a modern Jewish life.

Some reformers argued for radical change; others proposed more moderate action. The debate carried over to America's shores where Reform was organized into a national movement by Isaac Mayer Wise. The texts presented here are primarily representative of contemporary Reform, which more closely identifies with the proponents of moderation in ritual change. Nonetheless, in matters of broad doctrine, the texts reflect the Reform movement as a whole.

Reform has often led the way instituting change in Jewish prayer and ritual. From its inception, Reform argued for the equality of women in all religious matters, and the movement began ordaining women rabbis and cantors in the 1970s. By then the ceremony of bat mitzvah, as identical to bar mitzvah, had won widespread acceptance. Early on Reform introduced changes designed to enhance the esthetics of religious worship: prayer in the vernacular and musical accompaniment. Spurred by its identification with the prophetic heritage of the Bible, Reform advocated involvement in the general community's efforts to achieve social justice.

Not a few Reform decisions, however, remain bones of contention in the Jewish community. Among Reform's most controversial changes of late was the decision to accept patrilineal descent as a basis for determining whether a child is Jewish; previously, matrilineal descent was the only acceptable determinant. Reform's decision has led to the situation in which children born of a non-Jewish mother and Jewish father are considered Jewish by one segment of the Jewish community, the Reform community, but not by the others.

Reform congregations are members of the Union of American Hebrew Congregations (UAHC). Rabbis, cantors, educators, and communal service workers are trained at the Hebrew Union College—Jewish Institute of Religion (HUC–JIR), with campuses in New York, Cincinnati, Los Angeles, and Jerusalem. The Reform rabbinical organization is known as the Central Conference of American Rabbis (CCAR). Approximately 40 to 45 percent of the affiliated Jewish community identifies as Reform.

CONSERVATIVE JUDAISM

The Conservative position is popularly characterized as occupying the middle ground between Orthodox and Reform. Its roots lie in dissatisfaction with early Reform coupled with a dissent from strict Orthodoxy. Some scholars link the beginning of the new movement with Zechariah Frankel's decision to walk out of a Reform rabbinical conference in Germany. The conference had decided that the use of the Hebrew language in much of the synagogue service was not necessary. Frankel considered this too great a break with tradition, and along with other rabbis dissatisfied with Reform, he founded a new school which would be more traditional in outlook, the Jewish Theological Seminary of Breslau. Others see the protest by some American rabbis over Reform's Pittsburgh Platform as the genesis of Conservative Judaism. As with Frankel, this protest led to the creation of a school, the Jewish Theological Seminary of New York. In America, the Conservative movement, under the direction of Solomon Schechter and others, flourished organizationally and ideologically.

The Conservative movement has attempted to articulate a unique school of thought which incorporates allegiance to *halachah* while at the same time admitting cautious change. The new unified Conservative platform, *Emet Ve-Emunah* (1988), reveals efforts to define consensus among diversity of opinion on even the most basic theological points.

Conservative Judaism's inherent caution and internal diversity have led to extensive debate on all proposed changes in ritual and law. Many of the decisions adopted by the majority have been resisted by a minority. In the mid-1980s the Conservative movement accepted the ordination of women rabbis. This followed acceptance of women as leaders of prayer, as Torah readers, and as participants in a minyan. Not all Conservative congregations accept these practices, however. After the ordination vote, a group of professors and rabbis broke from the mainstream Conservative movement to form their own, more traditional, organization. Some of these same individuals were opposed to a decision more than two decades earlier that permitted travel on the Sabbath for appropriate purposes.

The congregational arm of the Conservative movement is known as the United Synagogue of America (USA). Rabbis are trained at the Jewish Theological Seminary of America in New York (JTS), and become members of the Rabbinical Assembly (RA). Along with its West Coast affiliate, the University of Judaism, the Jewish Theological Seminary also trains cantors, educators, and communal service workers. Some 40 to 45 percent of the affiliated Jewish community are part of the Conservative movement.

Reconstructionist Judaism

The Reconstructionist movement, dwarfed in membership by the other branches, nevertheless occupies a distinct position on the Jewish spectrum. Its importance further transcends its size because of the influence it has exerted upon many individuals in Reform and Conservative Judaism. The only movement with exclusively American origins, Reconstructionism embodies the philosophy of one of this century's seminal Jewish thinkers, Mordecai Kaplan.

In essence, Kaplan proposed two new theses for what he termed the reconstruction of modern Judaism. The first might be called sociological, for it argued that Judaism should be viewed in much broader terms than doctrinal religion. Judaism needed to be evaluated in a new light, as the "civilization," or full cultural expression of a people. Religion was perhaps the most important component of Jewish civilization but by no means the exclusive one. Kaplan argued that our religious institutions should embody the whole of our civilization's heritage.

Kaplan's other thesis was theological, involving a bold new conception of God that drew inspiration from the insights of twentieth-century anthropology and philosophy. As will become apparent, Mordecai Kaplan strove to articulate a view of God in harmony with the rationalistic thinking characteristic of the modern era.

Given its cultural sensitivity and liberal theology, Reconstructionism has often led the way in introducing change in the Jewish world, despite its brief history. Many people are unaware, for example, that important innovations concerning the participation of women in the synagogue service actually began in the Reconstructionist movement, including the first bat mitzvah ceremony (of Kaplan's own daughter).

Reconstructionism, like Reform, is a strong advocate of ritual creativity and social involvement in the larger society. In fact, the Jewish Community Center as an institution owes a great deal to Kaplan's original conceptions in the 1920s and 1930s. In addition, the increase in educational and social programming by synagogues of all kinds was another response to the teachings of Kaplan.

Kaplan's Society for the Advancement of Judaism in New York (created in 1921) was the spiritual center of Reconstructionism for decades, but it was only in the 1960s that the movement achieved a distinct organizational identity. Today the Reconstructionists, like the other movements, have a congregational entity, called the Federation of Reconstructionist Congregations and Havurot (FRCH), a rabbinical seminary in Philadelphia known as the Reconstructionist Rabbinical College (RRC), and a rabbinical organization, the Reconstructionist Rabbinical Association (RRA). A very small percentage of the affiliated Jewish community is Reconstructionist.

Part I
GOD

What a movement believes about God will profoundly influence its entire ideological stance. Judaism has traditionally maintained that God is not only the creator of the world, but the revealer of law and wisdom, and the guiding hand of human affairs. What one believes about God will thus shape how one understands revelation (the sacred texts of Judaism) and history (including the mission and destiny of the people Israel).

Judaism has consistently professed a belief in one God, expressed by the central affirmation of Jewish worship, the Shema. Beyond this fundamental assumption, however, the texts that follow reveal widely varying views on such important issues as the extent of God's power, the ways in which God is involved with us, and the ways in which we are involved with God. What is more, it should become apparent that at least two of America's major religious movements deliberately refrain from articulating a specific dogma about God.

Theological debate and uncertainty notwithstanding, the quest for God through prayer, study, and deeds remains the primary spiritual concern of Judaism's religious movements. Above the ark in many synagogues throughout the country is the simple Hebrew sentence which proclaims: "Know Before Whom You Stand."

An Orthodox Perspective

APPROACHING THE TEXT
The Nineteen Letters of Ben Uzziel

Samson Raphael Hirsch's statement reflects much of the traditional Jewish doctrine concerning God. The text underscores these characteristics of God's nature:

God is One
God is eternal
God is omnipotent   (all-powerful)
God is omniscient   (all-knowing)
God is beneficent   (doing good)
God is transcendent   (above nature)

Although Hirsch's statement deals primarily with God as Creator, traditional Jewish doctrine also speaks of God as Revealer (Giver of Torah) and Redeemer. This view maintains that God is continually active in the world, as opposed to the view (called deism) that God creates the world and then leaves it to run by natural law alone. Hirsch is adamant that all laws and forces are expressions of the Divine will. God is the source of whatever order we perceive, and the source of miracles that seemingly defy the natural order.

Two great questions arise from this conception of God. The first is the question of theodicy (*theo-*, God; *dicy*, justice: the problem of God's justice). If God is all-good and all-powerful, why is there evil in the world? Although there are various responses to this problem, the traditional response most often heard is that God's will is inscrutable. As the Book of Job asks: Who are we, mere mortals, to cast judgment on God's plan? For others, this kind of reply is insufficient. It is inconceivable that pain and suffering could be intentional on the part of the Divine. Individuals with such views often search out alternative conceptions of God. After the Holocaust, the question of theodicy is perhaps the greatest challenge to traditional Jewish conceptions of God.

The second great question arising from traditional theological speculation about God is one of providence. If God is all-powerful and all-knowing, do human beings have free will? Traditional Judaism responds with the idea that every individual is responsible for his or her own actions. Free will is the basis for our ability to pursue good or evil; however, our actions do not escape God's attention and each of us is ultimately rewarded or punished according to our deeds.

THE TEXT

Samson Raphael Hirsch (1808–1888) was the leading figure of German Orthodox Judaism in the nineteenth-century. Although strict in his obedience to halachah, *he advocated secular study in addition to Jewish education. Hirsch's considerable writings include his popular* The Nineteen Letters of Ben Uzziel, *from which this text is excerpted.*

"There is One God, one omnipotent Creator," the Torah proclaims, "Through His word all that is was created." Heaven and earth are His handiwork; His are the light and air, sea and dry land; His are the plants and fishes, birds, insects and all beasts; His the sun, moon and stars. He spoke—vayehi—and it was. Now behold separately each creation, from the blade of grass to the vast orb of the sun, each with its special purpose and each specially adapted in its form and matter for that purpose by the same Almighty wisdom. This Divine wisdom called to the light, "Serve the day"; to darkness, "Serve the night"; to the firmament, "Be the heaven over the earth"; to the gathering of waters, "Be the ocean"; to the dry substance, "Become thou the earth, the soil of life and development"; to the planets, "Be rulers of the seasons." Divine wisdom determined the purpose, and, in accordance with the purpose, ordained form, force and dimensions. He spoke—vayehi ken, and it was as it is, infinitesimally small or infinitely great. All was created by the Word of God, determined by His will, formed by His finger. To God, the Universal Force, belong all the forces which are at work in nature and the universe and all the laws which regulate life: from the force and the law which govern the fall of the stone or the growth of the seed, to those which determine the orbit of the planets or the unfolding of the human mind.

PROBING THE TEXT

1. What is God's relationship to nature as described in this passage?

2. What other possible God-nature relationships can you describe?

3. If God is omnipotent, as Hirsch claims, how would Hirsch respond to the question of why there is evil in the world?

4. Why do you suppose God would choose to grant free will to human beings?

A Reform Perspective

APPROACHING THE TEXT
Columbus Platform
San Francisco Platform

To the extent that the rabbinic platforms represent the movement as a whole, Reform Judaism has consistently espoused the idea of belief in God as central to Judaism. In fact, the Columbus Platform (1937) reaffirms traditional notions of God as One, living (active), creating, lawgiving and redeeming. There is nothing in this brief statement that contradicts Orthodox Judaism! The differences are manifest in other categories examined in subsequent chapters of this book.

The tenor of the San Francisco Platform (1976), composed almost four decades after the Columbus Platform, is less self-assured in its declaration about God. The San Francisco Platform seeks to reaffirm belief in God as central, without specifying the content of that belief. It seeks to be as inclusive as possible, recognizing the widely varying God beliefs that typify the contemporary movement. The Platform recognizes that both recent history (especially the Holocaust) and "challenges to modern culture" have made it more difficult for some people to affirm God.

The texts as a whole might strike you as rather brief, vague, and incomplete. The Reform movement has not published a more comprehensive position. Even these words have been criticized for misrepresenting the supposed majority viewpoint of the movement. In the absence of survey data or published collective opinion, it is difficult to assess if a prevailing view about God exists at all. Individual essays abound, demonstrating that within Reform there can be found adherents of almost every theological orientation concerning God. On the basis of the platforms it can be concluded that Reform, while affirming belief in God, does not espouse a particular dogma about the nature of God.

THE TEXT

The three "Platforms of Reform Judaism" are the products of rabbinic gatherings of the movement in 1875 (Pittsburgh), 1937 (Columbus), and 1976 (San Francisco). While not official expressions of doctrine, they have been influential in determining the nature of Reform ideology and practice. The accompanying text is excerpted from the Columbus and San Francisco Platforms.

Columbus Platform 1937

The heart of Judaism and its chief contribution to religion is the doctrine of the One, living God, who rules the world through law and love. In Him all existence has its creative source and mankind its ideal of conduct. Through transcending time and space, He is the indwelling Presence of the world, we worship Him as the Lord of the universe and as our merciful Father.

San Francisco Platform 1976

The affirmation of God has always been essential to our people's will to survive. In our struggle through the centuries to preserve our faith we have experienced and conceived of God in many ways. The trials of our own time and the challenges to modern culture have made steady belief and clear understanding difficult for some. Nevertheless, we ground our lives, personally and continually, on God's reality and remain open to new experiences and conceptions of the Divine. Amid the mystery we call life, we affirm that human beings, created in God's image, share in God's eternality despite the mystery we call death.

PROBING THE TEXT

1. What do the authors mean by "the trials of our time and the challenges to modern culture"?

2. How have these "trials" and "challenges" affected some people's view of God?

3. What do the authors mean by the phrase "human beings ... share in God's eternality"?

4. In light of the San Francisco Platform, can a Reform Jew be an agnostic or an atheist?

A Conservative Perspective

APPROACHING THE TEXT
Emet Ve-Emunah

Emet Ve-Emunah is a very recent document. Like the most recent Reform platform, it seeks to be as inclusive as possible. The text recognizes the significant diversity of opinion within the Conservative movement. In the same spirit as Reform, it begins by affirming the critical importance of belief in God but explicitly acknowledges that Conservative Judaism does not "specify all the particulars." The statement then goes on to present two alternative views of God.

The first conception of God is basically the traditional view. It is linked with those who understand the Bible as God's revealed word. Most of the paragraph is devoted not to a description of divine attributes, but to an exposition of the grounds for maintaining such belief. They include all the classic arguments for the existence of a supreme Creator and Lawgiver.

The second conception of God is linked with more recent philosophical thinking. This section seems to be an attempt to acknowledge a significant Reconstructionist influence within Conservative Judaism. It should be noted that Reconstructionism initially began as a school of thought within Conservative Judaism and only later became a distinct movement. The breaking point was not so much Reconstructionism's new ideas about God, but its refusal to accept the unconditional binding authority of traditional Jewish law. The clue in this text to the influence of Reconstructionist theology (to be examined in the next section of this book) is the sentence: "[God is] present when we look for meaning in the world, when we work for morality, for justice, and for future redemption."

The Conservative statement may also be alluding to the thought of another important twentieth-century philosopher, Martin Buber. One of Buber's primary ideas was that God cannot be proven or rationalized. God can only be encountered. For Buber, the real content of religion emerged out of experiencing a profound relationship with another person or with God. Buber called the mundane kind of relationship that often exists between people and objects (animate or inanimate) "I-It." However, when people transcended that relationship with each other and with God, treating the other not as an object but as worthy of full concern and care, then the result was what he termed "I-Thou." The clue in the text to Buber's influence are the words, "the existence of God is not a 'fact' that can be checked against the evidence. Rather, God's presence is the starting point."

It is evident that the Conservative movement is willing to accept a wide range of views concerning God. The influence of a theologically diverse group of thinkers, most notably Mordecai Kaplan, Martin Buber, and Abraham Joshua Heschel (a traditionalist influence), has only widened the spectrum of views over the years. As with Reform, no one conception of God can be said to speak for the movement as a whole.

The Text

This text is from Emet Ve-Emunah, *subtitled:* Statement of Principles of Conservative Judaism. *It is the unified statement of the movement, published in 1988. Joining in the platform were all three major bodies of the Conservative movement: the Jewish Theological Seminary, the Rabbinical Assembly, and United Synagogue of America.*

Conservative Judaism affirms the critical importance of belief in God, but does not specify all the particulars of that belief. Certainly, belief in a trinitarian God, or in a capricious, amoral God can never be consistent with Jewish tradition and history. Valid differences in perspective, however, do exist.

For many of us, belief in God means faith that a supreme, supernatural being exists and has the power to command and control the world through His will. Since God is not like objects that we can readily perceive, this view relies on indirect evidence. Grounds for belief in God are many. They include the testimony of Scripture, the fact that there is something rather than nothing, the vastness and orderliness of the universe, the sense of command that we feel in the face of moral imperatives, the experience of miraculous historical events, and the existence of phenomena which seem to go beyond physical matter, such as human consciousness and creativity. All of these perceptions are encounters that point beyond us. They reinforce one another to produce an experience of, and thus a belief in, a God who, though unperceivable, exists in the usual sense of the word. This is the conception of God that emerges from a straightforward reading of the Bible.

Some view the reality of God differently. For them, the existence of God is not a "fact" that can be checked against the evidence. Rather, God's presence is the starting point for our entire view of the world and our place in it. Where is such a God to be found and experienced? He is not a being to whom we can point. He is, instead, present when we look for meaning in the world, when we work for morality, for justice, and for future redemption. A description of God's nature is not the last line of a logical demonstration: It emerges out of our shared traditions and stories as a community. God is, in this view as well, a presence and a power that transcends us, but His nature is not completely independent of our beliefs and experiences. This is a conception of God that is closer to the God of many Jewish philosophers and mystics.

The two views broadly characterized here have deep roots in the Bible and in the rest of Jewish tradition. They are both well represented in Conservative Jewish thought.

PROBING THE TEXT

1. According to the text, what are the two primary conceptions of God?

2. What are the six arguments for the existence of God advanced here? Can you develop a line of reasoning supporting each one?

3. Can we pray and refer to God in personal terms if, as the second view suggests, "He is not a being to whom we can point"?

4. What is meant by the statement, "His nature is not completely independent of our beliefs and experiences"?

A Reconstructionist Perspective

Approaching the Text
The Meaning of God in Modern Jewish Religion

Mordecai Kaplan presents a conception of God that is radically different from that of traditional Judaism. Kaplan shies away from describing God in terms of a personal being, preferring instead the word "force" or "power." In this view God is not omnipotent and omniscient, but dependent, as it were, on our actions. God is present to the extent that we strive after our highest ideals. God remains the transcendent creative and moral force of the world. God is the source of human love, courage, morality, and creativity.

Kaplan's conception of God is often termed "religious naturalism" because it postulates a God that works through nature (trans-natural) and not above nature (super-natural). Although God is not the same as nature, God is manifest to us only through our experience of natural and moral law. In this sense, Reconstructionism does not accept ideas of revelation or miracles that contradict our understanding of the natural order.

The Reconstructionist view of God, as set forth by Kaplan, has been severely criticized by traditionalists on a number of grounds. First and foremost is the argument that any attempt to limit God's power and providence flies in the face of rabbinic teaching. According to traditional doctrine, God, as the creator of the universe, can act independent of the laws of nature at will. Any attempt to limit God's dominion, from an Orthodox perspective, would seem to suggest an alternative power to God's. So controversial was Kaplan's new theology that soon after his first works were published he was excommunicated by a group of Orthodox rabbis.

A second criticism of Kaplan's theology is the perception that his rationalism lacks warmth and spirituality. A frequently heard question is: How can one pray to an idea or a force? In the same vein: How can a view of God that is so conceptual and impersonal engender the kind of human—God relationship that inspires and commands? If God is not the One who can respond to individual petition, why pray?

THE TEXT

Mordecai Kaplan (1881–1983), one of the twentieth-century's most influential Jewish philosophers, founded the Reconstructionist movement in the 1940s. His ideas are contained in more than a dozen books, among them: Judaism as a Civilization *(1934) and* The Meaning of God in Modern Jewish Religion *(1937), from which this text is excerpted.*

But it is an undeniable fact that there is something in the nature of life which expresses itself in human personality, which evokes ideals, which sends men on the quest of personal and social salvation. By identifying that aspect of reality with God, we are carrying out in modern times the implications of the conception that man is created in God's image. For such an identification implies that *there is something divine in human personality, in that it is the instrument through which the creative life of the world effects the evolution of the human race.* The corollary of the thought of man's likeness to God has always been the sense of the sacredness of human personality, of its inherent worth.

This should not be interpreted as implying that the belief in God is purely subjective, a figment of the imagination rather than an interpretation of reality. One might as well say that, since the awareness of color is a subjective experience, it is entirely a creation of the eye, and that no objective reality is responsible for the eye experiencing color, as to say that, since our idea of God is determined wholly by our own limited experience of life's values, there is no objective reality which is responsible for the values which we experience. *The word "God" has thus come to be symbolically expressive of the highest ideals for which men strive and, at the same time, points to the objective fact that the world is so constituted as to make for the realization of those ideals.*

PROBING THE TEXT

1. How would you define God from a Reconstructionist viewpoint?

2. What can God do, and not do according to such a view?

3. What is problematic about this conception of God?

4. In light of the Reconstructionist view of God, how would you describe the purpose of prayer?

Part II
TORAH

The idea of one God is shared by other religious traditions. So too is the general notion of Divine revelation. Unique to Judaism, however, is the concept of Torah.

Originally, Torah was taken to mean the written law (Tanach) alone. Rabbinic Judaism expanded the concept of Torah to include the so-called oral law (Talmud). Even though the Talmud was acknowledged to have been written by later sages, they were said to have acted under a prophetic inspiration that stemmed from the original revelation to Moses at Sinai. According to the Talmud, prophecy and the authority to establish new law ceased as the Talmud was being completed. In other words, the Sages put self-closure on the process of revelation by contending that they were the last generations to receive the dictates of Divine will. Although the movements of modern Judaism differ on what constitutes Torah, how it was created, and the extent of its authority, all agree that it is the foundation of Judaism.

It will become apparent in this chapter that the great debate among the movements of Judaism is whether the Torah is the directly revealed word of God or the indirectly revealed (humanly written, divinely inspired) word of God. Not to be overlooked, however, is the fact that Torah, however defined and understood, remains a kind of blueprint for the observance of Judaism. Some may adopt the blueprint as it was once drawn, others may modify specifications, but the basic plan remains in use.

AN ORTHODOX PERSPECTIVE

APPROACHING THE TEXT
The Condition of Jewish Belief

There are essentially two basic views of revelation in Judaism: Orthodox and liberal. To a large extent, which school you subscribe to is determined by how you answer the question: Who wrote the Torah?

This text presents the Orthodox response. Norman Lamm is unequivocal in the belief that the Torah is God-given. God's revelation of the Torah took place at one time, in one place, to one people—Israel—standing at the foot of Mount Sinai. According to Lamm, one need not comprehend precisely how God communicates with Moses to hold this view. The process of revelation is not given to rational explanation. Nor does holding the view that the Torah is God-given mean that the Torah text is subject to only a literal interpretation. As Lamm points out, language is an imperfect instrument, though still the best means of collective communication. All written language must be interpreted by the reader. The crucial point is that whatever the interpretation, the text is still viewed as an explicit expression of God's will.

Orthodox Torah commentary does not employ the critical/scientific approach that is common to modern scholarship. The reason is not hard to understand. Most modern biblical scholarship rests on the assumption of human authorship of the Torah and suggests that the Torah is a collection of many different sources and documents edited together. It suggests that these texts have changed over time. Orthodox Judaism, on the other hand, holds that the Torah is immutable, unchanging and unchangeable for all time.

THE TEXT

Norman Lamm has long been a leading figure in the modern Orthodox community. He is president of Yeshiva University and has authored numerous books and articles. This text is taken from The Condition of Jewish Belief, *a symposium compiled by the editors of* Commentary *magazine in 1966.*

I believe the Torah is divine revelation in two ways: in that it is God-given and in that it is godly. By "God-given," I mean that He willed that man abide by His commandments and that that will was communicated in discrete words and letters. Man apprehends in many ways: by intuition, inspiration, experience, deduction—and by direct instruction. The divine will, if it is to be made known, is sufficiently important for it to be revealed in as direct, unequivocal, and unambiguous a manner as possible, so that it will be understood by the largest number of the people to whom this will is addressed. Language, though so faulty an instrument, is still the best means of communication to most human beings.

Hence, I accept unapologetically the idea of the verbal revelation of the Torah. I do not take seriously the caricature of this idea which reduces Moses to a secretary taking dictation. Any competing notion of revelation, such as the various "inspiration" theories, can similarly be made to sound absurd by anthropomorphic parallels. Exactly how this communication took place no one can say: it is no less mysterious than the nature of the One who spoke. The divine—human encounter is not a meeting of equals, and the *kerygma* that ensues from this event must therefore be articulated in human terms without reflecting on the mode and form of the divine *logos*. *How* God spoke is a mystery; how *Moses* received this message is an irrelevancy. *That* God spoke is of the utmost significance, and *what* He said must therefore be intelligible to humans in a human context, even if one insists upon an endlessly profound mystical overplus of meaning in the text. To deny that God can make His will clearly known is to impose upon him a limitation of dumbness that would insult the least of His human creatures.

PROBING THE TEXT

1. How does Norman Lamm understand the way in which the Torah was communicated to us?

2. According to Lamm, is the Torah perfect?

3. Why does Lamm accept varying interpretations of Torah if it is God's word?

4. What objections would a rationalist have with this view of revelation?

A Reform Perspective

APPROACHING THE TEXT
The Growth of Reform Judaism

At the very outset of the text in this section, Julian Morgenstern defines the central theological difference between Orthodox and Reform Judaism: does one believe that the Torah was dictated by God or by humans? Morgenstern contends that any process of reform is predicated on viewing the Torah as a human document. Otherwise, in his opinion, there is no justification for making any change in God's revelation.

Morgenstern articulates a view of Torah that might be termed "indirect revelation," in contrast to Orthodoxy's doctrine of "direct revelation." Indirect revelation acknowledges the role of Divine inspiration in the composition of Torah. While the Torah may not be the direct word of God, it is nevertheless inspired by God.

The concept of Divine inspiration is referred to consistently in Reform Judaism but is often employed ambiguously. Just what does Divine inspiration mean? Just what parts of the Bible are inspired? Morgenstern does not associate inspiration with prophecy, which would be in keeping with traditional Jewish understanding. Rather, he understands Torah as the record of a people's encounter with God. It is Israel's diary, as it were: a people's thoughts about God, feelings about God, and attempts to be godlike. In this sense much of the Torah is a unique source of moral and spiritual instruction.

Like every human document, however, the written Torah is imperfect and subject to the inherent limitations of particular individuals writing at particular times. The Torah's commandments, therefore, should not be viewed as eternally authoritative edicts. Reform maintains that the Torah reflects one particular stage in Jewish evolution. Divine inspiration is not limited to the written or oral law. Reform argues that we continue to gain insight about God's intention in every generation so that Revelation should be understood as an ongoing process rather than a single event.

THE TEXT

Julian Morgenstern (1881–1976) was president of the Reform movement's rabbinical seminary, Hebrew Union College, for three decades. He was a noted biblical scholar who championed a modern critical approach to Scripture.

"Is the Torah, in the literal sense in which our fathers understood it, divinely revealed; that is, were its laws actually established by God and communicated, whether in writing or orally, by Him to Moses and through Moses to Israel?" If the answer be "Yes," then the only conclusion possible is that the laws of the Torah, one and all, are eternally and indissolubly binding upon all Israel. Only if the answer to the question be "No," only if, after careful, earnest, conservative and reverent research, we are forced to conclude that the laws of the Torah are of altogether human origin, and that only for certain, easily comprehended, historical reasons were they represented as having been given by God to Moses, are we justified in abrogating or altering even the least of these laws. Otherwise no reform is justifiable, even under the plea of historical necessity or "the spirit of the age." Either we hold the Torah to be, as our fathers believed, in the most literal sense of divine origin, and therefore all its laws eternally binding upon all Israel, and all reform in Judaism, which would entail disregard or abrogation of even a single one of these laws, out of the question; or else we must hold the firmly established and absolutely irrefutable conclusion that the Torah and the entire Bible are, in the literal sense at least, the result of human effort, human knowledge and human religious insight, inspiration and revelation. Logically reform in Judaism may only follow, and never precede, this conclusion.

Nor does Biblical Science deny, as so many of its opponents claim, the inspiration of the Bible. On the contrary, it feels therein a larger and fuller measure of inspiration than the traditionalist can ever conceive of. For it interprets the Bible as the record of Israel's thinking about God and feeling after Him and of the knowledge of Him which was revealed to it, and which it, therefore, discovered and came to possess, through a thousand or more years of its early history. In this light, not merely the laws, and not merely a certain few of the stories, and not merely the Torah, are inspired, but every book, every story, every chapter. For all bespeak something of Israel's search after God and record something of the knowledge of God which has been revealed to Israel. In this sense Israel was indeed God's chosen people, His inspired people, upon whom His spirit truly rested, whose entire history, therefore, was guided and inspired by Him. And certainly the record of this history, the only record preserved to us of all Israel's ancient literature, is truly inspired too. It is no mere ordinary, human record or book. It is in no sense like any other book. It is the inspired and inspiring record of God, working with His people and leading them on to an ever higher, fuller and truer knowledge of Himself.

PROBING THE TEXT

1. Why does Morgenstern believe that the Reform view of Torah "feels therein a larger and fuller measure of inspiration than the traditionalist can ever conceive of"?

2. According to the Reform view, is it possible to claim with certainty that any particular command of the Torah is God's will?

3. What authority does Torah have from a Reform perspective?

4. What do you think the early reformers meant by the term "progressive revelation"?

A Conservative Perspective

Approaching the Text
Emet Ve-Emunah

While Conservative Jews do not necessarily agree about the extent of human involvement in the giving of the Torah, they view it as more than Moses recording God's communication. For many, the Torah is a Divinely inspired but humanly written document. This premise is not unlike the inspiration-based beliefs of some more traditionally minded Reform thinkers. Admitting a human component in the content of revelation, as opposed to the belief in a completely Divine creation, is the divide that separates liberal from Orthodox Judaism.

Conservative Judaism understands revelation as a continuous process. While it terms Sinai the "greatest event," the statement stresses that revelation is ongoing. Orthodox Judaism, it will be remembered, limits the content of revelation to the Bible and Talmud. Conservative Judaism contends that God's communication "remains alive in the Codes and Responsa to the present day."

It should also be noted that the Conservative text's final paragraph introduces an idea that is essentially Reconstructionist in nature. Recall that in the Conservative statement about God we also identified an effort to include Reconstructionist thought within the ranks of acceptable Conservative doctrine. Here the key sentence is: "Others among us conceive of revelation as the continuing discovery, through nature and history, of truths about God and the world." As the next text will demonstrate, Reconstructionist Judaism understands revelation more as our discovery of wisdom and truth than as miraculous disclosures of Divine will through prophecy. This view of revelation presents Torah as one of many possible sources of Divine truth.

THE TEXT

This text is from Emet Ve-Emunah, *subtitled:* Statement of Principles of Conservative Judaism. *It is the unified statement of the movement, published in 1988. Joining in the platform were all three major bodies of the Conservative movement: the Jewish Theological Seminary, the Rabbinical Assembly, and United Synagogue of America.*

Conservative Judaism affirms its belief in revelation, the uncovering of an external source of truth emanating from God. This affirmation emphasizes that although truths are transmitted by humans, they are not a human invention. That is why we call the Torah *torat emet*. The Torah's truth is both theoretical and practical, that is, it teaches us about God and about our role in His world. As such, we reject relativism, which denies any objective source of authoritative truth. We also reject fundamentalism and literalism, which do not admit a human component in revelation, thus excluding an independent role for human experience and reason in the process.

The nature of revelation and its meaning for the Jewish people have been understood in various ways within the Conservative community. We believe that the classical sources of Judaism provide ample precedents for these views of revelation.

The single greatest event in the history of God's revelation took place at Sinai, but was not limited to it. God's communication continued in the teaching of the Prophets and the biblical Sages, and in the activity of the Rabbis of the Mishnah and the Talmud, embodied in Halakhah and the Aggadah (law and lore). The process of revelation did not end there; it remains alive in the Codes and Responsa to the present day.

Some of us conceive of revelation as the personal encounter between God and human beings. Among them there are those who believe that this personal encounter has propositional content, that God communicated with us in actual words. For them, revelation's content is immediately normative, as defined by rabbinic interpretation. The commandments of the Torah themselves issue directly from God. Others, however, believe that revelation consists of an ineffable human encounter with God. The experience of revelation inspires the verbal formulation by human beings of norms and ideas, thus continuing the historical influence of this revelational encounter.

Others among us conceive of revelation as the continuing discovery, through nature and history, of truths about God and the world. These truths, although always culturally conditioned, are nevertheless seen as God's ultimate purpose for creation. Proponents of this view tend to see revelation as an ongoing process rather than as a specific event.

PROBING THE TEXT

1. In what way does this statement differ from that of Orthodox Judaism?

2. In what way does it differ from that of Reform Judaism?

3. What are the possible consequences of so much diversity of opinion within the Conservative movement?

4. Do you think there is a uniquely Conservative conception of Torah?

A Reconstructionist Perspective

Approaching the Text
The Reconstructionist Prayer Book

Reconstructionist Judaism unequivocally identifies with the liberal view of the Torah as a humanly written document. In Kaplan's words: "The truth is not that God revealed the Torah to Israel, but that the Torah has...revealed God to Israel." In actuality, Reconstructionist Judaism could not have it any other way. Mordecai Kaplan's philosophy, which remains the guiding approach of the movement, denies that God acts in supernatural ways. Consequently, revelation can be no more, or less, than the discovery of religious truths through our own natural powers of perception. Kaplan explicitly calls this process of discovery revelation. Revelation is real because there are truths to be discovered and the human ability to accomplish the task.

Without the benefit of supernatural Divine communication, however, a series of questions arise that apply to all liberal Judaism and their views on revelation:

> What really happened at Sinai?
> Which parts of the Torah represent genuine religious truth, and which do not?
> Who decides the above question?
> Which commandments should be observed?
> Why should the commandments be observed?

Like Reform, Reconstructionist Judaism emphasizes the continuing significance of Torah, even if its authority can no longer be considered absolute. As a repository of wisdom about Israel's search for God, it is unrivaled. The reading and study of Torah spur our own spiritual quest. In these historical and spiritual senses, the Torah is inspirational and sacred. Since the discovery of religious truth is never ending, we too add our part to Torah.

THE TEXT

Mordecai Kaplan (1881–1983), one of the twentieth-century's most influential Jewish philosophers, founded the Reconstructionist movement in the 1940s. His ideas are contained in more than a dozen books, among them Judaism as a Civilization *(1934) and* The Meaning of God in Modern Jewish Religion *(1937). This statement is excerpted from the introductory section of the* Reconstructionist Prayer Book *(1945), edited by Kaplan and a group of his early disciples.*

Tradition affirms that God supernaturally revealed the Torah in its present text, to Moses on Mount Sinai. But the critical analysis of the text by modern scholars and the scientific outlook on history render this belief no longer tenable. We now know that the Torah is a human document, recording the experience of our people in its quest for God during the formative period of its history. The sacredness of the Torah does not depend upon its having been supernaturally revealed. The truth is not that God revealed the Torah to Israel, but that the Torah has, in every successive generation, revealed God to Israel. It can still reveal God to us. Though we no longer assume that every word in the text is literally or even figuratively true, the reading of the Torah enables us to relive, in imagination, the experiences of our fathers in seeking to make life conform to the will of God, as they understood it. We thus make this purpose of theirs our own and are inspired to seek God also in our own experiences. And those who seek God find Him. Our discovery of religious truth is God's revelation to us.

The study of Torah in this spirit is properly the central act of worship. It is, moreover, indispensable to our survival and growth as a people. The Torah so conceived is indeed a "tree of life" everlasting, planted within us. But it cannot serve this purpose as long as the Synagogue bases the authority of the Torah on the dogma of supernatural revelation, which the modern mind rejects. We have, accordingly, deemed it necessary to stress the sacredness of the Torah in other ways than by affirming that it was supernaturally revealed to Moses on Mount Sinai.

PROBING THE TEXT

1. What does Kaplan mean when he writes, "The truth is not that God revealed the Torah to Israel, but that the Torah has, in every successive generation, revealed God to Israel"?

2. If the sacredness of the Torah does not depend upon its having been supernaturally revealed, what does make the Torah sacred?

3. Are there any differences between the Reform and Reconstructionist views of Torah?

4. What does Kaplan mean when he states, "Our discovery of religious truth is God's revelation to us"?

Part III
HALACHAH

Many Jews argue that allegiance to *halachah*, more than anything else, has sustained Judaism and the Jewish people. *Halachah* is the traditional Jewish law contained in the Torah and the Talmud. The word *halachah* actually comes from the Hebrew root meaning "to go" or "to walk." *Halachah* is the way, or path, that a Jew is commanded to follow.

Halachah was intended to govern all aspects of life; it is what we would consider today as civil and religious law. The body of regulations that comprise *halachah* deal with everything from agriculture and business to prayer and charity. In previous eras, rabbis and leaders of the Jewish community were charged with enforcing *halachah* throughout the community.

The question of *halachah*'s authority is naturally linked to one's view of Torah and is thus very much a subject of debate in the Jewish community. Two of Judaism's four major movements accept the binding nature of *halachah*, and two do not. But the questions concerning *halachah* are not limited to authority. They extend to who should determine what *halachah* says, and how. On these issues the movements disagree not only with each other, but within themselves!

When considering the issue of *halachah* from a comparative denominational perspective, three questions are crucial:

> Is *halachah* binding upon the Jewish people?
> Can *halachah* be changed if need be?
> Who should interpret *halachah*, and how?

This trio of questions on authority, change, and interpretation, are the issues most responsible for the denominational divisions in contemporary Judaism. Almost everyone would agree, however, that the accumulated wisdom of more than 2,000 years of *halachah* is the starting point for informed Jewish decision making.

An Orthodox Perspective

APPROACHING THE TEXT
The Condition of Jewish Belief

Orthodox Judaism defines *halachah* to mean Jewish law derived from the Torah (Tanach, or Bible, and Talmud). Given the Orthodox view of revelation already examined, it should come as no surprise that Berkovits views *halachah* as eternally binding.

According to Orthodoxy, no change in *halachah* is permissible, as God's word is eternally valid. Human beings cannot presume to tamper with Divinely revealed law. Maimonides made clear that one is not allowed to add or subtract even a single command. At most, we can only interpret, or apply, *halachah*. Berkovits notes that Judaism presents a rich tradition of Torah interpretation. That is why some Orthodox thinkers argue that there is no Jewish fundamentalism. Even the Talmudic Sages recognized meanings in the text beyond the literal, although the law itself, however understood, remains immutable.

Orthodox Judaism greatly limits who is qualified to interpret halachah, and in what way. In the ultra-Orthodox community, only a handful of venerable experts offer *halachic* opinions. Even then, a particular individual or ruling may not be acceptable to all. In the modern Orthodox community, the number of individuals rendering *halachic* judgments is greater, though still restricted to rabbis with advanced training.

THE TEXT

Eliezer Berkovits is a leading Orthodox theologian. He has served as chairman of the Jewish Philosophy Department of the Hebrew Theological College, and he is the author of a number of volumes addressing issues of modern Jewish thought. This text is from The Condition of Jewish Belief, *a symposium compiled by the editors of* Commentary *magazine in 1966.*

But if this is the case, would not any commandment of God, because it expresses His will, have the same religious significance or effect? The answer to this old theological question is Yes: no matter what the contents of the commandments were, man would still be obligated to submit to the will of God and obey them. But it so happened that God revealed and commanded this Torah and not another one, because of His concern for man. As to the meaning of the commandments, even those that apparently have neither ethical nor doctrinal content, one must—as always—refer to the oral tradition, as well as to the continually developing philosophy and theology of Judaism. One may explain the ritual commandments according to Saddia's hedonism, or according to Yehuda Halevi's quasi-mysticism; according to Maimonides's rationalism, or Kabbalistic mysticism, or according to some more sophisticated modern religious philosophy or theology. The commandments, however, remain unchangeably binding.

PROBING THE TEXT

1. From an Orthodox perspective, are all the commandments of equal significance?

2. Does reason have a role in revelation or in the observance of *halachah*?

3. How does one decide a *halachic* question on a matter of new technology where there is apparently no precedent?

4. Does Orthodox Judaism reflect a fundamentalist approach to Torah and *halachah*?

A Reform Perspective

Approaching the Text
Pittsburgh Platform
San Francisco Platform

The premise of Reform Judaism, that Torah is a humanly written document, has profound implications regarding its view of *halachah*. Orthodox Judaism recognizes the supreme authority of *halachah* because it is God's revealed will. Reform makes no such argument and so has viewed *halachah* differently in various periods of its history.

The Pittsburgh Platform makes a distinction between two kinds of commandments, ethical and ritual. Ethical commandments are generally those involving actions between people. Ritual commandments are usually those involving actions between the individual and God. Of course, there are certain commandments, such as observing the Sabbath, that touch upon both realms. The Pittsburgh Platform looked upon the ethical commandments of the Torah as binding and upon the ritual commandments as conditional on the times. Since ritual commandments had to pass the test of relevance, it is no surprise that early Reform judged many Jewish customs dating from the biblical and rabbinic eras as no longer meaningful. In particular, it scorned rules of attire (such as *kippot* and *tallit*), diet (*kashrut*), and personal status (priestly regulations, purity, *ketubah*, *get*, etc.).

A marked softening of early Reform's negative attitude toward ritual can be detected in the Columbus and San Francisco Platforms. While the significance of ethics is not diminished, the importance of ritual life is elevated. It is fair to say that the Columbus and San Francisco Platforms recognize that ritual, so long as it evolves, remains central to Judaism.

Even though Reform came to appreciate the place of ritual observance, it maintains a number of crucial distinctions in the observance of *halachah*. Most important, the individual Jew at home, and each community of Jews in their congregation, are free to shape their own pattern of observance. Reform contends that as a humanly created system of law, *halachah* is not infallible. Through study, the wisdom of the collective tradition can be appreciated, but it must be weighed against other considerations including issues of individual conscience, insights from other ethical traditions, and exigencies of time and place. This process of informed decision making is as true for the individual as it is for the congregation. Reform thus maintains that *halachah* can, and should, evolve.

Reform's support of individual autonomy in ritual decisions has been rather severely criticized by traditional Jews on two grounds. The first is that such individual liberty is contrary to the Torah, which obligates all Jews to follow its law. The second objection is that offering freedom to each individual to do as he or she sees fit leads to religious anarchy. Opponents of Reform argue that this kind of anarchy seriously divides the Jewish people and leads to significant assimilation. Proponents of Reform, on the other hand, praise its recognition of individual autonomy as the only true democratic approach to Judaism in the modern age. They generally see the ideological divisions within Judaism as constant and inevitable, and they view Reform not as encouraging, but as preventing, assimilation.

THE TEXT

The three "Platforms of Reform Judaism" are the products of rabbinic gatherings of the movement in 1875 (Pittsburgh), 1937 (Columbus), and 1976 (San Francisco). While not official expressions of doctrine, they have been influential in determining the nature of Reform ideology and practice. The accompanying text is excerpted from the Pittsburgh and San Francisco Platforms.

Pittsburgh Platform 1875

We recognize in the Mosaic legislation a system of training the Jewish people for its mission during its national life in Palestine, and today we accept as binding only the moral laws and maintain only such ceremonies as elevate and sanctify our lives, but reject all such as are not adapted to the views and habits of modern civilization.

We hold that all such Mosaic and Rabbinical laws as regulate diet, priestly purity and dress originated in ages and under the influence of ideas altogether foreign to our present mental and spiritual state. They fail to impress the modern Jew with a spirit of priestly holiness; their observance in our day is apt rather to obstruct than to further modern spiritual elevation.

San Francisco Platform 1976

Torah results from the relationship between God and the Jewish people. The records of our earliest confrontations are uniquely important to us. Lawgivers and prophets, historians and poets gave us a heritage whose study is a religious imperative and whose practice is our chief means to holiness. Rabbis and teachers, philosophers and mystics, gifted Jews in every age amplified the Torah tradition.

Judaism emphasizes action rather than creed as the primary expression of a religious life, the means by which we strive to achieve universal justice and peace. Reform Judaism shares this emphasis on duty and obligation. Our founders stressed that the Jew's ethical responsibilities, personal and social, are enjoined by God. The past century has taught us that the claims made upon us may begin with our ethical obligations but they extend to many other aspects of Jewish living, including: creating a Jewish home centered on family devotion; lifelong study; private prayer and public worship; daily religious observance; keeping the Sabbath and the holy days; celebrating the major events of life; involvement with the synagogue and community; and other activities which promote the survival of the Jewish people and enhance its existence. Within each area of Jewish observance Reform Jews are called upon to confront the claims of Jewish tradition, however differently perceived, and to exercise their individual autonomy, choosing and creating on the basis of commitment and knowledge.

PROBING THE TEXT

1. How do Reform Jews go about making their own decision on a point of *halachah*?

2. What factors account for the change in Reform attitudes toward ritual observance between the Pittsburgh Platform of 1875 and the San Francisco Platform of 1976?

3. When deciding which *halachah* to observe, what other factors besides traditional law should be taken into account, and what relative weight in the decision-making process should they occupy?

4. Can you give examples of Reform practice in each of the categories of ritual observance specified in the 1976 Platform?

A Conservative Perspective

APPROACHING THE TEXT
Emet Ve-Emunah

While Conservative Judaism shares with Reform the conviction that Torah is a humanly written document, the Conservative approach to *halachah* is significantly different. Reform does not accept *halachah* as binding; the ultimate decision concerning ritual observance is left to the individual or congregation. Conservative Judaism, to the contrary, does view *halachah* as binding.

A major difference between the two movements is the way in which *halachah* can be changed or modified. Careful reading of the text will reveal that the Conservative movement restricts the agents of *halachic* change to the rabbis. While the voice of their constituency may be important, the decision-making process remains a rabbinic prerogative. The specific body within the Conservative movement that issues *halachic* opinions is the Committee on Jewish Laws and Standards of the Rabbinical Assembly. Those individuals selected to offer *halachic* judgments may come to opposing verdicts. As in the Talmud, the normative judgment usually follows the majority. While procedures have changed over the years, of late the rule has been that if a position is held by all but two or fewer members, it is binding. If three or more oppose, then the minority position is also considered a legitimate option for the Conservative movement.

The voice of the laity can have an important influence on the deliberations of the Conservative rabbinate. Two important and controversial decisions of recent decades were taken in part due to the groundswell of support that emerged among the general membership. In neither case was acceptance of these decisions unanimous. In the first case, the Law Committee voted to permit travel on the Sabbath for the purpose of attending synagogue services. In the second case, the Law Committee agreed to ordain women as rabbis. This followed a series of earlier decisions, going back to the 1950s, that allowed women to be called to the Torah, to be counted in a minyan, and to serve as witnesses in legal proceedings. In almost every controversial case, dissenting minority opinions (of three or more votes) have been offered and thus remain a Conservative option.

THE TEXT

This text is from Emet Ve-Emunah, *subtitled:* Statement of Principles of Conservative Judaism. *It is the unified statement of the movement, published in 1988. Joining in the platform were all three major bodies of the Conservative movement: the Jewish Theological Seminary, the Rabbinical Assembly, and the United Synagogue of America.*

We in the Conservative community are committed to carrying on the rabbinic tradition of preserving and enhancing Halakhah by making the appropriate changes in it through rabbinic decision. This flows from our conviction that Halakhah is indispensable for each age. As in the past, the nature and number of adjustments of the law will vary with the degree of change in the environment in which Jews live. The rapid technological and social change of our time, as well as new ethical insights and goals, have required new interpretations and applications of Halakhah to keep it vital for our lives; more adjustments will undoubtedly be necessary in the future. These include additions to the received tradition to deal with new circumstances and, in some cases, modifications of the corpus of Halakhah.

While change is both a traditional and a necessary part of Halakhah, we, like our ancestors, are not committed to change for its own sake. Hence, the thrust of the Jewish tradition and the Conservative community is to maintain the law and practices of the past as much as possible, and the burden of proof is on the one who wants to alter them. Halakhah has responded and must continue to respond to changing conditions, sometimes through alteration of the law and sometimes by standing firm against passing fads and skewed values. Moreover, the necessity for change does not justify any particular proposal for revision. Each suggestion cannot be treated mechanically but must rather be judged in its own terms, a process which requires thorough knowledge of both Halakhah and the contemporary scene as well as carefully honed skills of judgment.

PROBING THE TEXT

1. What reasons account for the changes in *halachah* that the Conservative movement feels compelled to make?

2. Why is the right to make such changes restricted to rabbis?

3. By what authority does the Conservative movement feel that it is justified in permitting travel on the Sabbath and ordaining women rabbis?

4. How does the Conservative view of adapting *halachah* to contemporary life differ from that of Reform?

A Reconstructionist Perspective

APPROACHING THE TEXT
Exploring Judaism: A Reconstructionist Approach

Reconstructionism shares a liberal view of revelation in many ways consistent with Reform. As Alpert and Staub state: "Transnaturalism rejects the belief that the words of Torah come from divine revelation at Sinai or that the mitzvot are each divinely ordained commandments." Torah as a humanly written document is the only logical conclusion of Reconstructionist doctrine. Thus it is to be expected that Reconstructionism agrees with Reform on the nonbinding nature of *halachah* and the concept of individual and congregational autonomy.

In fact, Alpert and Staub use the term "Post-*Halachic* Judaism" to describe the Reconstructionist approach. Reform and Reconstructionism have often been criticized for the anarchy that can result from individual freedom to determine ritual observance. Yet as many liberal Jews see it, this is the inescapable predicament of modern times. In the words of one Kaplan disciple, there can be "no retreat from reason."

At the same time, Reconstructionism has always accorded merit to the preservation of ritual life. Although *halachah* requires voluntary consent and should undergo evolutionary change, Kaplan recognized the importance of ritual in Jewish civilization. He called the commandments *sancta:* the means by which a people invested their lives with symbolic and transcendent meaning. In this context we can understand Milton Steinberg's claim that "presumption is always in favor of the tradition." *Halachah* represents the accumulated cultural wisdom of a people over the ages. Tradition can and should be emended, but for good reason.

Alpert and Staub offer the lighting of the Sabbath candles as an example of the abiding significance of ritual. Not only do the candles symbolize the special nature of the Sabbath, they also express the different meanings Jews have attached to them throughout the ages. Some see the light as an invocation of God's presence. Others look upon the candle lighting as ushering in the added soul, or dimension of spirituality, associated with the Sabbath. Today many point to the way in which observing this ritual brings families together.

Before rejecting the past, Alpert and Staub urge that we ask ourselves a series of questions which are designed to "hear the voices of our ancestors" but at the same time to "hear our own voices." Making informed decisions on matters of religious observance is never easy. All the movements of Judaism that admit autonomous decision making require the individual and community to struggle with tradition and change, with the claims of the past and those of the present.

THE TEXT

Rebecca T. Alpert is Dean of Students at the Reconstructionist Rabbinical College in Philadelphia. Jacob J. Staub is editor of the Reconstructionist magazine and Director of the Department of Medieval Civilization at the Reconstructionist Rabbinical College. Together, they coauthored a popular summary of Reconstructionist thought, Exploring Judaism: A Reconstructionist Approach, *from which this text is excerpted.*

From a transnaturalist viewpoint, God is not an omnipotent commander who rewards and punishes. What then is the rationale for obeying Jewish laws? What does it mean, for example, to address God as the one who commands us to light Shabbat candles? In what sense are we commanded?

The answer to this question is found in our initial definition of what it means to see oneself as part of the Jewish people. We behave as Jews because we value our connections to Jewish people, past and present. Jewish rituals have a sacred history that reflect inherited wisdom as well as group renewal. They should not be discarded casually. Otherwise, each generation could begin anew rather than reconstruct.

We often choose to retain the traditional forms of Jewish practice, even when we no longer mean what our ancestors meant when they spoke those words or performed those actions. We do so because such rituals both enrich us and sustain us—leading to our salvation in terms of our own values. Sanctified by the intentionality of our ancestors, the ritual forms themselves are permeated with a sacred aura that is ideally suited to help us deepen our connections to the divine presence.

Thus, when we light the Shabbat candles, we do more than symbolize the beginning of the day of rest devoted to our ultimate values. The flickering candles themselves possess a power to transform us because of the *kavvanot* (meanings) that past generations attributed to those candles.

Kaplan insisted that we preserve and observe Jewish customs and values as long as they continue to serve as a vehicle towards salvation—the enhancement of the meaning and purposefulness of our existence.

When a particular Jewish value or custom is found wanting in this respect, it is our obligation as Jews to find a means to reconstruct it—to adopt innovative practices or find new meanings in old ones.

That the past has a vote means that we must struggle to hear the voices of our ancestors. What did this custom or that idea mean to them? How did they see the presence of God in it? How can we retain or regain its importance in our own lives? That the past does not have a veto means that we must struggle to hear our own voices as distinct from theirs. What might this custom or that idea mean to us today? As participants in a secular civilization, how can we incorporate our values into our lives as Jews?

PROBING THE TEXT

1. What criteria would a Reconstructionist employ to judge the importance and continued relevance of a particular commandment, such as the lighting of Sabbath candles?

2. What is the power, and the limitation, of tradition according to the Reconstructionist view?

3. In what way is the Reconstructionist view of *halachah* different from that of Conservative Judaism?

4. How do Alpert and Staub understand Kaplan's famous dictum that *halachah* "has a vote, not a veto"?

Part IV
ISRAEL

Eretz Yisrael, the land of Israel, has always occupied a prominent position in Jewish religious thought. In the Bible, the land of Israel is promised to the descendants of Abraham. For almost a thousand years a Jewish state persisted in the Land of Israel. Surviving wars and outlasting imperial oppression, the people of Israel kept Jerusalem as their capital and Judaism as their religion. Jews returned to Israel after each exile, and a small community clung to the land from the time of the Roman destruction of the Temple in 70 C.E. to the present. During almost two thousand years of Diaspora existence, Jews remembered Israel in their prayers and literature. A movement to reestablish a Jewish state gained momentum in the late 1800s, largely under the leadership of Theodor Herzl. Vision became reality in 1948 when the modern State of Israel was born.

The creation of the State of Israel in 1948 has posed two great questions for contemporary Judaism. The first concerns the nature of the relationship between Israel and the Diaspora. One might think that support for a Jewish state has always been strong and united. Happily today such support for a sovereign Israel is almost unanimous in the Jewish community. But from the beginning of the political Zionist movement until the Holocaust, significant elements in both the Reform and Orthodox communities did not favor the establishment of a new Jewish state. The reasons for their objections will be examined in the texts that follow. But even today, when all four movements recognize Israel's essential place in their own ideology, the exact nature of Israel's place is still at issue. Should Israel be the sole or primary focus of Jewish life? Should *aliyah* (making one's home in Israel) be encouraged? Should Jews in the Diaspora publicly oppose policies of the Jewish state when they think they are wrong?

The other central question involving Israel is: What role should Judaism play in the life of a modern democratic nation which is at the same time the historic Jewish homeland? In particular, what role should *halachah*, traditional Jewish law, assume in a country where the clear majority of Jews do not classify themselves as traditionally observant? These questions have assumed dramatic importance due to the influence of Orthodox parties on the Israeli political process during the last decades. To this day, any Jewish citizen in Israel wishing to marry or divorce, or any individual wishing to convert, must do so according to Orthodox procedures.

In the 1970s and 1980s, the other three Jewish movements became increasingly vocal about what they perceived as the unfair Orthodox monopoly on these matters. The three liberal movements began to protest Orthodoxy's attempts to thwart their growth by denying them governmental funds and building permits. They vigorously opposed legislation introduced by the Orthodox parties which, to their minds, represented religious coercion. Most notable was the campaign by the liberal movements to prevent an amendment to Israel's Law of Return, in regard to Jewish converts, which would have required evidence of conversion according to *halachah* for purposes of citizenship. While this amendment was not instituted, progress in limiting the power of Orthodoxy in other areas is modest or nonexistent. The issue of religious equality and pluralism in the Jewish state remains controversial.

AN ORTHODOX PERSPECTIVE

APPROACHING THE TEXT
The Mizrachi Manifesto

Although the Mizrachi Manifesto dates back to the early nineteenth-century, it remains representative of Orthodox Zionist thinking. Like Reform, part of the Orthodox community initially displayed hostility toward Theodor Herzl and the Zionist enterprise. With the Holocaust and creation of the State of Israel, however, the anti-Zionist school diminished. Today only a few ultra-Orthodox sects remain opposed to the State.

Initial Orthodox opposition grew out of two concerns. The first was the belief that a new Israel should come about by Divine, not mortal, initiative. In other words, when God saw fit to establish a third commonwealth, well and good; in the meantime it was necessary to wait and endure. The second factor was fear of what a non-*halachic* state might bring. Even today many Orthodox Jews are dismayed that Torah enjoys only a limited role in Israel's judicial system.

The Manifesto itself envisions an Israel that will be a "secure fortress for our Torah." Not all Orthodox Jews agree that this goal is realizable. They understand that Israel is home to a majority of Jews who call themselves secular as well as to a significant non-Jewish population. Neither do all Orthodox Jews agree with the Manifesto's contention that full Jewish expression is possible only in Israel. Orthodox Jews living in the Diaspora commonly endorse the justification of Diaspora existence expressed in the three other statements of this chapter.

The Text

Mizrachi is a religious Zionist movement founded in Vilna in 1902. It is guided by the motto: "The land of Israel for the people of Israel according to the Torah of Israel". Mizrachi has remained an important Zionist faction throughout Israel's history. This excerpt, in translation, is from its Manifesto.

In the lands of the Diaspora the soul of our people—our Holy Torah—can no longer be preserved in its full strength, nor can the commandments, which comprise the entire spiritual life of the people, be kept in their original purity.

Against his will each loses his Jewish self in the (non-Jewish) majority, for only in their midst can he fulfill all those secular requirements which the times demand of him. The people have found one remedy for this affliction—to direct their hearts to that one place which has always been the focus of our prayers, that place wherein the oppressed of our people will find their longed-for respite: Zion and Jerusalem. We have always been united by that ancient hope, by the promise which lies at the very roots of our religion, namely, that only out of Zion will the Lord bring redemption to the people of Israel. The emancipation which our German brethren so desired did much to divide us and keep us scattered in the countries of our dispersion. When the limbs are dispersed, the body disintegrates, and when there is no body, the spirit has no place to dwell in this world.

It has therefore been agreed by all those who love the spirit of their people and are faithful to their God's Torah, that the reawakening of the hope of the return to Zion will provide a solid foundation as well as lend a special quality to our people. It will serve as a focus for the ingathering of our spiritual forces and as a secure fortress for our Torah and its sanctity.

PROBING THE TEXT

1. What is the problem of Diaspora existence according to the Manifesto?

2. What way will the return to Israel effect spiritual renewal for the Jewish people?

3. What role does religion play in the State of Israel as envisioned by Mizrachi?

4. What aspects of Mizrachi's viewpoint might other Orthodox groups find objectionable?

A Reform Perspective

Approaching the Text
San Francisco Platform

The evolution of thought in the San Francisco Platform is rather remarkable. It reflects the dramatic change that transpired as Reform responded to the sweep of Jewish history in this century. While today many might take Reform support of Zionism and Israel for granted, it was not always the case.

The Pittsburgh Platform of 1875 bluntly stated Reform's initial objection to the idea of a Jewish state:

> We consider ourselves no longer a nation, but a religious community, and therefore expect neither a return to Palestine nor the restoration of any of the laws concerning the Jewish state.

Classical Reform stressed the universalistic, ethical impulse of Judaism. Nationalism had little place in that scheme. Ironically, Reform in Germany allied itself with Orthodox circles to oppose the early Zionist Congress gatherings. In all fairness, it should be added that both in Europe and America some individual rabbis remained staunch Zionists even while their respective organizations publicly opposed Zionist activities.

The Columbus Platform of 1937, on the eve of the Holocaust, already reveals a changed movement:

> In the rehabilitation of Palestine, the land hallowed by memories and hopes, we behold the promise of renewed life for many of our brethren. We affirm the obligation of all Jewry to aid in its upbuilding as a Jewish homeland.

The platform goes on to describe Israel as "homeland" in the sense of physical refuge, but also in the sense of a spiritual and cultural center for the Jewish people. Two prominent Reform rabbis, Stephen S. Wise and Abba Hillel Silver, were leading Zionists of their day. Their role in influencing American opinion in support of the newly emerging Jewish state was crucial.

Reform's latest platform enlarges upon the Columbus declaration in three ways. The San Francisco Platform goes as far as to encourage *aliyah* for those in the Reform community who are so inclined. At the same time, it strongly defends the right of Jews to maintain communities wherever they choose. The platform makes explicit the possibility of experiencing a full Jewish life in the Diaspora. Also noteworthy is the call for unconditional recognition of Reform Judaism in Israel. Even today, Israeli law provides that all Jewish religious matters of personal status are under the jurisdiction of the Orthodox rabbinate in Israel. As a result, marriages, conversions, and related ceremonies officiated by non-Orthodox rabbis are not recognized by the State. Neither, for that matter, are civil ceremonies allowed. The fledgling Reform movement in Israel has attempted to contest this arrangement in court, to almost no avail.

THE TEXT

The three "Platforms of Reform Judaism" are the products of rabbinic gatherings of the movement in 1875 (Pittsburgh), 1937 (Columbus) and 1976 (San Francisco). While not official expressions of doctrine, they have been influential in determining the nature of Reform ideology and practice. The accompanying text is excerpted from the San Francisco Platform.

San Francisco Platform 1976

We are privileged to live in an extraordinary time, one in which a third Jewish commonwealth has been established in our people's ancient homeland. We are bound to that land and to the newly reborn State of Israel by innumerable religious and ethnic ties. We have been enriched by its culture and ennobled by its indomitable spirit. We see it providing unique opportunities for Jewish self-expression. We have both a stake and a responsibility in building the State of Israel, assuring its security and defining its Jewish character. We encourage aliyah for those who wish to find maximum personal fulfillment in the cause of Zion. We demand that Reform Judaism be unconditionally legitimized in the State of Israel.

At the same time that we consider the State of Israel vital to the welfare of Judaism everywhere, we reaffirm the mandate of our tradition to create strong Jewish communities wherever we live. A genuine Jewish life is possible in any land, each community developing its own particular character and determining its Jewish responsibilities. The foundation of Jewish community life is the synagogue. It leads us beyond itself to cooperate with other Jews, to share their concerns, and to assume leadership in communal affairs. We are therefore committed to the full democratization of the Jewish community and to its hallowing in terms of Jewish values.

The State of Israel and the diaspora, in fruitful dialogue, can show how a people transcends nationalism even as it affirms it, thereby setting an example for humanity which remains largely concerned with dangerously parochial goals.

PROBING THE TEXT

1. What are the "innumerable religious and ethnic ties" that bind the Jewish people to Israel, as referred to in the platform statement?

2. In what way does this statement distinguish itself from classic Zionism?

3. Why is there a specific call for Reform Judaism to be unconditionally recognized in Israel?

4. Why was early Reform Judaism antagonistic toward Zionism?

_____
_____
_____
_____
_____
_____
_____
_____
_____
_____
_____
_____
_____
_____
_____
_____
_____
_____

A CONSERVATIVE APPROACH

APPROACHING THE TEXT
Emet Ve-Emunah

The section of the Conservative platform entitled "The State of Israel and the Role of Religion" acknowledges the State as homeland and haven. Israel is called "a distinctively Jewish state fostering Jewish religious and cultural values." At the same time, however, it is conceived as fully democratic. In the words of the platform: "We do not view Israel as just another state or political entity; rather we envision it as an exemplar of religious and moral principles, of civil, political and religious rights for all citizens."

The Conservative vision articulates what many consider to be a unique, and certainly a challenging and problematic, aspect of modern Israel. On the one hand, Israel aspires to be a full democracy. On the other hand, Israel is not an officially secular state, like most democratic nations. The United States, for example, is constitutionally required to maintain, in Jefferson's words, a wall of separation between church and state. Difficult questions arise from Israel's predicament. Can Israel be fully democratic and at the same time be a "distinctively Jewish state"? What should the role of religion be in matters of government?

This is the backdrop for a strongly worded appeal in the Conservative platform against religious coercion, discrimination, and intolerance in the State of Israel. As with the Reform movement, the status of liberal Judaism in Israel is of major concern to the Conservative movement. The Conservative movement maintains some 30 congregations in Israel, numbering a few thousand individuals. Conservative rabbis are unable to perform marriages and funerals. Like Reform, Conservative Judaism is regularly denigrated by members of Israel's Orthodox community and denied funds provided to the Orthodox establishment. The Conservative movement has been working to change the status quo, but the statement admits that the balancing of democratic and Jewish goals, including equal treatment not only for liberal Jews but for fully secular Jews and non-Jews, "presents a constant challenge."

The second section of the Conservative platform, entitled "Israel and the Diaspora," affirms the attachment of the Jewish people to the land of Israel throughout its long history. Israel's past and present role in Jewish life is described as central. The presence of the Conservative movement within Israel is proudly stressed, yet a clear justification of Diaspora Jewish life is also presented. The platform describes Jewish religion as "land-centered but never land-bound." It reiterates what it sees as the vital role Diaspora centers have played in Jewish history. It calls for a relationship of mutual support and enrichment. Remember that the Reform, Conservative, and Reconstructionist statements included here are products of American movements. It should come as no surprise that their ideologies support their own continued existence!

THE TEXT

This text is from Emet Ve-Emunah, *subtitled:* Statement of Principles of Conservative Judaism. *It is the unified statement of the movement, published in 1988. Joining in the platform were all three major bodies of the Conservative movement: the Jewish Theological Seminary, the Rabbinical Assembly, and United Synagogue of America.*

We rejoice in the existence of *Medinat Yisrael* (the State of Israel) in *Eretz Yisrael* (the Land of Israel) with its capital of Jerusalem, the Holy City, the City of Peace. We view this phenomenon not just in political or military terms; rather, we consider it to be a miracle, reflecting Divine Providence in human affairs. We glory in that miracle; we celebrate the rebirth of Zion.

We staunchly support the Zionist ideal and take pride in the achievement of the State of Israel in the gathering of our people from the lands of our dispersion and in rebuilding a nation. The State of Israel and its well-being remain a major concern of the Conservative movement, as of all loyal Jews. To be sure, the Conservative movement has not always agreed with Israel's positions on domestic and foreign affairs. We have often suffered from discriminatory policies, but we remain firm and loving supporters of the State of Israel economically, politically, and morally.

We view it as both a misinterpretation of Jewish history and a threat to Jewish survival to negate the complementary roles of *Eretz Yisrael* and the Diaspora. Currently there are various important centers of Jewish life in the Diaspora. Diaspora Jewry furnishes vital economic, political and moral support to Israel; Israel imbues Diaspora Jewry with a sense of pride and self-esteem. Some see the role of *Medinat Yisrael* as the cultural and religious center of world Jewry. Others insist that since the days of the Prophets, various foci or centers of Jewish life and civilization, in both Israel and the Diaspora, have sustained the creative survival of *Am Yisrael* and *Torat Yisrael*.

PROBING THE TEXT

1. How is this statement similar to that of the Reform platform?

2. How do Israel and the Diaspora mutually support each other?

3. What is meant by the term "miracle" in this passage?

4. What "discriminatory policies" by the State of Israel against the Conservative Movement are being alluded to in this statement?

A Reconstructionist Perspective

APPROACHING THE TEXT
Tradition and Change

Milton Steinberg offers two basic rationales for the direct link he perceives between Zionism and Reconstructionism. Each one appeals to an aspect of Reconstructionism's broad view of Judaism not only as an institutional religion but as a complete civilization. Like Conservative Judaism, but unlike Reform and Orthodox, the Reconstructionist movement was Zionist oriented from its inception and did not have within its ranks a dissenting school.

The first rationale for the Reconstructionist's tie to Zionism is ethnic in nature. Israel is a refuge for Jews around the world. It is the second largest community of Jews in the world; anyone concerned with the welfare of the Jewish people is necessarily supportive of Israel's well-being. Like any other people the Jews have every right to their own homeland and the basic security that derives from such a place.

The second rationale is historical and cultural in nature. Characteristic of Jewish history is the presence of the Jewish people in the land of Israel. Even after Jewish sovereignty was denied and the Jewish people dispersed, the land of Israel and the hope for regained sovereignty remained part of Jewish liturgy, law, and lore. Jewish civilization, as history demonstrates, is not wholly dependent on land but is intimately tied to it. Given the hardships imposed upon the flowering of Jewish culture, even in our day, the imperative for a Jewish homeland remains as strong as ever. As Steinberg puts it: "Somewhere in the world it [Jewish culture] must be the dominant concern of Jews."

Steinberg concludes in a fashion similar to the Reform and Conservative statements by disassociating Reconstructionism from those Zionists who negate the Diaspora. Mordecai Kaplan had argued from the beginning of the movement that Diaspora Jews could flourish Jewishly in America. He noted that doing this would entail shouldering the burden of living in two civilizations: secular American democracy and sectarian Jewish culture. But Kaplan pointed out that this fact of existence could give rise to a creative tension, of the kind that had contributed immensely to Jewish thought and culture throughout the 2,000-year history of the Diaspora. Like Reform and Conservative thinkers, Kaplan claimed that the historical study of Judaism revealed a religion and culture in continuous dynamic interaction with cultures around it. Judaism, according to this theory, survived because it was able to absorb and evolve. The Diaspora, according to Kaplan, should remain a spiritual center, like the reborn Jewish State, for the rejuvenation of Judaism.

The Reconstructionist movement, small even in the United States, does not have an organizational structure in Israel, save for one congregation that has long been sympathetic to the Reconstructionist outlook. Joining with its sister liberal Jewish movements, however, the Reconstructionists have supported close ties with the Jewish State and at the same time protested the inequality among the movements of Judaism in Israel.

THE TEXT

Milton Steinberg (1903–1950) was a congregational rabbi, author, and leading figure in the young Reconstructionist movement. Like others of his generation, he was trained in the Conservative movement and, although profoundly influenced by Kaplan, differed with him at times.

To put the matter bluntly, Reconstructionism leads directly to Zionism. Given the premises of the first, the second follows relentlessly.

1) No program for the perpetuation of Judaism can be indifferent to the welfare of the people who are its bearers. Palestine has saved the lives of myriad Jews in the past, it promises to redeem many more in the future. On this score, alone, Reconstructionism must indorse Zionism.

2) There is in Reconstructionism a heavy bias in favor of the historical in Judaism. The love of Zion, the hope of its rebuilding, the dream of the restoration there of at least a part of the Jewish people are etched deep and indelible in the consciousness of the Jewish traditionalist. In effect, it is next to impossible to accept the Jewish civilization without embracing Zionism at the same time.

3) The Jews constitute, as we have seen, not only a religious communion and a culture group but a people also. And every people ought to have some place in the world where its peoplehood can find total expression.

4) Reconstructionism implies Zionism because of the needs of Judaism, because of the persistent disadvantages we have just surveyed under which Jewish culture operates everywhere. The second civilization of Jews, Judaism is constantly under the necessity of refreshing itself from a free-flowing source. Somewhere in the world it must be the dominant concern of Jews. In other words, a Jewish Homeland must be established.

By the same token, Reconstructionism offers no sympathy or asylum to the Zionism that sees only Palestinian Jewry and no other. There is a Zionist who is so thoroughly absorbed in his distant task that he forgets his Jewish obligations nearer to home. There is another Zionist who despairs of the possibility of Jewish life outside Palestine. Convinced that Diaspora Judaism is doomed, he concentrates his energies on the only Jewry that appears to him to have a chance. With such pessimism, Reconstructionism has no patience. It has confidence in the future of Judaism throughout the world. It objects to the notion that Palestine and the Diaspora are competitive and mutually exclusive. It holds such an alternative to be false and to obscure the job of modern Jews which is not a matter of "either ... or" but of "both."

PROBING THE TEXT

1. According to Steinberg, why is Reconstructionism inherently Zionist?

2. Which of the reasons—ethnic, historical, or cultural—do you find most compelling?

3. What concerns does this statement share with the Reform and Conservative positions already examined?

4. What does it mean to describe Israel as a cultural or spiritual center?

_____
_____
_____
_____
_____
_____
_____
_____
_____
_____
_____
_____
_____
_____
_____
_____
_____
_____
_____
_____

Conclusion

Our study of the sources in this book lead to some broad conclusions. Before stating them, however, it is worthwhile to remember the following caveats:

- not everyone will agree that these texts accurately represent their movement.
- no one text may be able to represent an entire movement.
- individuals within one branch of Judaism may hold widely divergent viewpoints.
- all sources can be interpreted in different ways.
- all conclusions tend toward oversimplification, and are open to dispute.

Keeping in mind all these cautions, my own conclusions are as follows:

God

On the issue of God, the Jewish ideological spectrum is framed by two basic positions:

The first can be termed (rather awkwardly) "theosupernaturalism," belief in a God who is above nature and who creates and rules the world.

The second conception can be called (also clumsily) "theotransnaturalism," belief in a God who works through nature and who is not considered to be infinitely powerful.

Orthodox Judaism adheres to the former position. Reconstructionist Judaism clearly espouses the latter. Reform and Conservative Judaism generally abstain from officially siding with either view; their members include adherents of both schools.

Torah

On the issue of Torah, the Jewish ideological spectrum is also framed by two basic positions:

The first view holds that the Torah is God-given and restricted to the revelation at Sinai.

The second view holds that the Torah is humanly written and part of an ongoing process of revelation or discovery.

Orthodox Judaism champions the former idea. Conservative, Reform, and Reconstructionist Judaism uphold the latter notion of Torah. Remember, however, that the conclusions the movements draw from their shared liberal view of revelation vary.

HALACHAH

On the issue of *halachah*, the Jewish ideological spectrum is framed by three basic positions:

The first posits the absolute authority of *halachah*, which is subject to no change and limited rabbinic interpretation.

The second position upholds the continuing authority of *halachah*, which is subject to cautious change and broader rabbinic interpretation.

The third position supports the conditional authority of *halachah*, which is subject to considerable change and the autonomous decision making of individual Jews.

Orthodox Judaism identifies with the first position. Conservative Judaism has staked out a position reflected by the second view. Reform and Reconstructionist Judaism advocate the third position.

ISRAEL

On the issue of Zionism and Israel, the Jewish ideological spectrum is framed by a unanimity of opinion. This unanimity does not mean that the various branches accept the classical Zionist position that Israel is the only legitimate place for the Jewish people. It does mean, however, that the branches of contemporary American Judaism view Israel as a Jewish homeland and a spiritual center. Of course, no unanimity of opinion exists concerning the extent to which Israel should be governed by civil law or *halachah*.

This book has been written because I believe it is important to recognize our differences in belief, in order to understand and tolerate our diversity of opinion and action. Yet it is also important to recognize our common ground, in order to appreciate what binds us together as a people.

Having explored and learned, it is now time to determine what you believe, and what you will do.

LIST OF SOURCES

1. Samson Raphael Hirsch, *The Nineteen Letters of Ben Uzziel*. New York: Feldheim, 1969, p. 31. Reprinted by permission.

2. *An Overview Of Reform Judaism*. New York: Union of American Hebrew Congregations, 1983, pp. 16, 24. The platforms were originally published in various editions of the Central Conference of American Rabbis Yearbook. Reprinted by permission.

3. *Emet Ve-Emunah: Statement of Principles of Conservative Judaism*. New York: Rabbinical Assembly (with the Jewish Theological Seminary and United Synagogue of America), 1988, p.18. Reprinted by permission.

4. Mordecai Kaplan, *The Meaning Of God In Modern Jewish Religion*. New York: Reconstructionist Press, 1962 (1937), p. 89. Reprinted by permission.

5. Norman Lamm, in *The Condition of Jewish Belief*. New York: Macmillan Publishing Co., 1967, p. 124. Reprinted by permission.

6. Julian Morgenstern, in *The Growth of Reform Judaism*. New York: World Union for Progressive Judaism, 1965, p. 231. Reprinted by permission.

7. *Emet Ve-Emunah*, pp. 19—20.

8. *Reconstructionist Prayer Book* as quoted in *Tradition and Change*. New York: Rabbinical Assembly, 1958, p. 346. Reprinted by permission.

9. Eliezer Berkovits, in *The Condition of Jewish Belief*, p. 25.

10. *An Overview of Reform Judaism*, pp. 11, 12, 16, 17, 19, 24, 25.

11. *Emet Ve-Emunah*, pp. 23, 24.

LIST OF SOURCES (Continued)

12. Rebecca T. Alpert and Jacob J. Staub, *Exploring Judaism: A Reconstructionist Approach*. New York: Reconstructionist Press, 1985, pp. 23, 31. Reprinted by permission.

13. The Mizrachi Manifesto, in *The Jew in the Modern World*. New York: Oxford University Press, 1980, p. 436. Reprinted by permission.

14. *An Overview of Reform Judaism*, pp. 25, 26.

15. *Emet Ve-Emunah*, pp. 37–39.

16. Milton Steinberg, in *Tradition and Change*. pp. 259-260.

NORWEGIAN
in 10 minutes a day®

by Kristine K. Kershul, M.A., University of California, Santa Barbara

Consultants: Katrine V. Grove • Troy Storfjell • Henning C. Boe

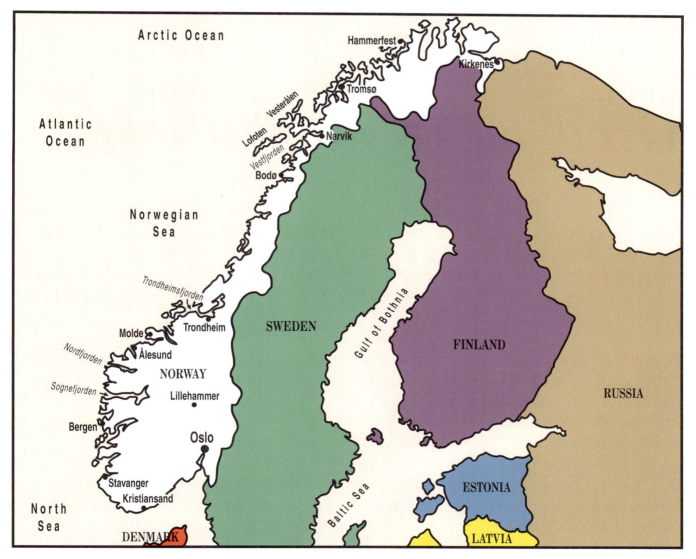

Bilingual Books, Inc.
1719 West Nickerson Street, Seattle, WA 98119
Tel: (206) 284-4211 Fax: (206) 284-3660
www.10minutesaday.com • www.bbks.com

ISBN: 978-1-931873-08-6   Third printing, May 2013

Copyright © 2007, 2005, 1998, 1988, 1982 Bilingual Books, Inc., Seattle, WA.   Fifth edition.   All rights reserved.

Can you say this?

(vah) *(het-air)* *(deh)*
Hva heter det?
what   is called   that

(deh) *(het-air)* *(en)* *(krahb-eh)*
Det heter en krabbe.
that   is called   a   crab

(vee) *(vil)* *(hah)* *(en)* *(krahb-eh)* *(tahk)*
Vi vil ha en krabbe, takk.
we   would   like   a   crab   please

If you can say this, you can learn to speak Norwegian. You will be able to easily order beer, lunch, theater tickets, pastry, or anything else you wish. With your best Norwegian accent, you simply ask **"Hva heter det?"** *(vah) (het-air) (deh)* and, upon learning what it is, you can order it with **"Vi vil ha det, takk,"** *(vee) (vil) (hah) (deh) (tahk)*. Sounds easy, doesn't it?

The purpose of this book is to give you an **immediate** speaking ability in Norwegian. Using the acclaimed **"10 minutes a day®"** methodology, you will acquire a large working vocabulary that will suit your needs, and you will acquire it almost automatically. To help you, this book offers a unique and easy system of pronunciation above each word which walks you through learning Norwegian.

If you are planning a trip or moving to Norway, you will be leaps ahead of everyone if you take just a few minutes a day to learn the easy key words that this book offers. Start with Step 1 and don't skip around. Each day work as far as you can comfortably go in those 10 minutes. Don't overdo it. Some days you might want to just review. If you forget a word, you can always look it up in the glossary. Spend your first 10 minutes studying the map on the previous page. And yes, have fun learning your new language.

As you work through the Steps, always use the special features which only this Series offers. This book contains sticky labels and flash cards, free words, puzzles and quizzes. When you have completed this book, cut out the menu guide and take it along on your trip.

1 Alfabetet
(ahl-fah-bate-eh)
alphabet the

Throughout this book you will find an easy pronunciation guide above all new words. Refer to this Step whenever you need help, but remember, spend no longer than 10 minutes a day.

Most letters in Norwegian are identical to those in English and are pronounced in just the same way.

(b)	(c)	(d)	(f)	(h)	(l)	(m)	(n)	(p)	(q)	(t)	(v)	(x)
b	c	d	f	h	l	m	n	p	q	t	v	x

Here is a guide to help you learn the sounds of the Norwegian letters which are pronounced somewhat differently. Practice these sounds with the examples given which are mostly towns or areas you might wish to visit. You can always refer back to these pages if you need to review.

Norwegian letter	English sound	Examples	Write it here
a	ah	**St**a**vanger** *(stah-vahng-air)*	
	uh	**Glomm**a *(glohm-uh)* Norway's longest river	
au	ow (as in how)	**H**au**gesund** *(how-geh-suhn)*	
d	often silent	**Kristiansan**d *(krist-yahn-sahn)*	
e	eh (as in vet)	**Mold**e *(mohl-deh)*	*Molde, Molde, Molde*
	ay (as in day)	**T**e**lemark** *(tay-leh-mark)*	
ei, eg	ay	**Trondh**ei**m** *(trohn-haym)*	
er (before ei, i, y)	air (as in yes)	**B**er**gen** *(bairg-en)*	
g	y	**G**ei**ranger** *(yay-rahng-air)*	
g	g	**G**ol *(gohl)*	
gj	y	**Gj**øvik *(yuhr-vik)*	
i	ih	**L**i**llehammer** *(lil-leh-hahm-air)*	
	ee	**Sver**i**ge** *(svair-ree-eh)* Sweden	
j	y (breathe hard)	**J**ostedalsbreen *(yoh-steh-dahls-bray-en)*	
k	hy (breathe hard)	} **K**ir**kenes** *(hyeer-ken-es)*	
	k		
kj	hy	**Kj**øbenhavn *(hyuh-pen-hahvn)* Copenhagen	
o	oh	**O**s**lo** *(oh-shloh)*	
r	r (slightly rolled)	**R**øros *(ruh-rohs)*	

Letter	Sound	Example	Write it here
s	sh	no**rs**k *(norshk)* Norwegian	_____
	s	**S**andnes *(sahn-nes)*	_____
sj (before i, j, y, ø)	sh	Kara**sj**ok *(kah-rah-shohk)*	_____
sk	sh	**Sk**ien *(shee-en)*	_____
sk	sk (breathe hard)	**Sk**agerak *(skah-gair-ahk)*	_____
tj	hy	**Tj**eldsund *(hyel-suhn)*	_____
u	uh	Kristians**u**nd *(krist-yahn-suhn)*	_____
	oo	Ringeb**u** *(ring-eh-boo)*	_____
w	v (elongated)	**w**eekendtur *(veek-end-toor)* weekend trip (something you'll do a lot)	_____
y	ee (as in new)	Str**y**n *(streen)*	_____
	ew/oo	M**y**rdal *(mewr-dahl)*	_____
z	s	**z**oo *(soh)*	_____

In addition to the sounds above, Norwegian has three additional letters. Each of these three letters represent two letters which have been combined into a new letter.

(o+e) **ø**	uh	Tro**ms**ø *(trohm-suh)*	_____
(a+o/a+a) **å**	oh	**Å**lesund *(oh-leh-suhn)*	_____
(a+e) **æ**	air	V**æ**røy *(vair-uh-oy)*	_____

Notes:
- Frequently **"d," "g"** and **"h"** are silent.

  (lahn) **lan**d — land   *(vik-tee)* **vikti**g — important   *(vah)* **h**va — what

- When **et** is used as "a" or "an" in front of a word it is pronounced "*et*," but when **et** is used to mean "the" it is tacked on to the end of the word and it is pronounced "*eh*."

  (et) **et** a   *(hoh-tel)* **hotell** hotel   *(hoh-tel-eh)* **hotellet** hotel the   *(et)* **et** a   *(tohg)* **tog** train   *(tohg-eh)* **toget** train the

Sometimes the phonetics may seem to contradict your pronunciation guide. Don't panic! The easiest and best possible phonetics have been chosen for each individual word. Pronounce the phonetics just as you see them. Don't over-analyze them. Speak with a Norwegian accent and, above all, enjoy yourself!

2 Key Question Words

When you arrive in **Norge** *(nor-geh)* [Norway], the very first thing you will need to do is ask questions — "Where is the bus stop?" (**hvor** *(vor)* [where]) "**Hvor** *(vor)* [where] can I exchange money?" "**Hvor** *(vor)* [where] is the lavatory?" "**Hvor** is a restaurant?" "**Hvor** do I catch a taxi?" "**Hvor** is a good hotel?" "**Hvor** is my luggage?" — and the list will go on and on for the entire length of your visit. In Norwegian, there are EIGHT KEY QUESTION WORDS to learn. For example, the eight key question words will help you find out exactly what you are ordering in a restaurant before you order it — and not after the surprise (or shock!) arrives. Notice that all but one question **ord** *(oor)* [word] begin with "**hv**." Don't confuse them! Take a few minutes to study and practice saying the eight key question words listed below. Then cover the Norwegian with your hand and fill in each of the blanks with the matching **norsk ord** *(norshk) (oor)* [Norwegian word].

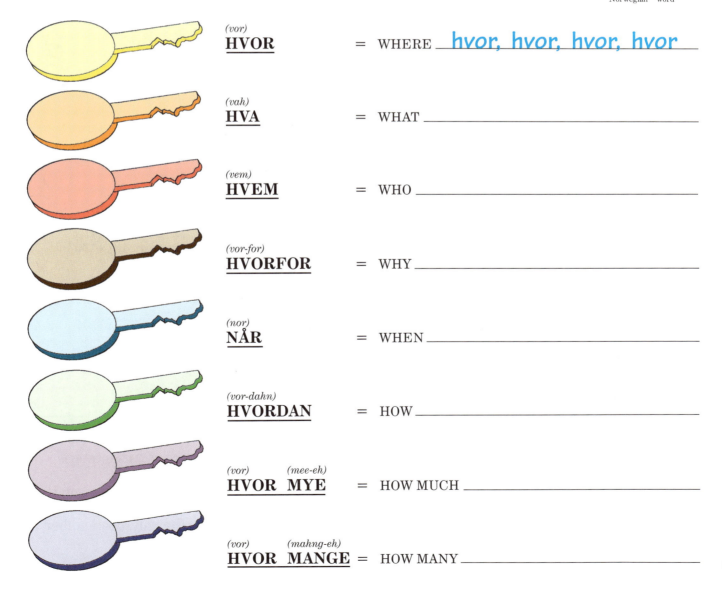

(vor) **HVOR**	= WHERE	_hvor, hvor, hvor, hvor_
(vah) **HVA**	= WHAT	
(vem) **HVEM**	= WHO	
(vor-for) **HVORFOR**	= WHY	
(nor) **NÅR**	= WHEN	
(vor-dahn) **HVORDAN**	= HOW	
(vor) (mee-eh) **HVOR MYE**	= HOW MUCH	
(vor) (mahng-eh) **HVOR MANGE**	= HOW MANY	

Now test yourself to see if you really can keep these **ordene** *(oor-en-eh)* / words straight in your mind. Draw lines between the **norske** *(norshk-eh)* / Norwegian **og** *(oh)* / and English equivalents below.

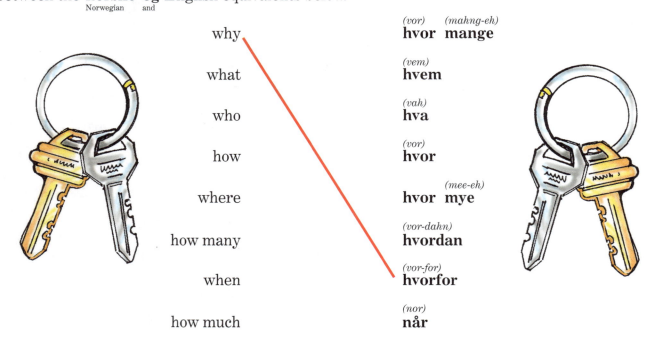

English	Norwegian
why	**hvor mange** *(vor) (mahng-eh)*
what	**hvem** *(vem)*
who	**hva** *(vah)*
how	**hvor** *(vor)*
where	**hvor mye** *(vor) (mee-eh)*
how many	**hvordan** *(vor-dahn)*
when	**hvorfor** *(vor-for)*
how much	**når** *(nor)*

Examine the following questions containing these **ordene**. Practice the sentences out loud **og** *(aw)* / and then practice by copying the Norwegian in the blanks underneath each question.

Hva er galt? *(vah) (ar) (gahlt)*
what — is — wrong

_____

Hvordan er salaten? *(vor-dahn) (ar) (sah-lah-ten)*
how — is — salad the

_____

Hvem er det? *(vem) (ar) (deh)*
who — is — it

Hvem er det?

Når kommer toget? *(nor) (kohm-air) (tohg-eh)*
when — comes — train the

_____

Hvor mye er det? *(vor) (mee-eh) (ar) (deh)*
how much — is — it

_____

Hvor er telefonen? *(vor) (ar) (tay-leh-fohn-en)*
where — is — telephone the

_____

"**Hvor**" *(vor)* will be your most used question **ord**. Say each of the following Norwegian sentences aloud. Then write out each sentence without looking at the example. If you don't succeed on the first try, don't give up. Just practice each sentence until you are able to do it easily. Remember the "h" in "**hv**" is silent.

(vor) (ar) (toh-ah-let-eh)
Hvor er toalettet?
where is toilet the

(vor) (ar) *(en) (droh-sheh)*
Hvor er { en drosje?
where is   a
              (tahx-ee)
           en taxi?

(vor) (ar) (boos)
Hvor er en buss?
where is a bus

_____   _____   _Hvor er en buss?_

(vor) (ar) (res-tuh-rahng)
Hvor er en restaurant?

(vor) (ar) (bahnk)
Hvor er en bank?
            a bank

(vor) (et) (hoh-tel)
Hvor er et hotell?
           a hotel

_____   _____   _____

(yah)
Ja, you can see similarities between **engelsk** and **norsk** if you look closely. You will be amazed at
yes   *(eng-elsk)* *(norshk)*
                                          English   Norwegian

the number of **ord** which are identical (or almost identical) in both languages. Of course, they do
                words

not always sound the same when spoken by a Norwegian speaker, but the similarities will

                          (oh)
certainly surprise you **og** make your work here easier. Listed below are five "free" **ord** beginning
                        and

       (ah)   *(oh)*   *(norshk-eh)*
with " **a** " to help you get started. Be sure to say each **ord** aloud **og** then write out the **norske**

ord in the blank to the right.

☑ **absolutt** *(ahp-soh-loot)* .... absolutely		_absolutt, absolutt, absolutt_
☐ **en adresse** *(ah-dres-eh)* .... address		_____
☐ **et aerogram** *(air-oh-grahm)* .... aerogram	**a**	_____
☐ **akkurat** *(ah-kooh-raht)* .... accurate, exactly		_____
☐ **alkohol** *(ahl-koh-hohl)* .... alcohol		_____

Free **ord** like these will appear on the following pages in a yellow color band. They are easy —

enjoy them! Remember, **norsk** has three extra letters – **æ, ø** and **å** which come at the end of the

alphabet.

3   Odds 'n Ends

(norshk)
Norsk has multiple **ord** for "the," and "a," but they are very easy.
Norwegian   words

(en) (guht)	*(ay) (yen-teh)*	*(et) (hoos)*
en gutt a boy	**ei jente** a girl	**et hus** a house
(stohl)	*(ay) (bohk)*	*(tohg)*
en stol a chair	**ei bok** a book	**et tog** a train

These endings are tacked on the end of an **ord** and mean "the."

These words also mean "the" and are added in front as well when an adjective is used.

(en)	*(eh)*	*(uh)*	*(en-eh)*
- en	**- et**	**- a**	**- ene**

(den)	*(deh)*	*(dee)*
den	**det**	**de**

(guh-ten)
gutten
boy the

(hoos-eh)
huset
house the

(yen-tuh)
jenta
girl the

(hoos-en-eh)
husene
houses the

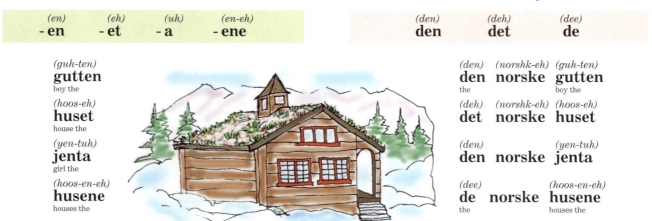

(den) (norshk-eh) (guh-ten)
den norske gutten
the   boy the

(deh) (norshk-eh) (hoos-eh)
det norske huset
the   house the

(den) (yen-tuh)
den norske jenta
the   girl the

(dee) (hoos-en-eh)
de norske husene
the   houses the

This might appear difficult, but only because it is different from *(eng-elsk)* **engelsk**. Just remember you will be understood whether you say "**en** *(guht)* **gutt**" or "**et** *(guht)* **gutt**." Soon you will automatically select the right one without even thinking about it.

In Step 2 you were introduced to the Key Question Words. These words are the basics, the most essential building blocks for learning Norwegian. Throughout this book you will come across keys asking you to fill in the missing question word. Use this opportunity not only to fill in the blank on that key, but to review all your question words. Play with the new sounds, speak slowly and have fun.

❏	**allerede** *(ahl-eh-red-eh)*	already	_____
❏	**en ambassadør** *(ahm-bah-sah-dur)*	ambassador	_____
❏	**Amerika** *(ah-mair-ih-kuh)*	America **a**	_____
❏	**– en amerikaner** *(ah-mair-ih-kahn-air)*	American	_____
❏	**en appetitt** *(ah-peh-teet)*	appetite	_____

4   Look Around You

Before you proceed **med** *(meh)* [with] this Step, situate yourself comfortably in your living room. Now look around you. Can you name **tingene** *(ting-en-eh)* [things the] that you see in this **rom** *(rohm)* [room] in Norwegian? You can probably guess **lampa** *(lahm-puh)* [lamp the] and maybe even **sofaen** *(soh-fah-en)* [sofa the]. Let's learn the rest of them. After practicing these **ordene** out loud, write them in the blanks below.

(ay) (lahm-peh) (lahm-puh)
ei lampe / lampa _____
a   lamp   lamp the

(en) (soh-fah) (soh-fah-en)
en sofa / sofaen _____
a   sofa   sofa the

(stohl) (stohl-en)
en stol / stolen _____
    chair   chair the

(et) (tep-eh) (tep-eh)
et teppe / teppet _____
a   carpet   carpet the

(boor) (boor-eh)
et bord / bordet   bordet, bordet
    table   table the

(ay) (dur) (dur-uh)
ei dør / døra _____
    door   door the

(klohk-eh) (klohk-uh)
ei klokke / klokka _____
    clock   clock the

(gar-deen) (gar-deen-en)
en gardin / gardinen _____
    curtain   curtain the

(tay-leh-fohn) (tay-leh-fohn-en)
en telefon / telefonen _____
    telephone   telephone the

(et) (vin-doo) (vin-doo-eh)
et vindu / vinduet
a   window   window the
_____

(et) (bild-eh) (bild-eh)
et bilde / bildet
a   picture   picture the
_____

You will notice that the correct form of "the" **og** *(oh)* "a" is given **med** *(meh)* [with] each noun. Now open your book to the sticky labels on page 17 and later on page 35. Peel off the first 11 labels **og** *(oh)* proceed around the **rom** *(rohm)* [room], labeling these items in your home. This will help to increase your Norwegian **ord** [word] power easily. Don't forget to say each **ord** as you attach the label.

Now ask yourself, **"Hvor er lampa?"** *(vor)(ar)(lahm-puh)* [where is lamp the] **og** point at it while you answer, **"Der er lampa."** *(dair)(ar)(lahm-puh)* [there is lamp the]
Continue on down **lista** *(list-uh)* [list the] above until you feel comfortable **med** *(meh)* [with] these new **ordene**.

❐	**en aprikos** *(ah-pree-kohs)*	apricot	_____
❐	**april** *(ah-preel)*	April	_____
❐	**en arm** *(arm)*	arm **a**	_____
❐	**august** *(ow-goost)*	August	_____
❐	**en automat** *(ow-toh-maht)*	vending machine	_____

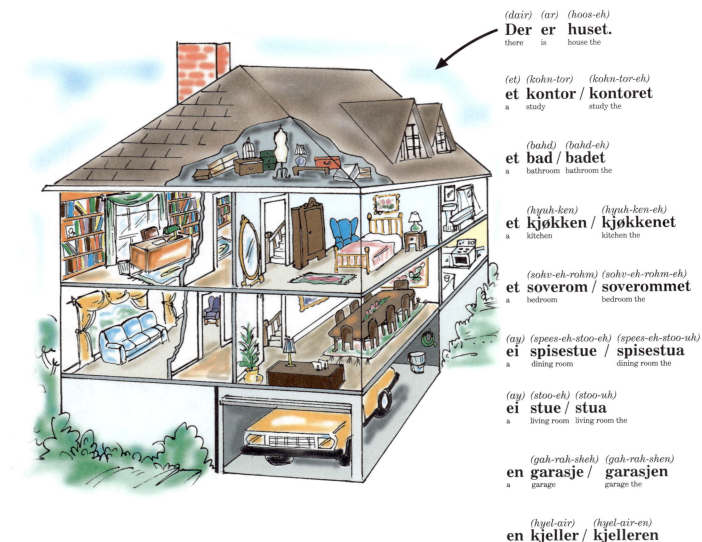

(hoos-uh)
huset = the house

(dair) (ar) (hoos-eh)
Der er huset.
there is house the

(et) (kohn-tor) (kohn-tor-eh)
et kontor / kontoret
a study study the

(bahd) (bahd-eh)
et bad / badet
a bathroom bathroom the

(hyuh-ken) (hyuh-ken-eh)
et kjøkken / kjøkkenet
a kitchen kitchen the

(sohv-eh-rohm) (sohv-eh-rohm-eh)
et soverom / soverommet
a bedroom bedroom the

(ay) (spees-eh-stoo-eh) (spees-eh-stoo-uh)
ei spisestue / spisestua
a dining room dining room the

(ay) (stoo-eh) (stoo-uh)
ei stue / stua
a living room living room the

(gah-rah-sheh) (gah-rah-shen)
en garasje / garasjen
a garage garage the

(hyel-air) (hyel-air-en)
en kjeller / kjelleren
a basement basement the

(oor-en-eh)
While learning these new **ordene,** let's not forget:
words

(beel) (beel-en)
en bil / bilen
a car car the

(moh-tor-seek-el) (moh-tor-seek-el-en)
en motorsykkel / motorsykkelen
a motorcycle motorcycle the

(seek-el) (seek-el-en)
en sykkel / sykkelen
a bicycle bicycle the

_____ _____ _____

❐	**bagasje** *(bah-gah-sheh)*	luggage, baggage
❐	**et bakeri** *(bah-kair-ee)*	bakery
❐	**en balkong** *(bahl-kohng)*	balcony
❐	**en banan** *(bah-nahn)*	banana
❐	**en bank** *(bahnk)*	bank

b

(kaht) *(kaht-en)*
en katt / katten
a cat   cat the

(hah-geh) *(hah-gen)*
en hage / hagen
a garden   garden the

(blohm-sten-eh)
blomstene
flowers the

_____   *en hage / hagen*   _____

(hoon) *(hoon-en)*
en hund / hunden
dog   dog the

(post-kah-seh) *(post-kah-sen)*
en postkasse / postkassen
mailbox   mailbox the

(post-en)
posten
mail the

_____   _____   _____

Peel off the next set of labels **og** *(oh)* wander through your **hus** *(hoos)* learning these new **ordene.** It will be somewhat difficult to label **katten,** *(kaht-en)* **blomstene** *(blohm-sten-eh)* **og** *(oh)* **hunden,** *(hoon-en)* but be creative. Practice by asking yourself, "**Hvor** *(vor)* **er** *(ar)* **bilen?** *(beel-en)*" and reply, "**Der** *(dair)* **er bilen.** *(beel-en)*"
                                                             car the   there   is

(vor) *(ar)* *(hoos-eh)*
Hvor er huset?

☐	**en benk** *(benk)*	bench
☐	**best** *(best)*	best
☐	**en biff** *(bif)*	beef, steak
☐	**blå** *(bloh)*	blue
☐	**ei bok** *(bohk)*	book

b

5   En, To, Tre!
(en)   *(too)*   *(tray)*
one   two   three

Consider for a minute how important numbers are. How could you tell someone your *(tay-leh-fohn-num-air)* **telefonnummer,** your *(ah-dres-eh)* **adresse** *(el-air)* **eller** your *(hoh-tel-rohm)* **hotellrom** if you had no *(num-air)* **nummer?** *(oh)* **Og** think of how

telephone number   address   or   hotel room   numbers

difficult it would be if you could not understand the time, the price of **et** *(ep-leh)* **eple** *(el-air)* **eller** the correct

an   apple   or

(boos) **buss** to take. When practicing *(num-ren-eh)* **numrene** below, notice the similarities which have been

bus   numbers the

underlined for you between *(tray)* **tre** and *(tret-ten)* **tretten,** *(fem)* **fem** and *(fem-ten)* **femten og** so on.

three   thirteen   five   fifteen

0	*(nool)* **null**		10	*(tee)* **ti**
1	*(en) (et)* **en, ett**		11	*(elv-eh)* **elleve**
2	*(too)* **to**		12	*(tohl)* **tolv**
3	*(tray)* **tre**		13	*(tret-ten)* **tretten**
4	*(fear-eh)* **fire**		14	*(fyor-ten)* **fjorten**
5	*(fem)* **fem**		15	*(fem-ten)* **femten**
6	*(sex)* **seks**		16	*(sigh-ten)* **seksten**
7	*(shoe)* **sju**	sju, sju, sju, sju, sju	17	*(suh-ten)* **sytten**
8	*(oh-teh)* **åtte**		18	*(ah-ten)* **atten**
9	*(nee)* **ni**		19	*(neet-ten)* **nitten**
10	*(tee)* **ti**		20	*(hyoo-eh)* **tjue**

☑ **britisk** *(brih-tisk)* . . . . British   britisk, britisk, britisk, britisk
☐ **en bror** *(bror)* . . . . brother
☐ **brun** *(broon)* . . . . brown, tanned   **b**
☐ **et brød** *(bruh)* . . . . bread
☐ **en buss** *(boos)* . . . . bus

Use these **numrene** *(num-ren-eh)* on a daily basis. Count to yourself **på** *(poh)* **norsk** *(norshk)* when you brush your teeth,
numbers   in

exercise **eller** commute to work. Fill in the blanks below according to **numrene** *(num-ren-eh)* given in
numbers the

parentheses. Now is also a good time to learn these **to** *(too)* very important phrases.
two

Jeg vil ha..., takk. *(yay) (vil) (hah) (tahk)* _____
I would like please

Vi vil ha..., takk. *(vee) (vil) (hah) (tahk)* _____
we would like please

Jeg vil ha _____(1)_____ **brevkort, takk.** *(brave-koort) (tahk)* **Hvor mange?** _____(1)_____ *(vor) (mahng-eh)*
I would like   postcard   how many

Jeg vil ha _____(7)_____ **frimerker, takk.** *(free-mair-kair) (tahk)* **Hvor mange?** _____(7)_____
stamps   how many

Jeg vil ha __*åtte*__ **frimerker, takk.** **Hvor mange?** _____(8)_____
(8)   stamps

Jeg vil ha _____(5)_____ **frimerker, takk.** **Hvor mange?** __*fem*__
(5)

Vi vil ha _____(9)_____ **brevkort, takk.** *(brave-koort)* **Hvor mange?** _____(9)_____
we   postcards

Vi vil ha _____(10)_____ **brevkort, takk.** **Hvor mange?** _____(10)_____
we

Jeg vil ha _____(1)_____ **billett, takk.** *(bil-let)* **Hvor mange?** _____(1)_____
ticket

Jeg vil ha _____(4)_____ **billetter, takk.** *(bil-let-air)* **Hvor mange?** _____(4)_____
tickets

Vi vil ha _____(11)_____ **billetter, takk.** **Hvor mange?** _____(11)_____

Jeg vil ha _____(3)_____ **kopper te, takk.** *(kohp-air) (tay)* **Hvor mange?** _____(3)_____
cups (of) tea

Vi vil ha _____(4)_____ **glass vann, takk.** *(glahs) (vahn)* *(how many)* _____(4)_____
glasses (of) water

Norsk itself has no "c's" so you will note that these free **ordene** are taken into **norsk** from other languages.

☐ **en campingplass** *(kam-ping-plahs)* .... campground _____
☐ **en CD-plate** *(say-day-plaht-eh)* .... CD   **c**   _____
☐ **en CD-spiller** *(say-day-spil-air)* .... CD player _____
☐ **et centigram** *(sen-tih-grahm)* .... centigram   _____

Now see if you can translate the following thoughts into **norsk** *(norshk)* / *norwegian*. The **svar** *(svar)* / *answers* are provided upside down at the bottom of **sida** *(seed-uh)* / *page the*.

1. I would like seven postcards, please.
   _____

2. I would like nine stamps, please.
   _____

3. We would like four cups of tea, please.
   _____

4. We would like three bus tickets, please.
   _____

Review **numrene** *(num-ren-eh)* / *numbers the* 1 **til** *(til)* / *to* 20. Write out your telephone number, fax number **og** *(oh)* / *and* cellular number. Then write out a friend's telephone number and a relative's telephone number.

(2 0 6) 2 8 4 — 4 2 1 1

to null seks _____

(___ ___ ___) ___ ___ ___ — ___ ___ ___ ___

_____

(___ ___ ___) ___ ___ ___ — ___ ___ ___ ___

SVAR

1. Jeg vil ha sju brevkort, takk.
2. Jeg vil ha ni frimerker, takk.
3. Vi vil ha fire kopper te, takk.
4. Vi vil ha tre billetter, takk.

6 *(farg-air)* **Farger**
colors

(far-gair) *(ar)* *(ee)(nor-geh)* *(ee)(ah-mair-ih-kuh)* *(nahvn)*
Farger **er** the same **i** **Norge** as they are **i** **Amerika** — they just have different **navn**. You can
colors are   in Norway   in   names

(puhr-puhr) *(broon)* *(far-gen-eh)*
easily recognize **purpur** as purple **og brun** as brown. Let's learn the basic **fargene** so when you
                                                                              colors the

(hoos) *(oh)* *(far-gen-eh)*
are invited to someone's **hus og** you want to bring flowers, you will be able to order **fargene** you
house   colors the

want. Once you've learned these **fargene**, quiz yourself. What color are your shoes? Your eyes?

Your hair? Your house?

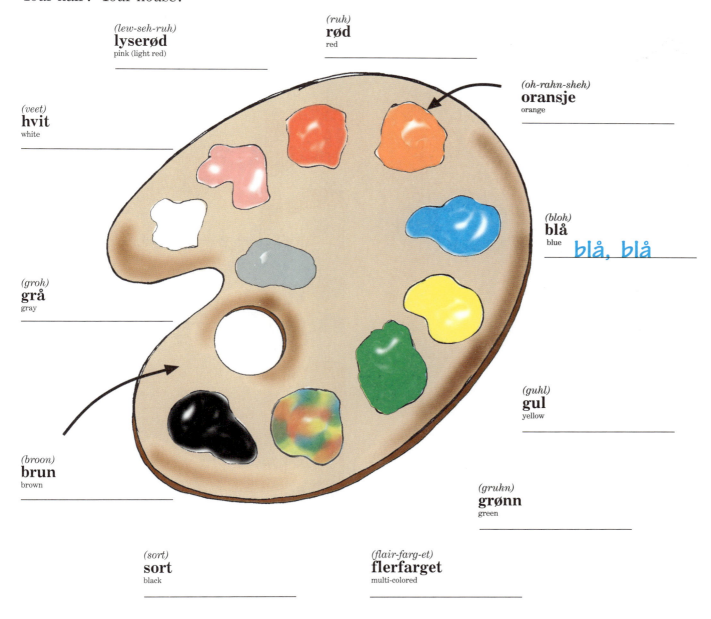

(lew-seh-ruh) **lyserød** — pink (light red)

(ruh) **rød** — red

(oh-rahn-sheh) **oransje** — orange

(veet) **hvit** — white

(bloh) **blå** — blue   *blå, blå*

(groh) **grå** — gray

(guhl) **gul** — yellow

(broon) **brun** — brown

(gruhn) **grønn** — green

(sort) **sort** — black

(flair-farg-et) **flerfarget** — multi-colored

❒	**en champagne** *(shahm-pahn-yeh)*	champagne
❒	**en chanse** *(shang-seh)*	chance
❒	**en choke** *(shohk)*	choke (in car) **c**
❒	**en clutch** *(kluhtsh)*	clutch (in car)
❒	**en cocktail** *(kohk-tail)*	cocktail

Peel off the next group of labels **og** proceed to label these **farger** *(farg-air)* in your **hus** *(hoos)* (house). Identify the **to** *(too)* **eller** *(or)* **tre** *(tray)* dominant **farger** in the flags below.

Flag	Country
	Norway
	Russia
	Germany
	Italy
	Finland
	Iceland
	the Netherlands
	Poland
	Belgium
	Canada
	France
	Denmark
	Luxembourg
	Sweden
	Switzerland
	Spain

_____ (where) _____ (where) **er en taxi?** *(tahx-ee)*

_____ (what) _____ (what) **er galt?** *(ar)* *(gahlt)* (is wrong)

- ☐ **en dag** *(dahg)* .... day
- ☐ **Danmark** *(dahn-mark)* .... Denmark   **d**
- ☐ – **hvor de snakker dansk** *(dahnsk)* .... where they speak Danish
- ☐ **en dans** *(dahns)* .... dance
- ☐ **ei datter** *(daht-air)* .... daughter

(lahmp-eh) ei **lampe**	*(beel)* en **bil**	*(lew-seh-ruh)* **lyserød**	*(veen-en)* **vinen**
(soh-fah) en **sofa**	*(moh-tor-seek-el)* en **motorsykkel**	*(ruh)* **rød**	*(uhl-eh)* **ølet**
(stohl) en **stol**	*(seek-el)* en **sykkel**	*(veet)* **hvit**	*(melk-en)* **melken**
(tep-eh) et **teppe**	*(kaht)* en **katt**	*(oh-rahn-sheh)* **oransje**	*(smur-eh)* **smøret**
(boor) et **bord**	*(hah-geh)* en **hage**	*(groh)* **grå**	*(sahl-teh)* **saltet**
(dur) ei **dør**	*(blohm-sten-eh)* **blomstene**	*(bloh)* **blå**	*(pep-air-en)* **pepperen**
(klohk-eh) ei **klokke**	*(hoon)* en **hund**	*(broon)* **brun**	*(veen-glahs-eh)* **vinglasset**
(gar-deen) en **gardin**	*(post-kah-seh)* en **postkasse**	*(guhl)* **gul**	*(glahs-eh)* **glasset**
(tay-leh-fohn) en **telefon**	*(post-en)* **posten**	*(sort)* **sort**	*(ah-vees-uh)* **avisa**
(vin-doo) et **vindu**	*(nool)* 0 **null**	*(gruhn)* **grønn**	*(kohp-en)* **koppen**
(bild-eh) et **bilde**	*(en)* 1 **en**	*(flair-farg-et)* **flerfarget**	*(sair-vee-et-en)* **servietten**
(hoos) et **hus**	*(too)* 2 **to**	*(go) (mor-en)* **god morgen**	*(gah-fel-en)* **gaffelen**
(kohn-tor) et **kontor**	*(tray)* 3 **tre**	*(go) (dahg)* **god dag**	*(tahl-air-ken-en)* **tallerkenen**
(bahd) et **bad**	*(fear-eh)* 4 **fire**	*(go) (et-tair-mid-ahg)* **god ettermiddag**	*(kneev-en)* **kniven**
(hyuh-ken) et **kjøkken**	*(fem)* 5 **fem**	*(go) (kvel)* **god kveld**	*(shay-en)* **skjeen**
(sohv-eh-rohm) et **soverom**	*(sex)* 6 **seks**	*(go) (naht)* **god natt**	*(skahp-eh)* **skapet**
(spees-eh-stoo-eh) ei **spisestue**	*(shoe)* 7 **sju**	*(hah) (deh) (brah)* **ha det bra**	*(tay-en)* **teen**
(stoo-eh) ei **stue**	*(oh-teh)* 8 **åtte**	*(vor-dahn) (har) (doo)(deh)* **Hvordan har du det?**	*(kahf-en)* **kaffen**
(gah-rah-sheh) en **garasje**	*(nee)* 9 **ni**	*(hyul-eh-skahp-eh)* **kjøleskapet**	*(bruh-eh)* **brødet**
(hyel-air) en **kjeller**	*(tee)* 10 **ti**	*(kohm-few-ren)* **kohmfyren**	*(tahk)* **takk**

STICKY LABELS

This book has over 150 special sticky labels for you to use as you learn new words. When you are introduced to one of these words, remove the corresponding label from these pages. Be sure to use each of these unique self-adhesive labels by adhering them to a picture, window, lamp, or whatever object they refer to. And yes, they are removable! The sticky labels make learning to speak Norwegian much more fun and a lot easier than you ever expected. For example, when you look in the mirror and see the label, say

(spail)
"et speil."
mirror

Don't just say it once, say it again and again. And once you label the refrigerator, you should never again open that door without saying

(kyul-eh-skahp-eh)
"kjøleskapet."
refrigerator the

By using the sticky labels, you not only learn new words, but friends and family learn along with you! The sooner you start, the sooner you can use these labels at home or work.

7 Penger
(peng-air)
money

Before starting this Step, go back **og** *(oh)* review Step 5. It is important that you can count to **tjue** *(hyoo-eh)* twenty without looking at **boka** *(bohk-uh)* book the. Let's learn the larger **numrene** *(num-ren-eh)* now. After practicing aloud **de** *(dee)* the **norske** *(norshk-eh)* **numrene** *(num-ren-eh)* numbers the 10 through 1,000 below, write these **numrene** *(num-ren-eh)* in the blanks provided. Again, notice the similarities (underlined) between **numrene** *(num-ren-eh)* such as **fem** *(fem)* (5), **femten** *(fem-ten)* (15) og **femti** *(fem-tee)* (50).

10	**ti** *(tee)*	_____
20	**tjue** *(hyoo-eh)*	_____
30	**tretti** *(tret-tee)*	_____
40	**førti** *(fur-tee)*	_____
50	**femti** *(fem-tee)*	*femti, femti, femti, femti, femti, femti, femti*
60	**seksti** *(sex-tee)*	_____
70	**sytti** *(soo-tee)*	_____
80	**åtti** *(oh-tee)*	_____
90	**nitti** *(neet-tee)*	_____
100	**hundre** *(huhn-dreh)*	_____
500	**fem hundre** *(fem) (huhn-dreh)*	_____
1,000	**tusen** *(too-sen)*	_____

Here are **to** *(too)* important phrases to go with all these **numrene** *(num-ren-eh)*. Say them out loud over and over and then write them out twice as many times.

jeg har *(yay) (har)* _____
I   have

vi har *(vee) (har)* _____
we have

❒ **desember** *(des-em-bair)* .... December _____
❒ **en dessert** *(des-airt)* .... dessert _____
❒ **en drikk** *(drik)* .... drink   **d**   _____
❒ **dum** *(doom)* .... dumb _____
❒ **dyp** *(dewp)* .... deep _____

The unit of currency **i** *(ee)* **Norge** *(nor-geh)* **er** *(ar)* **norske** *(norshk-eh)* **kroner,** *(krohn-air)* abbreviated "**Nkr.**" eller "**kr.**" Let's learn the various kinds of **mynter** *(mewnt-air)* (or **småpenger** *(smoh-peng-air)*) **og sedler** *(sed-lair)*. Always be sure to practice each **ord** out loud. You might want to exchange some money **nå** *(naw)* so that you can familiarize yourself **med** the various types of **penger** *(peng-air)*.

Sedler *(sed-lair)*
bills

Mynter *(mewnt-air)*
coins

femti *(fem-tee)* **kroner** *(krohn-air)*
50   krones

en *(en)* **krone** *(krohn-eh)*
one   krone

hundre *(huhn-dreh)* **kroner**

fem kroner *(krohn-air)*
   krones

to hundre kroner

fem hundre kroner *(fem)*

ti kroner *(tee)*

tjue kroner *(hyoo-eh)*

tusen kroner *(too-sen)*
1,000

- ☐ **et egg** *(egg)* .... egg
- ☐ **et eksempel** *(ek-sem-pel)* .... example
- ☐ **en eksport** *(ek-sport)* .... export   **e**
- ☐ **ekstra** *(ek-strah)* .... extra
- ☐ **elektrisk** *(el-ek-trisk)* .... electric

Review **numrene** *(num-ren-eh)* **ti** *(tee)* through **tusen** *(too-sen)* again. **Nå,** *(noh)* **hvordan** *(vor-dahn)* do you say "twenty-two" **eller** *(el-air)* "fifty-three" **på** *(poh)* **norsk?** *(norshk)* It's just like **på engelsk** *(eng-elsk)* except that **nummer** *(num-air)* up to 100 are written as one **ord**. See if you can say **og** *(oh)* write out **numrene** *(num-ren-eh)* on this **side**. *(seed-eh)* **Svarene** *(svar-en-eh)* **er** *(ar)* at the bottom of **sida**. *(seed-uh)*

- *in* — på
- *Norwegian* — norsk
- *English* — engelsk
- *page* — side
- *answers the* — Svarene
- *are* — er
- *page the* — sida
- *now* — Nå
- *how* — hvordan
- *or* — eller

1. _____ (25 = 20 + 5)

2. _____ (83 = 80 + 3)

3. _____ (47 = 40 + 7)

4. **nittiseks, nittiseks** (96 = 90 + 6)

Now, how would you say the following **på norsk?** *(norshk)*

5. _____ (I have 80 krones.)

6. _____ (We have 72 krones.)

To ask how much something **koster** *(kohst-air)* **på** *(poh)* **norsk,** *(norshk)* one asks — **Hvor** *(vor)* **mye** *(mee-eh)* **koster** *(kohst-air)* **det?** *(deh)*
- *costs* — koster
- *how* — Hvor
- *much* — mye
- *costs* — koster
- *that* — det

Nå *(noh)* you try it. _____ (How much does that cost?)
now

Answer the following questions based on the numbers in parentheses.

7. **Hvor** *(vor)* **mye** *(mee-eh)* **koster** *(kohst-air)* **det?** *(deh)* **Det** *(deh)* **koster** *(kohst-air)* _____ **kroner.** *(krohn-air)* (10)
   - *costs* — koster; *that* — det; *it* — Det; *costs* — koster

8. **Hvor** **mye** *(mee-eh)* **koster** *(kohst-air)* **billetten?** *(bil-let-en)* **Billetten koster** *(bil-let-en)* _____ **kroner.** (20)
   - *costs* — koster; *ticket the* — billetten

9. **Hvor** **mye** *(mee-eh)* **koster boka?** *(bohk-uh)* **Boka koster** *(bohk-uh)* _____ **kroner.** (17)
   - *book the* — boka

10. **Hvor mye koster filmen?** *(kohst-air) (film-en)* **Filmen koster** *(film-en)* _____ **kroner.** (30)

SVAR

1. tjuefem
2. åttitre
3. førtisju
4. nittiseks
5. Jeg har åtti kroner.
6. Vi har syttito kroner.
7. ti
8. tjue
9. sytten
10. tretti

8   I Dag, I Morgen og I Går
(ee) (dahg) today, *(ee) (mor-en)* tomorrow *(oh)* and *(ee) (gor)* yesterday

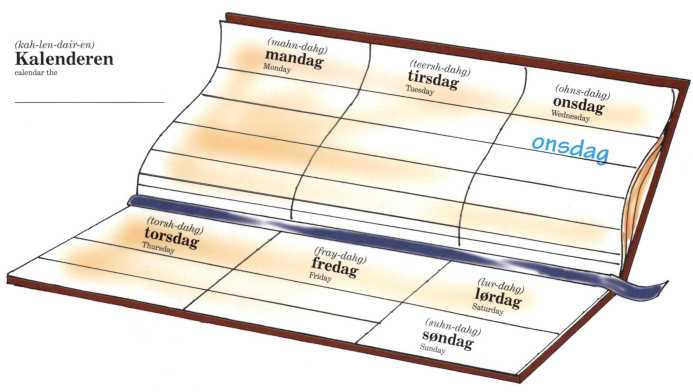

(kah-len-dair-en)
Kalenderen
calendar the

(mahn-dahg) **mandag** Monday
(teersh-dahg) **tirsdag** Tuesday
(ohns-dahg) **onsdag** Wednesday
onsdag
(torsh-dahg) **torsdag** Thursday
(fray-dahg) **fredag** Friday
(lur-dahg) **lørdag** Saturday
(suhn-dahg) **søndag** Sunday

Learn **dagene** *(dahg-en-eh)* days the of the week by writing them in **kalenderen** *(kah-len-dair-en)* calender the above **og** then move on to the **fire** *(fear-eh)* four parts to each **dag.** *(dahg)* day

(mor-en)
morgen
morning

(et-tair-mid-ahg)
ettermiddag
afternoon

(kvel)
kveld
evening

(naht)
natt
night

❑ **en familie** *(fah-meel-yeh)* . . . . family
❑ **fantastisk** *(fahn-tahs-tisk)* . . . . fantastic
❑ **en far** *(far)* . . . . father   **f**
❑ **en fasong** *(fah-sohng)* . . . . fashion, clothes style
❑ **en feber** *(fay-bair)* . . . . fever

22

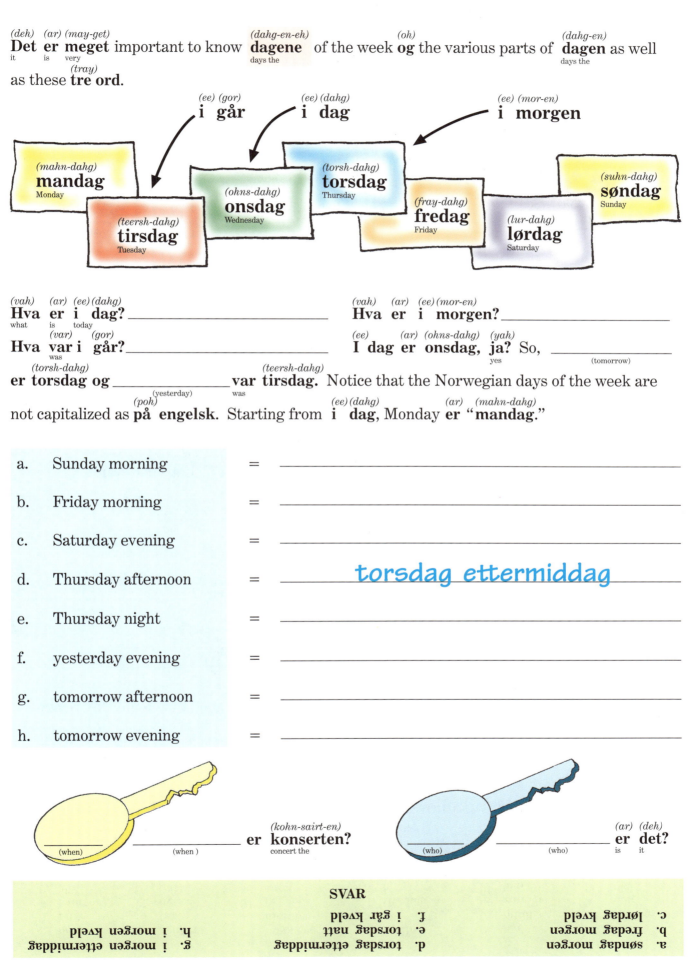

Knowing the parts of **dagen** ^(dahg-en) will help you to learn the various **norske** ^(norshk-eh) greetings below. Practice
_{day the}

these every day until your trip.

god ^(go) **morgen** ^(mor-en) _____
_{good   morning}

god ^(go) **dag** ^(dahg) _____
_{good   day / hello}

god ^(go) **ettermiddag** ^(et-tair-mid-ahg) _____
_{good   afternoon}

god ^(go) **kveld** ^(kvel) _____
_{good   evening}

god ^(go) **natt** ^(naht) _____
_{good   night}

ha ^(hah) **det** ^(deh) **bra** ^(brah) / **ha** ^(hah) **det** ^(deh) _____
_{good-bye}

Take the next group of labels **og** stick them on **de** ^(dee) appropriate **tingene** ^(hoos) in your **hus**. Make sure
_{the   things   house}

you attach them to the correct items, as they are only **på** ^(poh) **norsk** ^(norshk). How about the bathroom

mirror **for** ^(for) "**god** ^(go) **morgen**" ^(mor-en)? **Eller** your alarm clock for "**god** ^(go) **natt**" ^(naht)? Let's not forget,
_{for   or}

Hvordan ^(vor-dahn) **har** **du** ^(doo) **det** ^(deh)? _____
_{how are you}

Now for some "**ja**" ^(yah) or "**nei**" ^(nay) questions –
_{yes   no}

Are your eyes **blå**? ^(bloh) _____   Are your shoes **brun**? ^(broon) _____

Is your favorite color **rød**? ^(ruh) _____   Is today **lørdag**? ^(lur-dahg) _____

Do you own **en hund**? ^(hoon) _____   Do you own **en katt**? ^(kaht) _____

You **er** ^(ar) about one-fourth of your way through this **bok** ^(bohk) **og det** ^(deh) **er** ^(ar) a good time to quickly review
_{are   book   it   is}

ordene ^(oor-en-eh) you **har** learned before doing the crossword puzzle on the next **side**. ^(seed-eh) **God** ^(go) **fornøyelse** ^(for-nuh-oy-el-seh)
_{words the   have   have fun}

og lykke ^(loo-keh) **til**! ^(til)
_{good luck}

SVAR TO THE CROSSWORD PUZZLE (KRYSSORD OPPGAVE)

ACROSS
3. natt
5. bilde
7. hvorfor
8. blå
9. egg
10. fire
12. er
13. hvor
14. penger
15. takk
17. og
20. gul
22. posten
24. i går
26. ord
29. postkasse
41. rød
42. grå

DOWN
1. kjeller
2. vi
4. tirsdag
5. bil
6. øre
8. brevkort
10. førtito
11. lørdag
13. har
16. hund
18. garasje
19. hvit
21. lampe
23. norsk
25. god
27. bord
28. jente
30. onsdag
31. eller
32. i morgen
33. klokke
34. ni
35. kveld
36. sort
37. atten
38. to
39. ettermiddag
40. dør

CROSSWORD PUZZLE (KRYSSORD OPPGAVE)
(krees-oor) *(ohp-gah-veh)*

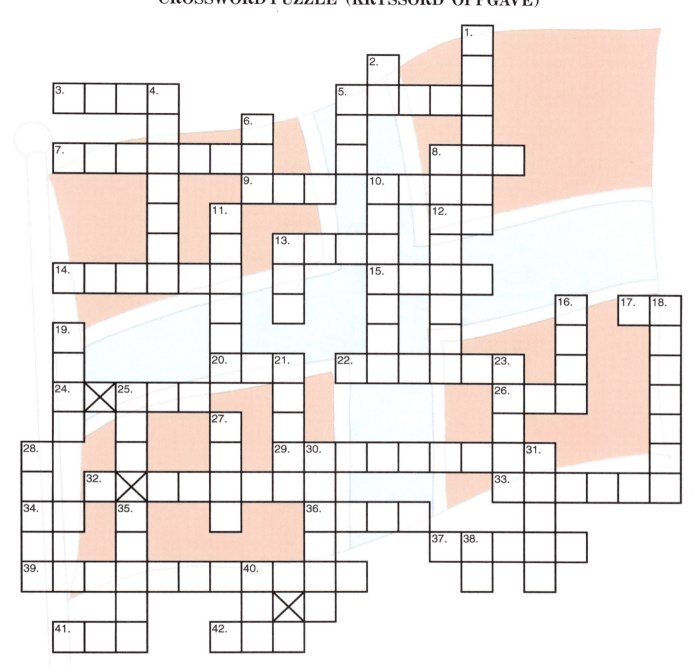

ACROSS

- 3. night
- 5. picture
- 7. why
- 8. blue
- 9. egg
- 10. four
- 12. is
- 13. where
- 14. money
- 15. thank you
- 17. and
- 20. yellow
- 22. the mail
- 24. yesterday
- 26. word
- 27. mailbox
- 32. morning
- 33. clock
- 34. nine
- 36. black
- 37. eighteen
- 39. afternoon
- 41. red
- 42. grey

DOWN

- 1. basement
- 2. we
- 4. Tuesday
- 5. car
- 6. ore (monetary unit)
- 8. postcard
- 10. 42
- 11. Saturday
- 13. have
- 16. dog
- 18. garage
- 19. white
- 21. lamp
- 23. Norwegian
- 25. good
- 27. table
- 28. girl
- 30. Wednesday
- 31. or
- 35. evening
- 38. two
- 40. door

- ❒ **februar** *(fay-broo-ar)* .... February
- ❒ **fersk** *(fairshk)* .... fresh
- ❒ **en fest** *(fest)* .... festival, party   **f**
- ❒ **fet** *(fet)* .... fat
- ❒ **en film** *(film)* .... film, movie

9   I, På, Under...
               (ee) (poh) (oon-air)
               in   on   under

(norshk-eh) **Norske** prepositions (words like "in," "on," "through" and "next to") *(ar)* **er** easy to learn *(oh)* **og** they allow you to be precise **med** a minimum of effort. Instead of having to point *(sex)* **seks** times at a piece of yummy pastry you would like, you can explain precisely which one you want by saying *(deh) (ar)* **det er** behind, in front of, next to **eller** under the piece of pastry that the salesperson is starting to pick up. Let's learn some of these little **ord.**

(oon-air) **under** _____ under

(oh-vair) **over** _____ over

(mel-ohm) **mellom** _mellom, mellom, mellom_ between

(veh) (seed-en) (ahv) **ved siden av** _____ next to

(poh) **på** _____ on / at / in

(ee) **i** _____ in

(in-eh) (ee) **inne i** _____ inside

(in) (ee) **inn i** _____ into

(for-ahn) **foran** _____ in front of

(bahk) **bak** _____ behind / in back of

(oot) (ahv) **ut av** _____ out of / from

(bahk-vairk) **bakverk** _____ pastry!

Fill in the blanks on the next *(seed-eh)* **side** with the correct prepositions.

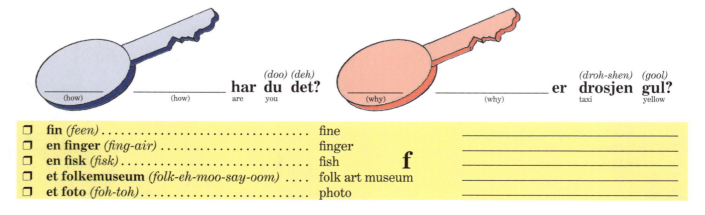

____ (how) ____ (how) **har du det?** *(doo) (deh)* are you

____ (why) ____ (why) **er drosjen gul?** *(droh-shen) (gool)* taxi yellow

☐	**fin** *(feen)*	fine
☐	**en finger** *(fing-air)*	finger
☐	**en fisk** *(fisk)*	fish **f**
☐	**et folkemuseum** *(folk-eh-moo-say-oom)*	folk art museum
☐	**et foto** *(foh-toh)*	photo

(bahk-vairk-eh) *(ar)*   *(boor-eh)*   *(hoon-en)* *(ar)*   *(boor-eh)*
Bakverket er _____ **bordet.**   **Hunden er** _____ **bordet.**
pastry the   (on)   table the   dog the   (under)

(lay-gen)   *(deh)* *(go-eh)* *(hoh-tel-eh)*   *(vor)* *(ar)* *(lay-gen)*
Legen er _____ **det gode hotellet.**   **Hvor er legen?** _____
doctor the   (inside)   good

(mahn-en)   *(hoh-tel-eh)*   *(mahn-en)*
Mannen er _____ **hotellet.**   **Hvor er mannen?** _____
man the   (in front of)

(tay-leh-fohn-en)   *(bild-eh)*   *(tay-leh-fohn-en)*
Telefonen er _____ **bildet.**   **Hvor er telefonen?** _____
telephone the   (next to)   picture the

(noh)
Nå, fill in each blank on the picture below with the best possible one of these little **ord.** Do you
now
                     (hohl-men-kohl-en)
recognize the **Holmenkollen** below? It is one of the world's longest ski jumps **og** it is located

right in **Oslo.**

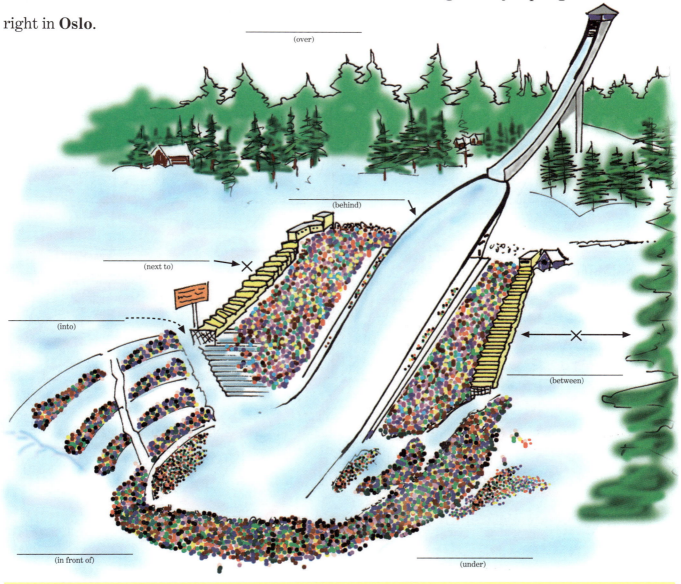

☐	**en fottur** *(foh-toor)*	hike, "foot tour"	_____
☐	**fra** *(frah)*	from	**f** _____
☐	**Frankrike** *(frahnk-reek-eh)*	France	_____
	– hvor de snakker fransk *(frahnsk)*	where they speak French	_____
☐	**fri** *(free)*	free	_____

	(yah-noo-ar)	(fay-broo-ar)	(marsh)
10	**Januar,**	**Februar,**	**Mars**
	January	February	March

You **har** learned **dagene** *(dahg-en-eh)* of **uken,** *(ook-en)* so **nå er** **det** *(deh)* time to learn **månedene** *(mohn-den-eh)* of **året og** *(or-eh)* all the different kinds of **vær.** *(vair)*

- have / days the / week the / it is / months the / year the / weather

(yah-noo-ar) **januar**

(fay-broo-ar) **februar**

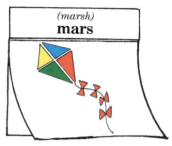
(marsh) **mars**

(ah-preel) **april**

(my) **mai**

(yoo-nee) **juni**

(yoo-lee) **juli**

(ow-goost) **august**

(sep-tem-bair) **september**

(ohk-toh-bair) **oktober**

(noh-vem-bair) **november**

(des-em-bair) **desember**

When someone asks, "**Hvordan** *(vor-dahn)* **er** *(ar)* **været** *(vair-eh)* **i** *(ee)* **dag?** *(dahg)*" you have a variety of answers. Let's learn them but first, does this sound familiar?

how / is / weather the / today

> September, **april,** *(ah-preel)* **juni** *(joo-nee)* **og** *(oh)* november har tretti **dager**... *(dahg-air)*
> days

- ❏ **en garasje** *(gah-rah-sheh)* .... garage
- ❏ **gin** *(jin)* .... gin
- ❏ **en gjest** *(yest)* .... guest   **g**
- ❏ **glad** *(glah)* .... glad, happy
- ❏ **et gram** *(grahm)* .... gram

(vor-dahn) *(vair-eh)* *(ee)* *(dahg)*
Hvordan er været i dag? _____
what   weather the   today

(deh) *(snur)* *(ee)*
Det snør i januar. _____
it   snows   in

(oh-soh) *(fay-broo-ar)*
Det snør også i februar. _____
           also

(rine-air) *(oh)* *(snur)*
Det regner og snør i mars. _____
it   rains

(rine-air)
Det regner i april. _____
it

(bloh-sair) *(my)*
Det blåser i mai. _____
      blows

(bloh-sair) *(oh-soh)* *(yoo-nee)*
Det blåser også i juni. _____
      blows

(varmt)
Det er varmt i juli. _____
        warm

(ow-goost)
Det er også varmt i august. _____

(pent) *(vair)*
Det er pent vær i september. _____
     nice   weather

(kahlt) *(ohk-toh-bair)*
Det er kaldt i oktober. _____
      cold

(oh-soh) *(kahlt)*
Det er også kaldt i november. _____

(dor-lee) *(vair)* *(des-em-bair)*
Det er dårlig vær i desember. _____
       bad

Hvordan er været i februar? _____
                in

(vair-eh)
Hvordan er været i april? *Det regner i april. Det regner i april.*

Hvordan er været i mai? _____

Hvordan er været i august? _____

❐ **en grapefrukt** *(grep-fruhkt)* .... grapefruit		
❐ **gresk** *(gresk)* .... Greek		
❐ **en gud** *(gewd)* .... God	**g**	
❐ **gull** *(guhl)* .... gold		
❐ **ei gås** *(gaws)* .... goose		

29

Nå for the seasons **i** *(ee)* **året** *(or-eh)* ...
in year the

(vint-air) **vinter** — winter

(sohm-air) **sommer** — summer

(hust) **høst** — autumn

(vor) **vår** — spring

(sel-see-oos) **Celsius** — Centigrade

(far-en-hite) **Fahrenheit** — Fahrenheit

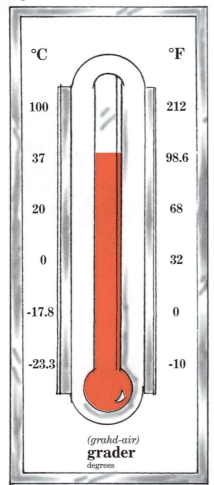

°C / °F
100 / 212
37 / 98.6
20 / 68
0 / 32
-17.8 / 0
-23.3 / -10

(grahd-air) **grader** — degrees

At this point, **det er en god** *(go)* **ide** *(ee-day)* to familiarize yourself **med europeiske** *(oy-roh-pay-isk-eh)* **temperaturer.** *(temp-air-ah-toor-air)*
Carefully study the thermometer because **temperaturer i Europa** *(temp-air-ah-toor-air) (oy-roh-puh)* are calculated on the basis of Centigrade (not Fahrenheit).

To convert °F to °C, subtract 32 and multiply by 0.55.

98.6 °F - 32 = 66.6 x 0.55 = 37 °C

To convert °C to °F, multiply by 1.8 and add 32.

37 °C x 1.8 = 66.6 + 32 = 98.6 °F

What is normal body temperature in **Celsius?**

What is the freezing point in **Celsius?**

- **halv** *(hahl)* .... half
- **en handlebag** *(hahn-leh-bayg)* .... shopping bag
- **hard** *(har)* .... hard   **h**
- **hardkokt** *(har-kohkt)* .... hard-boiled
- **en hatt** *(haht)* .... hat

11   Øst, Vest, Hjemme Best!
(ust) *(vest)* *(yem-meh)* *(best)*
east — west — at home — (is) best

Most **nordmenn** *(noor-men)* (Norwegians) tend to say, "**Øst, vest, hjemme best!**" Study the family tree below to help you to understand some of the basics of the **norske familie** *(norshk-eh) (fah-meel-yeh)* (family).

(fru Hansen)
Åse Hansen
bestemora — grandmother the

(herr Hansen)
Ole Hansen
bestefaren — grandfather the

(herr Hansen)
Per-Arne Hansen
faren — father the

(fru Solberg)
Turid Solberg
tanta — aunt the

(fru Hansen)
Astrid Hansen
mora — mother the

(Bjørn Solberg)
Bjørn Solberg
onkelen — uncle the

Tormod Hansen
sønnen — son the

(frøken Hansen)
Jorunn Hansen
dattera — daughter the

- ❏ **hei** *(hay)* .... hi, hello
- ❏ **en helligdag** *(hel-ee-dahg)* .... holiday
- ❏ **hjelp** *(yelp)* .... help, assistance
- ❏ **et hjem** *(yem)* .... home
- ❏ **en hydrofoilbåt** *(hee-droh-foil-boht)* ..... hydrofoil

h

Let's learn how to identify **familien** *(fah-meel-yen)* by **navn** *(nahvn)*. Study the following **eksempler** *(ek-sem-plair)* carefully.
family the   name   examples

(vah) *(het-air)* *(doo)*
Hva heter du? _____
what is your name / how are you called

(yay)
Jeg heter _____.
my name is / I am called   (your name)

(for-el-dren-uh)
foreldrene
parents the

(far-en)
faren _____
father the

(vah) *(het-air)*
Hva heter faren? Faren heter _____
what is called father the

(mor-uh)
mora _____
mother the

Hva heter mora? Mora heter _____
what mother the

(barn-uh)
barna
children the

(suhn-en) *(dah-tair-uh)* *(bror)* *(suhs-tair)*
Sønnen og dattera er bror og søster.
brother sister

(suhn-en)
sønnen _____
son the

(het-air) *(suhn-en)*
Hva heter sønnen? Sønnen heter _____

(dah-tair-uh)
dattera _____
daughter the

(dah-tair-uh)
Hva heter dattera? Dattera heter _____

(shlekt-ning-en-eh)
slektningene
relatives the

(best-eh-far-en)
bestefaren _____
grandfather the

(vah) *(best-eh-far-en)*
Hva heter bestefaren? Bestefaren heter ___

(best-eh-mor-uh)
bestemora _____
grandmother the

(best-eh-mor-uh)
Hva heter bestemora? Bestemora heter ___

Now you ask —

And answer —

_____
(How are you called? / What is your name?)

_____
(My name is . . .)

☐ **høy** *(huh-oy)* . . . . high, tall
☐ **ei hånd** *(hohn)* . . . . hand
☐ **håndbagasje** *(hohn-bah-gah-sheh)* . . . . hand baggage   **h**
☐ **et håndverk** *(hohn-vairk)* . . . . handwork, handicraft
☐ **hår** *(hor)* . . . . hair

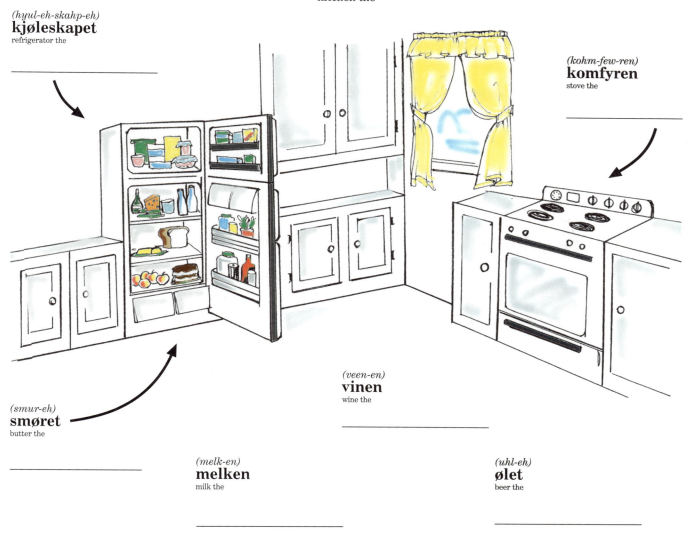

(hyuh-ken-eh)
Kjøkkenet
kitchen the

(hyul-eh-skahp-eh)
kjøleskapet
refrigerator the

(kohm-few-ren)
komfyren
stove the

(smur-eh)
smøret
butter the

(veen-en)
vinen
wine the

(melk-en)
melken
milk the

(uhl-eh)
ølet
beer the

Answer these questions aloud.

(ar) (uhl-eh)   *(hyul-eh-skahp-eh)*
Hvor er ølet? .... **Ølet er i kjøleskapet.**
        beer the   in

(ar)   *(ar)*
Hvor er melken?   **Hvor er vinen?**   **Hvor er smøret?**
                                                             wine the   butter the

(noh)   *(bohk) (seed-uh)*
Nå open your **bok** to **sida med** the labels **og** remove the next group of labels **og** proceed to
                               book   page the
                                         (poh) (hyuh-ken-eh)
label all these **tingene på kjøkkenet.**
                        things   kitchen the

☐ **en immigrant** *(im-ih-grahnt)*............. immigrant
☐ **immun** *(ih-moon)*....................... immune
☐ **en import** *(im-port)*..................... import   **i**
☐ **Italia** *(ee-tahl-ee-ah)*.................... Italy
   – hvor de snakker italiensk *(ee-tahl-ee-ensk)*.. where they speak Italian

(sahl-teh) **saltet** — salt the

(pep-air-en) **pepperen** — pepper

(veen-glahs-eh) **vinglasset** — wine glass

(glahs-eh) **glasset** — glass

(blohm-sten) **blomsten** — flower the

(kohp-en) **koppen** — cup the

(ah-vees-uh) **avisa** — newspaper

(shay-en) **skjeen** — spoon

(sair-vee-et-en) **servietten** — napkin

(gah-fel-en) **gaffelen** — fork

(tahl-air-ken-en) **tallerkenen** — plate

(kneev-en) **kniven** — knife

Og more . . .

(skahp-eh) **skapet** — cupboard the

(tay-en) **teen** — tea the

(vor) *(ar)* *(tay-en)* **Hvor er teen?** — is

(ee)(skahp-eh) **Teen er i skapet.**

(kahf-en) **kaffen** — coffee the

(kahf-en) **Hvor er kaffen?**

(bruh-eh) **brødet** — bread the

(bruh-eh) **Hvor er brødet?**

Don't forget to label all these things and do not forget to use every opportunity to say these **ord** out loud. *(deh)(ar)(may-get)(vik-tee)* **Det er meget viktig.** — very important

❏	**Japan** *(yah-pahn)*	Japan
	– **hvor de snakker japansk** *(yah-pahnsk)* . . .	where they speak Japanese
❏	**jazz** *(jahss)*	jazz
❏	**en jobb** *(yohb)*	job
❏	**en journalist** *(shuhr-nah-list)*	journalist

j

(vair) (shoh) (snil)
vær så snill

(un-shool)
unnskyld

(kles-skahp)
et **klesskap**

(seng)
ei **seng**

(poo-teh)
ei **pute**

(dee-neh)
ei **dyne**

(vek-kair-klohk-eh)
ei **vekkerklokke**

(spail)
et **speil**

(vahsk)
en **vask**

(hohn-klair-neh)
håndklærne

(toh-ah-let)
et **toalett**

(doosh)
en **dusj**

(blee-ahnt)
en **blyant**

(fyairn-seen)
et **fjernsyn**

(pen)
en **penn**

(bohk)
ei **bok**

(dah-tah)
en **data**

(bril-air)
briller

(pah-peer)
et **papir**

(pah-peer-koorv)
en **papirkurv**

(tee-skrift)
et **tidsskrift**

(brave)
et **brev**

(free-mair-keh)
et **frimerke**

(brave-koort)
et **brevkort**

(pahs)
et **pass**

(bil-let)
en **billett**

(kohf-airt)
en **koffert**

(hohn-vesk-eh)
ei **håndveske**

(lohm-eh-bohk)
ei **lommebok**

(peng-air)
penger

(kray-deet-koort-en-eh)
kreditkortene

(race-eh-shek-en-eh)
reisesjekkene

(foh-toh-grah-fee-ah-pah-raht)
et **fotografiapparat**

(film)
en **film**

(bahd-eh-drahkt)
ei **badedrakt**

(sahn-dahl-air)
sandaler

(sohl-bril-air)
solbriller

(tahn-bursh-teh)
en **tannbørste**

(tahn-krame)
en **tannkrem**

(sohp-eh)
såpe

(bar-bair-huh-vel)
en **barberhøvel**

(day-oh-doh-rahnt)
en **deodorant**

(kahm)
en **kam**

(rine-frahk)
en **regnfrakk**

(pah-rah-plee)
en **paraply**

(kohp-eh)
en **kåpe**

(hahn-skair)
hansker

(haht)
en **hatt**

(stuv-lair)
støvler

(skoh)
sko

(ten-is-skoh)
tennissko

(dres)
en **dress**

(shlips)
et **slips**

(short-eh)
en **skjorte**

(lohm-eh-tur-klay)
et **lommetørkle**

(yahk-eh)
ei **jakke**

(buhx-air)
bukser

(yay) (ar)
Jeg er amerikaner.

(yay) (veel) (lair-eh) (norshk)
Jeg vil lære norsk.

(yay) (het-air)
Jeg heter _____.

(shorts)
shorts

(tay-short-eh)
en **T-skjorte**

(oon-air-buhx-air)
underbukser

(oon-air-short-eh)
en **underskjorte**

(hyoh-leh)
en **kjole**

(bloos-eh)
en **bluse**

(shirt)
et **skjørt**

(gen-sair)
en **genser**

(oon-air-hyoh-leh)
en **underkjole**

(bay)(hoh)
en **B. H.**

(troos-air)
truser

(sohk-air)
sokker

(strump-air)
strømper

(pee-shah-mahs)
en **pyjamas**

(naht-short-eh)
en **nattskjorte**

(bahd-eh-kohp-eh)
en **badekåpe**

(tuf-lair)
tøfler

(ah-mair-ih-kahn-air)
amerikaner.

PLUS...

This book includes a number of other innovative features unique to the *"10 minutes a day®"* Series. At the back of this book, you will find twelve pages of flash cards. Cut them out and flip through them at least once a day.

On pages 116, 117 and 118 you will find a beverage guide and a menu guide. Don't wait until your trip to use them. Clip out the menu guide and use it tonight at the dinner table. Take them both with you the next time you dine at your favorite Norwegian restaurant.

By using the special features in this book, you will be speaking Norwegian before you know it.

(go) *(for-nuh-oy-el-seh)* *(loo-keh)* *(til)*
God fornøyelse og lykke til!
have fun   good luck

(reh-lih-gee-ohn-air)
Religioner
religions

(ee)(nor-geh) (ar) (deh)   *(reh-lih-gee-ohn-air)*   *(vee)(fin-air)*   *(hair) (ee) (ah-mair-ih-kuh)*
I Norge er det not the wide variety of **religioner** that **vi finner her i Amerika.**
religions   we   find   here   in

A person is usually one of the following.

(kah-tohlsk)
1. **katolsk** _____
Catholic

(proh-tes-tahn-tisk)
2. **protestantisk** _____
Protestant

(yuh-disk)
3. **jødisk** _____
Jewish

(hair)   *(hyeer-keh)*   *(nor-geh)*
Her er en kirke i Norge.
here   church

                        (hyeer-keh)
Er det en protestantisk kirke?
is   it

                (hyeer-keh)
Er det en katolsk kirke?

        (nee) (hyeer-keh)
Er det en ny kirke?
          new

       (gahm-el) (hyeer-keh)
Er det en gammel kirke?
          old

                                      (yay) (ar)
Nå, let's learn how to say "I am" **på norsk: jeg er** _____
now   I   am

                                        (seed-eh)
Test yourself – write each sentence on the next **side** for more practice. Add your own personal

variations as well.

                             (doo)   *(kohst-air) (deh)*
_____ _____ **er du i Norge?**   _____ _____ **koster det?**
(why)   (how much)   (how much)   does this cost

❏ **en kafé** *(kah-fay)* . . . . cafe   _____
❏ **en kakao** *(kah-kah-oh)* . . . . cocoa, hot chocolate   _____
❏ **Kanada** *(kah-nah-dah)* . . . . Canada   **k**   _____
❏ **kanadisk** *(kah-nah-disk)* . . . . Canadian   _____
❏ **en katedral** *(kah-tay-drahl)* . . . . cathedral   _____

(yay) (ar) (kah-tohlsk)
Jeg er katolsk. _____

I am Catholic

(yay) (proh-tes-tahn-tisk)
Jeg er protestantisk. _____

(yay) (yuh-disk)
Jeg er jødisk. _____

Jewish

(yay) (ay-vahn-gay-lisk-loo-tairshk)
Jeg er evangelisk-luthersk. _____

Evangelical Lutheran

(yay) (ee)(oy-roh-puh)
Jeg er i Europa. _____

(kah-nah-dyair)
Jeg er kanadier. _____

Canadian

(yay) (hyeer-ken)
Jeg er i kirken. _____

I am in church the

(yay) (hyuh-ken-eh)
Jeg er på kjøkkenet. _____

kitchen the

(yay) (nor-geh)
Jeg er i Norge. _____

(poh)(res-tuh-rahng-en)
Jeg er på restauranten. _____

in

(ah-mair-ih-kahn-air)
Jeg er amerikaner. _____

American

(hoh-tel-eh)
Jeg er på hotellet. _____

(suhl-ten)
Jeg er sulten. _____

hungry

(tursht)
Jeg er tørst. _____

thirsty

To negate any of these statements, simply add "**ikke**" *(ick-eh)* after the verb.

not / no

(yay) (ick-eh)
Jeg er ikke katolsk. _____

am not

(yay) (ick-eh) (nor-geh)
Jeg er ikke i Norge. _____

I

Go through and drill all these sentences again but with "**ikke.**"

Nå, take a piece of paper. Our **familie** *(fah-meel-yeh)* from earlier had a reunion. Identify everyone below by writing **det riktige norske ordet** *(deh) (rik-tee-eh) (oor-eh)* for each **menneske** *(men-es-keh)* — **mora, onkelen** *(mor-uh) (ohnk-el-en)* and so on. Don't forget **hunden!** *(hoon-en)*

right / correct word person

❐ **en kilo** *(hyee-loh)* . . . . kilo	
❐ **Kina** *(hyee-nah)* . . . . China	**k**
– **hvor de snakker kinesisk** *(hyee-nay-sisk)*	
❐ **klar** *(klar)* . . . . clear, ready	
❐ **en klasse** *(klahs-eh)* . . . . class	

12 Lære!
(lair-eh)
to learn

You **har** *(ahl-eh-red-eh)* **allerede** used **to** very important verbs: **jeg vil ha** and **jeg har**. Although you
have   already   *(yay)* *(vil)*   *(yay)*
                                                                I   would like   I   have

might be able to get by **med** only these verbs, let's assume you want to do **bedre**. First a quick
                                                                                (bed-reh)
                                                                                better
review.

How do you say **på norsk?** _____
              (norshk)

How do you say **på norsk?** _____

Compare these **to** charts very carefully **og** learn these **åtte** ord now.
              (too)   *(oh-tuh)*
                                                              eight

I = **jeg** *(yay)*	_____	we = **vi** *(vee)*	_____
you = **du** *(doo)*	_____	they = **de** *(dee)*	_____
he = **han** *(hahn)*	_____	it = **det** *(deh)*	_____
she = **hun** *(huhn)*	_____	it = **den** *(den)*	_____

Not too hard, is it? Draw lines between the matching **engelske og norske ordene** below to see
                                                     (eng-elsk-eh) *(norshk-eh)*
if **du** can keep these **ordene** straight in your mind.
   (doo)
   you

den *(den)*   I
vi *(vee)*   it
du *(doo)*   you
det *(deh)*   he
jeg *(yay)*   we
de *(dee)*   she
han *(hahn)*   they
hun *(huhn)*   it

☐	**en klubb** *(klub)*	club
☐	**et kne** *(knay)*	knee
☐	**et kompass** *(kohm-pahs)*	compass
☐	**en konge** *(kohng-eh)*	king
☐	**en konsert** *(kohn-sairt)*	concert

k

Nå close **boka og** write out both columns of this practice on **et stykke papir.** How did **du** do? *(stewk-eh) (pah-peer)* *(doo)*
a piece paper

(brah) *(dor-lee)* *(doo)* *(doo)*
Bra eller dårlig? Nå that **du** know these words, **du** can say almost anything **på norsk med**
well or badly you you

one basic formula: the "plug-in" formula.

(sex)
To demonstrate, let's take **seks** basic **og** practical verbs **og** see how the "plug-in" formula works.
six

(vairb-en-eh) *(doo)*
Write **verbene** in the blanks after **du har** practiced saying them out loud many times.
verbs the have

(oh) (snahk-eh) *(oh) (kohm-eh)*
å snakke _____ **å komme** _____
to speak to come

(oh) (lair-eh) *(oh) (beh-stil-eh)*
å lære _____ **å bestille** _____
to learn to order

(oh) (hyuhp-eh) *(oh) (het-eh)*
å kjøpe _____ **å hete** _____*hete, hete, hete*_____
to buy to be called

(doo)
Besides the familiar words already circled, can **du** find the above verbs in the puzzle below?

When **du** find them, write them in the blanks to the right.

P	H	L	M	E	S	N	D	Å	M	B
A	V	C	N	P	N	H	V	A	R	E
K	O	M	M	E	A	E	J	A	K	S
L	R	R	S	O	K	T	D	E	T	T
E	D	M	E	L	K	E	L	Ø	E	I
R	A	D	I	Æ	E	L	M	N	R	L
Æ	N	N	I	R	Y	B	D	Å	I	L
K	J	Ø	P	E	E	L	E	R	H	E

1. _____
2. _____
3. _____
4. _____
5. _____
6. _____

☐ **et konsulat** *(kohn-sue-laht)* . . . . consulate _____
☐ **kontaktlinser** *(kohn-tahkt-lin-sair)* . . . . contact lenses _____
☐ **korrekt** *(koh-rekt)* . . . . correct _____
☐ **krystall** *(krew-stahl)* . . . . crystal **k** _____
☐ **en kultur** *(kool-toor)* . . . . culture _____

Note: • With all these verbs, the first thing you do is drop the "**å**" *(oh)* preceding the verb. Now add an "**r**" to the basic verb form or stem. If the verb already ends in an "**r**" or an "**s**," no change is necessary.

• Notice **også** *(oh-soh)* that each verb has only one form. Easy? **Ja!** *(yah)*
  also   yes

jeg *(yay)* **han** *(hahn)* **hun** *(huhn)* **det/den** *(deh) (den)* it	**snakker** *(snahk-air)*	=	I *speak* _____ he/she *speaks*
	kjøper *(hyuhp-air)*	=	I *buy* _____ he/she *buys*
	lærer *(lair-air)*	=	I *learn* _____ he/she *learns*
	bestiller *(beh-stil-air)*	=	I *order* _____ he/she *orders*
	kommer *(kohm-air)*	=	I *come* _____ he/she *comes*
	heter *(het-air)*	=	I *am called* _____ he/she *is called*

De norske verbene er easy **og meget** useful. Try to use them all even if it takes a little extra
     (vairb-en-eh)   *(may-get)*
time to learn to say them correctly. **Og** remember - **nordmennene** *(noor-men-en-eh)* will be delighted that **du** *(doo)*
                                                        Norwegians the
have taken the time to learn their language.

Note: • Norwegian has two separate and very different ways of saying "you" whereas in English we only use one word.

• "**Du**" *(doo)* will be used throughout this book and will be appropriate for most
       you
situations. "**Du**" *(doo)* refers to one person in an informal sense.
              you

• "**De**" *(dee)* is a more formal form and is disappearing from use although you might still
       you
hear it used with older individuals or customers as a term of politeness. And yes, it sounds the same as the word for they – "**de**." The only difference is that it is written with a capital – **De** vs. **de.**
                                                                                   you   they

☐ **et lam** *(lahm)* .... lamb
☐ **et land** *(lahn)* .... land, country
☐ **en latter** *(laht-air)* .... laughter
  – en god latter forlenger livet .... a good laugh prolongs life
☐ **en legitimasjon** *(lay-gih-tih-mah-shohn)* ... legitimation, I.D. (card)

Again, notice that **vi,** *(vee)* **du,** *(doo)* **De** *(dee)* and **de** *(dee)* use the same verb form as **jeg,** *(yay)* **han,** *(hahn)* **hun,** *(huhn)* **det** *(deh)* and **den.** *(den)*
we / you / you / they / I / he / she / it / it

vi *(vee)*
du *(doo)*
De *(dee)*
de *(dee)*

- *(snahk-air)* **snakker** = we/you/they *speak* _____
- *(hyuhp-air)* **kjøper** = we/you/they *buy* _____
- *(lair-air)* **lærer** = we/you/they *learn* _____
- *(beh-stil-air)* **bestiller** = we/you/they *order* _____
- *(kohm-air)* **kommer** = we/you/they *come* _____
- *(het-air)* **heter** = we/you/they *are called* _____

Fill in the following blanks with the verb shown. Each time you write out the verb, be sure to say it aloud several times. **Det er meget viktig.**
(deh) (may-get) (vik-tee)
very / important

Her er seks more **verb.**
(hair) (sex) (vairb)
here / six / verbs

- *(oh) (leek-eh)* **å like** _____
  to / like
- *(oh) (blee)* **å bli** _____
  to / remain, stay
- *(boh)* **å bo** _____
  to / live, reside

- *(oh) (goh)* **å gå** _____
  to / go, walk
- *(hah)* **å ha** _____
  to / have
- *(treng-eh)* **å trenge** _____
  to / need

At the back of **boka, du** *(bohk-uh) (doo)* will find twelve pages of flash cards to help you learn these **nye** *(nee-eh)* new words. Cut them out; carry them in your briefcase, purse, pocket **eller** knapsack; **og** or review them whenever **du** *(doo)* have a free moment.

- ❏ **lenge** *(leng-eh)* .... long (time) _____
- ❏ **lik** *(leek)* .... alike, equal _____
- ❏ **en linje** *(lin-yeh)* .... line, phone extension _____
- ❏ **litt** *(lit)* .... a little, some _____
- ❏ **en litteratur** *(lit-air-ah-toor)* .... literature _____

Nå, it is your turn to practice what **du har** *(doo)* learned. Fill in the following blanks with the correct form of the verb. Each time **du** *(doo)* write out the sentence, be sure to say it aloud.

å snakke *(oh) (snahk-eh)*
to speak

Jeg snakker norsk.

Jeg _____ norsk. *(norshk)*
Du _____ engelsk. *(eng-elsk)*
Han / Hun / Det / Den _____ spansk. *(spahnsk)* Spanish
Vi _____ dansk. *(dahnsk)* Danish
De _snakker/_____ japansk. *(yah-pahnsk)* Japanese

å komme *(oh) (kohm-eh)*
to come

Jeg _kommer/_____ fra Amerika. *(frah)* from
Du _____ fra Norge. *(nor-geh)*
Han / Hun / Det / Den _____ fra Kanada. *(kah-nah-dah)*
Vi _____ fra Danmark. *(dahn-mark)*
De _____ fra Sverige. *(svay-ree-eh)*

å lære *(lair-eh)*
to learn

Jeg _____ norsk. *(norshk)*
Du _____ dansk. *(dahnsk)* Danish
Han / Hun / Det / Den _____ spansk. *(spahnsk)* Spanish
Vi _____ fransk. *(frahnsk)* French
De _____ engelsk.

å bestille *(beh-stil-eh)*
to order

Jeg _____ et glass vann. *(glahs) (vahn)*
Du _bestiller/_____ et glass vin. *(veen)*
Han / Hun / Det / Den _____ en kopp te. *(kohp) (tay)*
Vi _____ et glass melk.
De _____ en kopp kaffe. *(kahf-eh)*

å kjøpe *(hyuhp-eh)*
to buy

Jeg _____ ei bok. *(ay) (bohk)*
Du _____ salaten.
Han / Hun / Det / Den _____ en bil. *(beel)*
Vi _kjøper/_____ ei klokke. *(klohk-eh)*
De _____ åtte brevkort. *(oh-teh) (brave-koort)* postcards

å hete *(het-eh)*
to be called

Jeg heter Astrid.

Jeg _____ Helgerud. *(hel-guh-rood)*
Du _____ Bakke. *(bahk-eh)*
Han / Hun / Det / Den _____ Melhus. *(mel-hoos)*
Vi _heter/_____ Lønmo. *(luhn-moh)*
De _____ Pettersen. *(pet-tair-sen)*

❐ **logisk** *(loh-gisk)*	....	logical
❐ **lokal** *(loh-kahl)*	....	local
❐ **et losji** *(loh-shee)*	....	lodging
❐ **en luksus** *(luke-soos)*	....	luxury
❐ **en lunsj** *(luhnsh)*	....	lunch

l

Now take a break, walk around the room, take a deep breath **og** do the next **seks** verbs.

(oh) (leek-eh)
å like
to like

Jeg _____ vin. *(veen)*

Du **liker/** _____ melk.

Han / Hun / Det / Den _____ øl. *(uhl) beer*

Vi _____ te. *(tay)*

De _____ kaffe. *(kahf-eh)*

(oh) (goh)
å gå
to go, walk

Jeg _____ i parken. *(park-en)* in park the

Du **går/** _____ i parken.

Han / Hun / Det / Den _____ inn i hotellet. *(in) (ee) (hoh-tel-eh)* into

Vi _____ inn i banken. *(ee) (bahnk-en)*

De _____ inn i huset. *(hoos-eh)*

(blee)
å bli
to remain, stay

Jeg _____ fem dager til. *(dahg-air) (til)* more

Du **blir/** _____ tre dager til.

Han / Hun / Det / Den _____ i Norge.

Vi _____ i Europa. *(oy-roh-puh)*

De _____ åtte dager til. *(oh-teh)*

(hah)
å ha
to have

Jeg _____ fem kroner. *(krohn-air)*

Du _____ ti kroner. *(tee)*

Han / Hun / Det / Den _____ seks kroner. *(sex)*

Vi _____ sju kroner. *(shoe)*

De **har/** _____ hundre kroner. *(huhn-dreh)*

(boh)
å bo
to live, reside

Jeg **bor/** _____ i Norge. *(nor-geh)*

Du _____ i Amerika. *(ah-mair-ih-kuh)*

Han / Hun / Det / Den _____ i Spania. *(spah-nee-ah)*

Vi _____ i Europa. *(oy-roh-puh)*

De _____ i Japan. *(yah-pahn)*

(treng-eh)
å trenge
to need

Jeg **trenger/** _____ et rom. *(rohm)*

Du _____ et hotellrom. *(hoh-tel-rohm)*

Han / Hun / Det / Den _____ ei bok. *(ay) (bohk)*

Vi _____ et glass vann. *(glahs) (vahn)* water

De _____ en kopp te. *(kohp)* cup

- ❏ **en makrell** *(mah-krel)* . . . . mackerel
- ❏ **margarin** *(mar-gah-reen)* . . . . margarine
- ❏ **et marked** *(mar-ked)* . . . . market
- ❏ **marmelade** *(mar-mel-ah-deh)* . . . . marmalade
- ❏ **en maskin** *(mah-sheen)* . . . . machine

m

Ja, det er hard to get used to all those **nye** *(nee-eh)* **ordene.** Just keep practicing **og** before **du** *(doo)* know it, **du** will be using them naturally. **Nå er** a perfect time to turn to the back of **boka,** *(bohk-uh)* clip out your **verb** *(vairb)* flash cards **og** start flashing. Don't skip over your free **ord** either. Check them off in the box provided as **du lærer** *(lair-air)* each one. See if **du** can fill in the blanks below. **De riktige svarene** *(dee) (rik-tee-eh) (svar-en-eh)* **er** *(ar)* at the bottom of **sida.** *(seed-uh)*

1. _____ (I speak Norwegian.)
2. _____ (We learn Norwegian.)
3. _____ (She needs ten kroner.)
4. _____ (He comes from Canada.)
5. _____ (They live in Norway.)
6. _____ (You buy a book.)

In the following Steps, **du** *(doo)* will be introduced to more verbs **og du** should drill them in exactly the same way as **du** did in this section. Look up **de nye ordene** *(dee) (nee-eh) (oor-en-eh)* in your **ordbok** *(oor-bohk)* **og** make up your own sentences. Try out your **nye ord** *(nee-eh)* for that's how you make them yours to use on your holiday. Remember, the more **du** practice **nå,** the more enjoyable your trip will be.

Lykke til! *(loo-keh) (til)*
good luck

SVAR

1. Jeg snakker norsk.
2. Vi lærer norsk.
3. Hun trenger ti kroner.
4. Han kommer fra Kanada.
5. De bor i Norge.
6. Du kjøper ei bok.

13 Hvor mange er klokka?
(vor) (mahng-eh) (ar) (klohk-uh)
what time is it

Du know **hvordan** *(vor-dahn)* how to tell **dagene** *(dahg-en-eh)* days the **i uke** *(ook-en)* week the **og månedene** *(mohn-den-eh)* months the **i året,** *(or-eh)* year the so now let's learn to tell time.

As a traveler, **du** need to be able to tell time in order to make **reservasjoner,** *(res-air-vah-shohn-air)* reservations appointments **og** to catch **tog** *(tohg)* trains **og buss.** *(boos)* **Her** *(hair)* here **er** *(ar)* are the "basics."

What time is it?	=	**Hvor mange er klokka?** *(vor) (mahng-eh) (ar) (klohk-uh)* _____
	=	**Hvor mye er klokka?** *(mee-eh)* _____
hour	=	**time** *(teem-eh)* _____
before	=	**på** *(poh)* _____
after	=	**over** *(oh-vair)* _____
half	=	**halv** *(hahl)* _____
a quarter	=	**et kvarter** *(kvart-air)* _____
a quarter to	=	**kvart på** *(poh)* _____
a quarter after	=	**kvart over** *(oh-vair)* _____

Nå quiz yourself. Fill in the missing letters below.

half = h a _ _

after = _ v e r

a quarter to = k v _ _ t ✕ p _

hour = _ i m e

a quarter = _ t ✕ k v _ t _ _

and finally   when = n _ r

- ❏ **en medisin** *(med-ih-seen)* .... medicine _____
- ❏ **mest** *(mest)* .... most _____
- ❏ **en meter** *(may-tair)* .... meter   **m** _____
- ❏ **midnatt** *(mid-naht)* .... midnight _____
- ❏ **midtsommer** *(mid-sohm-air)* .... Midsummer (Day) _____

Nå, *(vor-dahn)* **hvordan er** these **ordene** used? Study **eksemplene** *(ek-sem-plen-eh)* below. When **du** *(doo)* think it through, it really is not too difficult. Just notice that the pattern changes after the halfway mark. Notice that the phrase "o'clock" is not used in Norwegian.

Den *(den)* **er** *(ar)* **fem.** — 5:00 — Den er fem. Den er fem.
it   is   five o'clock

Den er ti over *(oh-vair)* **fem.** — 5:10 — _____

Den er kvart *(kvart)* **over** *(oh-vair)* **fem.** — 5:15 — _____
a quarter

Den er tjue *(hyoo-eh)* **over** *(oh-vair)* **fem.** — 5:20 — _____

Den er halv *(hahl)* **seks.** *(sex)* — 5:30 — _____
half (of) six

Den er tjue *(hyoo-eh)* **på** *(poh)* **seks.** *(sex)* — 5:40 — _____
before

Den er kvart *(kvart)* **på seks.** — 5:45 — _____

Den er ti *(tee)* **på seks.** — 5:50 — _____

Den er seks. — 6:00 — _____

See how **viktig** *(vik-tee)* it is to learn **numrene**? *(num-ren-eh)* Answer the following **spørsmål** *(spursh-mohl)* based on **klokkene** below. **Hva er klokka?** *(klohk-uh)*
numbers the   questions   clocks the

1. 8:00 _____
2. 7:15 _____
3. 4:30 _____
4. 9:20 _____

SVAR

1. Den er åtte.
2. Den er kvart over sju.
3. Den er halv fem.
4. Den er tjue over ni.

When **du** answer a **"Når?"** *(nor)* question, say **"klokka"** before **du** give the **tid**. *(tee)*
when time

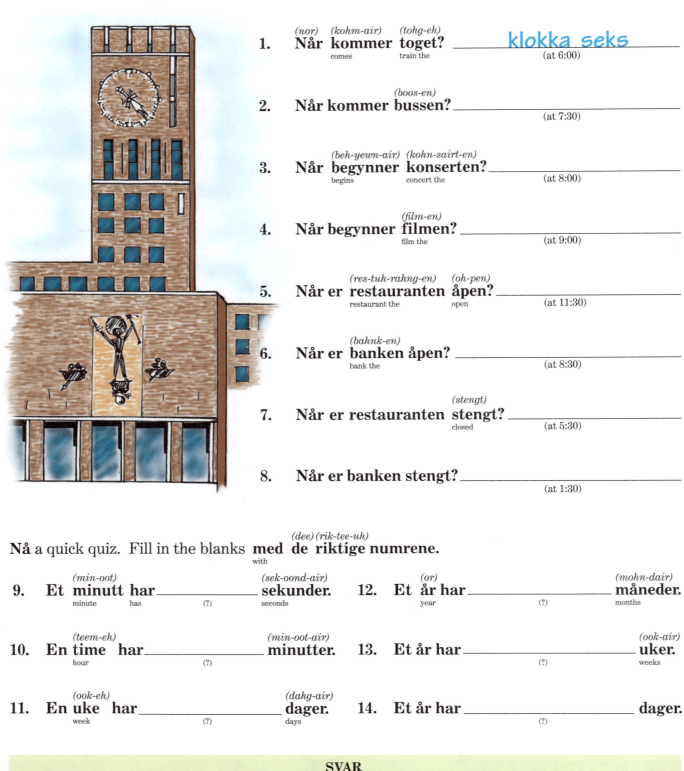

1. **Når kommer toget?** _klokka seks_
   (nor) (kohm-air) (tohg-eh)
   comes train the   (at 6:00)

2. **Når kommer bussen?** _____
   (boos-en)   (at 7:30)

3. **Når begynner konserten?** _____
   (beh-yewn-air) (kohn-sairt-en)
   begins concert the   (at 8:00)

4. **Når begynner filmen?** _____
   (film-en)
   film the   (at 9:00)

5. **Når er restauranten åpen?** _____
   (res-tuh-rahng-en) (oh-pen)
   restaurant the open   (at 11:30)

6. **Når er banken åpen?** _____
   (bahnk-en)
   bank the   (at 8:30)

7. **Når er restauranten stengt?** _____
   (stengt)
   closed   (at 5:30)

8. **Når er banken stengt?** _____
                                              (at 1:30)

Nå a quick quiz. Fill in the blanks **med de riktige numrene**.
(dee)(rik-tee-uh)
with

9. **Et minutt har** _____ **sekunder.**
   (min-oot) *(sek-oond-air)*
   minute has (?) seconds

12. **Et år har** _____ **måneder.**
    (or) *(mohn-dair)*
    year (?) months

10. **En time har** _____ **minutter.**
    (teem-eh) *(min-oot-air)*
    hour (?)

13. **Et år har** _____ **uker.**
    (ook-air)
    (?) weeks

11. **En uke har** _____ **dager.**
    (ook-eh) *(dahg-air)*
    week (?) days

14. **Et år har** _____ **dager.**
    (?)

SVAR

1. klokka seks
2. klokka halv åtte
3. klokka åtte
4. klokka ni
5. klokka halv tolv
6. klokka halv ni
7. klokka halv seks
8. klokka halv to
9. seksti
10. seksti
11. sju
12. tolv
13. femtito
14. tre hundre og sekstifem

(doo)
Do **du** remember your greetings from earlier? It is a good time to review them as they will always be **meget** *(may-get)* **viktige** *(vik-tee-eh)*.
very important

(klohk-uh) *(ohm)* *(mor-en-en)* *(see-air)* *(go)* *(mor-en)* *(froo)*
Klokka åtte om morgenen sier en, "**God morgen, fru Arnestad.**"
at   in morning the   says   one good morning Mrs.

(vah) *(see-air)*
Hva sier en? _____ God morgen, fru Arnestad. _____
what

(et-tair-mid-ahg-en) *(see-air)* *(go)* *(dahg)* *(hair)*
Klokka ett om ettermiddagen sier en, "**God dag, herr Christensen.**"
one   afternoon the   Mr.

(vah) *(see-air)*
Hva sier en? _____
what

(see-air) *(go)* *(fruhk-en)* *(byoh-nes)*
Klokka åtte om kvelden sier en, "**God kveld, frøken Bjånes.**"
evening the   Miss

Hva sier en? _____
what

(go) *(naht)*
Klokka ti om kvelden sier en, "**God natt.**"
night

Hva sier en? _____

Du har probably already noticed that plurals are formed in a variety of ways.

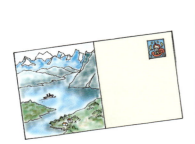
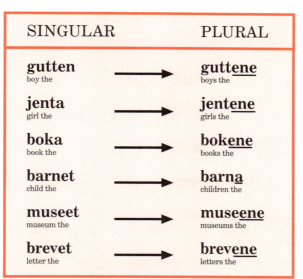
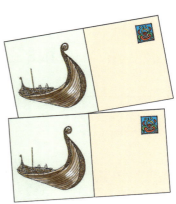

Know that **norske** words can change their ending in the plural so always listen for the core of the word.

- ❐ **mild** *(mil)*.................... mild
- ❐ **million** *(mil-yohn)*............. million
- ❐ **moderne** *(moh-dair-neh)*......... modern   **m**
- ❐ **et museum** *(moo-say-oom)*........ museum
- ❐ **musikk** *(moo-seek)*.............. music

Her er de nye verbene for Step 13.
(nee-eh) *(vairb-en-eh)*
new verbs

(oh) (spees-eh)
å spise
to eat

(oh) (drik-eh)
å drikke
to drink

(oh) (spees-eh)
å spise
to eat

(oh) (drik-eh)
å drikke
to drink

Jeg _____ **suppen.** *(suhp-en)* soup the

Du **spiser/** _____ **biff.** steak

Han / Hun / Det / Den _____ **mye.** *(mee-eh)* a lot

Vi _____ **ingenting.** *(ing-en-ting)* nothing

De _____ **fisken.** fish the

Jeg _____ **melken.** *(melk-en)* milk the

Du **drikker/** _____ **hvitvin.** *(veet-veen)* white wine

Han / Hun / Det / Den _____ **ølet.** *(uhl-eh)* beer

Vi _____ **et glass vann.** *(glahs) (vahn)* water

De _____ **teen.** *(tay-en)* tea the

Be sure to try the **smørbrød** *(smur-bruh)* **i Norge.** *(ee)* **Smørbrød** *(smur-bruh)* actually means "butter and bread" which open-faced sandwiches

does not do justice to these elaborate open-faced sandwiches. **Det er** *(deh) (ar)* so many types of

smørbrød *(smur-bruh)* that restaurants frequently have a separate **smørbrød** *(smur-bruh)* menu. Your **smørbrød** *(smur-bruh)* may be

topped with almost anything ranging from eggs to smoked salmon. **Er du** *(doo)* ready **å spise?** *(oh) (spees-eh)* to eat

❏ **naken** *(nah-ken)*	naked	
❏ **en nasjon** *(nah-shohn)*	nation	**n**
❏ **nasjonal** *(nah-shohn-ahl)*	national	
❏ **en natt** *(naht)*	night	
❏ **en natur** *(nah-toor)*	nature	

(doo) (har)
Du har learned a lot of material in the last few steps **og** that means it is time to quiz yourself.
Don't panic, this is just for you **og** no one else needs to know how **du** did. Remember, this is a chance to review, find out what **du** remember **og** what **du** need to spend more time on. After **du har** finished, check your **svar** in the glossary at the back of this **bok** *(bohk)*. Circle the correct answers.

have (under Du har); *book* (under bok)

kaffe	tea	coffee	**familie**	seven	family
ja	yes	no	**barn**	child	grandfather
tante	aunt	uncle	**melk**	butter	**milk** *(circled)*
eller	and	or	**salt**	pepper	salt
lære	to drink	to learn	**over**	under	over
natt	morning	night	**mann**	man	doctor
fredag	Friday	Tuesday	**juni**	June	July
snakke	to live	to speak	**kjøkken**	kitchen	religions
vinter	summer	winter	**jeg har**	I would like	I have
penger	money	page	**kjøpe**	to order	to buy
ti	nine	ten	**i går**	yesterday	tomorrow
mye	a lot	bread	**god**	good	yellow

(vor-dahn) *(doo) (deh)*
Hvordan har du det? <u>What time is it?</u> <u>How are you?</u> Well, how are you after this quiz?

❐ **et navn** *(nahvn)* .... name
❐ **neste** *(nest-eh)* .... next
❐ **en nevø** *(nev-uh)* .... nephew   **n**
❐ **en niese** *(nee-ay-seh)* .... niece
❐ **nær** *(nair)* .... near

14 Nord - Sør, Øst - Vest
(noor) *(sur)* *(ust)* *(vest)*
north — south — east — west

If **du** are looking at **et** *(kart)* **kart og du** see the following **ord**, it should *(ick-eh)* **ikke** be too difficult to figure out **hva de** mean. Take an educated guess.
(vah) (dee) — what they — *(kart)* map — *(ick-eh)* not

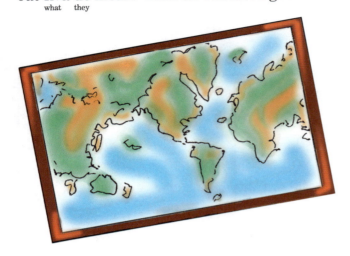

(noor-ah-mair-ih-kuh) **Nord-Amerika**

(sur-ah-mair-ih-kuh) **Sør-Amerika**

(noor-shuh-en) **Nordsjøen** sea

(ust-air-shuh-en) **Østersjøen** sea

(noor-pohl-en) **Nordpolen**

(sur-pohl-en) **Sørpolen**

(sur-ah-frih-kuh) **Sør-Afrika**

(vest-in-dee-ah) **Vestindia**

De norske ordene for "north," "south," "east," **og** "west" **er** easy to recognize due to their similarity to **engelsk**. These **ordene er meget** *(vik-tee-eh)* **viktige**. Learn them **i dag**!
(ee) (dahg) — are

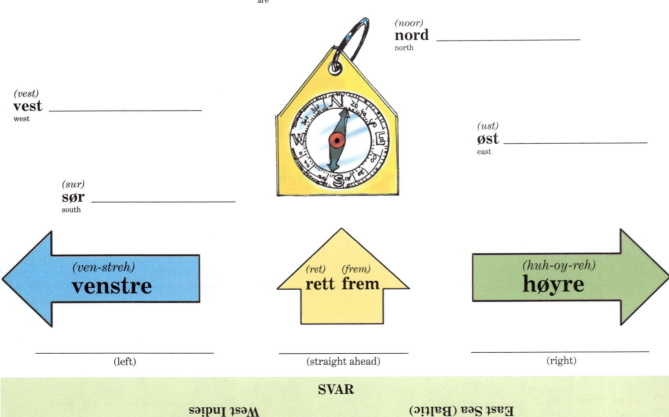

(noor) **nord** _____ north

(vest) **vest** _____ west

(ust) **øst** _____ east

(sur) **sør** _____ south

(ven-streh) **venstre** _____ (left)

(ret) (frem) **rett frem** _____ (straight ahead)

(huh-oy-reh) **høyre** _____ (right)

SVAR

North America — North Pole
South America — South Pole
North Sea — South Africa
East Sea (Baltic) — West Indies

These **ordene** can go a long way. Say them aloud each time you write them in the blanks below.

(tahk)
takk _____
please / thank you

(vair) (shoh) (snil)
vær så snil _____
please, be so kind

(un-shool)
unnskyld _____
excuse me

(vair) (shoh) (go)
vær så god _____
you're welcome / please, here you are / please go ahead

        (too) (too-pisk-eh) (sahm-tahl-air)
Her er to typiske samtaler for someone who is trying to find something. Write them out in
          two typical   conversations

the blanks below.

(hyeer-sten)   *(un-shool)*
Kirsten: **Unnskyld. Hvor er Grand Hotell?**

           Unnskyld. Hvor er Grand Hotell?

(knoot)   *(goh) (too) (gaht-air) (vee-dair-eh) (so) (til) (ven-streh) (so)*
Knut: **Gå to gater videre, så til venstre, og så rett frem.**
          go streets further then to left   then

                                 (ven-streh)
        Grand Hotell er til venstre.

(byurn)   *(folk-eh-moo-say-eh)*
Bjørn: **Unnskyld. Hvor er Folkemuseet?**
                                    folk art museum

(ah-stree)   *(goh)*   *(huh-oy-reh)*   *(goh) (so)*
Astrid: **Gå til høyre her; gå så rett frem fem meter.**
          go to

        (folk-eh-moo-say-eh)   *(huh-oy-reh)*
        Folkemuseet er til høyre.

❏ **ofte** *(ohf-teh)* .... often _____
❏ **en opera** *(oh-pair-ah)* .... opera _____
❏ **en operasjon** *(oh-pair-ah-shohn)* .... operation, surgery **O** _____
❏ **opp** *(ohp)* .... up _____
❏ **en optiker** *(ohp-tik-air)* .... optician _____

Are **du** lost? There is no need to be lost if **du har** learned the basic direction **ordene**. Do not try to memorize these *(sahm-tahl-en-eh)* **samtalene** (conversations) because **du** will never be looking for precisely these places. **En** (one) **dag, du** might need to ask for directions to "*(rohd-hoos-eh)* **Rådhuset**" (City Hall the) **eller** "*(vee-king-sheep-moo-say-eh)* **Vikingskipmuseet**" (Viking Ship Museum the) **eller** "*(sahs)* **SAS-hotellet**." Learn the key direction **ordene og** be sure **du** can find your destination. **Du** may want to buy a guidebook to start planning which places **du** would like to visit. Practice asking directions to these special places. **Hva** (what) if the person responding to your *(spursh-mohl)* **spørsmål** answers too quickly **for** you to understand the entire reply? Practice saying,

> *(un-shool)* **Unnskyld.** *(for-shtor)* **Jeg forstår** *(ick-eh)* **ikke.** *(see)* **Si** *(deh)* **det en** *(gahng)* **gang** *(til)* **til,** *(tahk)* **takk.**
> (understand) (not) (say) (one) (time) (more)

Nå, say it again **og** then write it out below.

_____
(Excuse me. I do not understand. Please say it again / repeat it, thank you.)

(yah) **Ja, det er** difficult at first but don't give up! *(nor)* **Når** (when) the directions **er** repeated, **du** will be able to understand if **du har** learned the key **ordene**. Let's review by writing them in the blanks below.

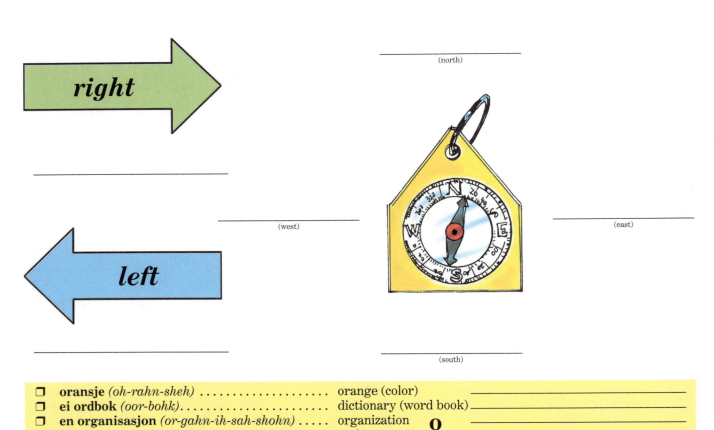

☐ **oransje** *(oh-rahn-sheh)* .... orange (color)	
☐ **ei ordbok** *(oor-bohk)* .... dictionary (word book)	
☐ **en organisasjon** *(or-gahn-ih-sah-shohn)* ..... organization	**o**
☐ **et orkester** *(or-kest-air)* .... orchestra	
☐ **en parfyme** *(par-few-meh)* .... perfume	**p**

Her er **fire** **nye** verb.
(fear-eh) *(nee-eh)*
new

å si *(oh) (see)* — to say

å selge *(sel-geh)* — to sell

å forstå *(oh) (for-shtoh)* — to understand

å si . . . en gang til *(see) (gahng) (til)* — to repeat (say one more time)

As always, say each sentence out loud. Say each **og** every **ord** carefully, pronouncing each **norsk** sound as well as **du** can.

å si *(see)*
to say

Jeg _sier/_____ "god morgen." *(go) (mor-en)*
Du _____ "god dag." *(dahg)*
Han / Hun / Det / Den _____ "nei." *(nay)* no
Vi _sier/_____ "ja."
De _____ ingenting. *(ing-en-ting)* nothing

å forstå *(for-shtoh)*
to understand

Jeg _forstår/_____ norsk. *(norshk)*
Du _____ fransk. *(frahnsk)*
Han / Hun / Det / Den _____ spansk. *(spahnsk)*
Vi _____ engelsk. *(eng-elsk)*
De _____ ikke. *(ick-eh)* not

å selge *(sel-geh)*
to sell

Jeg _____ frimerker. *(free-mair-kair)*
Du _____ brevkort. *(brave-koort)*
Han / Hun / Det / Den _____ blomster. *(blohm-stair)*
Vi _____ billetter. *(bil-let-air)* tickets
De _selger/_____ fisk. fish

å si .. en gang til *(see) (gahng) (til)*
to repeat

Hva? Hva? Hva?

Jeg __sier__ ordene _en gang til_.
Du _____ svarene _____.
Han / Hun / Det / Den _____ ingenting _____. *(ing-en-ting)*
Vi _____ "god morgen" _____. *(go) (mor-en)*
De _____ navnene _____. *(nahv-nen-eh)*

- ❏ **en parkeringsplass** *(par-kair-ings-plahs)* .... parking lot/space
- ❏ **en passasjer** *(pah-sah-share)* .... passenger
- ❏ **perfekt** *(pair-fekt)* .... perfect
- ❏ **personlig** *(pair-shohn-lee)* .... personally, personal
- ❏ **en pipe** *(pee-peh)* .... pipe

p

55

15   Ovenpå - Nede
                   (oh-ven-poh)   *(ned-eh)*
                   upstairs   downstairs

(lair-air) *(mayr)* *(hair)* *(ar)* *(hoos)* *(ee)* *(ee)* *(sohv-eh-rohm)* *(rohm-eh)*
Nå lærer du mer. Her er et hus i Norge. Gå inn i your **soverom og** look around **rommet.**
   learn   more   house   into   bedroom   room the

(nahv-nen-eh) *(sohv-eh-rohm-eh)* *(vee)*
Let's learn **navnene** of **tingene på soverommet,** just like **vi** learned the various parts of **huset.**
         names the   things the   we

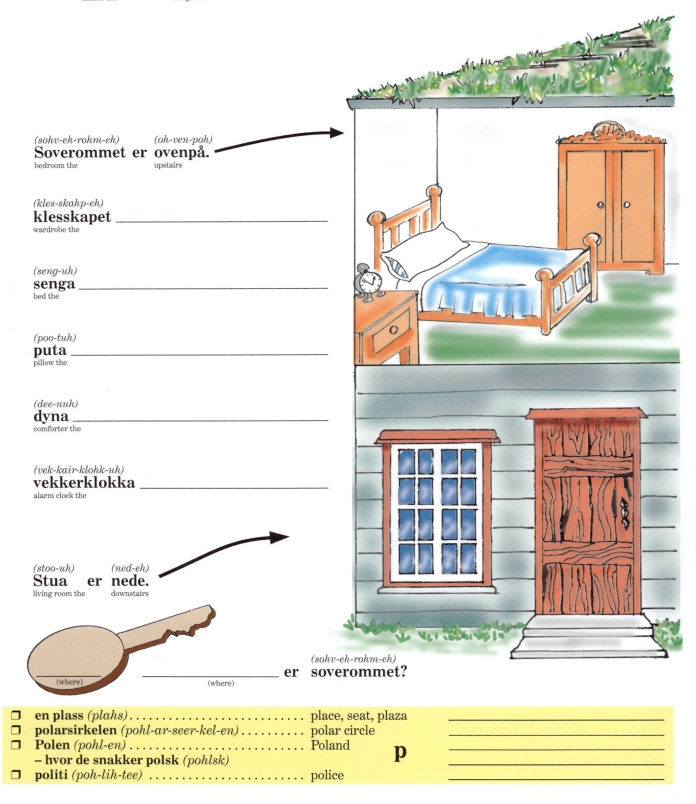

(sohv-eh-rohm-eh) *(oh-ven-poh)*
Soverommet er ovenpå.
bedroom the   upstairs

(kles-skahp-eh)
klesskapet _____
wardrobe the

(seng-uh)
senga _____
bed the

(poo-tuh)
puta _____
pillow the

(dee-nuh)
dyna _____
comforter the

(vek-kair-klohk-uh)
vekkerklokka _____
alarm clock the

(stoo-uh) *(ned-eh)*
Stua er nede.
living room the   downstairs

_____ (where)   _____ **er soverommet?**
                    (where)   *(sohv-eh-rohm-eh)*

❏ **en plass** *(plahs)* .... place, seat, plaza
❏ **polarsirkelen** *(pohl-ar-seer-kel-en)* .... polar circle
❏ **Polen** *(pohl-en)* .... Poland   **p**
    – **hvor de snakker polsk** *(pohlsk)*
❏ **politi** *(poh-lih-tee)* .... police

Nå, remove **de** *(dee)* **neste** *(nest-eh)* **fem** stickers **og** label these **tingene** in your **bad** *(bahd)*. Let's move **inn i** *(ee)*
the next things into
badet *(bahd-eh)* **og** do the same **ting**. Remember, **badet** *(bahd-eh)* means a room to bathe in. If **du er på en**
bathroom
restaurant og du trenger *(treng-air)* to use the lavatory, **du** want to ask for **toalettet** *(toh-ah-let-eh)* *not* for **badet** *(bahd-eh)*.
need

Restrooms may be marked with pictures **eller** simply with the letters <u>**D**</u> **eller** <u>**H**</u>.
or

Don't confuse them!

<u>**D**</u> = **Damer** *(dah-mair)*
ladies' (restroom)

<u>**H**</u> = **Herrer** *(hair-air)*
men's (restroom)

Badet *(bahd-eh)* **er også** *(oh-soh)* **ovenpå** *(oh-ven-poh)*.
bathroom the also

speilet *(spail-eh)* _____
mirror the

vasken *(vahsk-en)* _____
sink the

håndklærne *(hohn-klair-neh)* _____
towels the

toalettet *(toh-ah-let-eh)* _____
toilet the

dusjen *(doosh-en)* _____
shower the

Kontoret *(kohn-tor-eh)* **er også** *(oh-soh)* **nede** *(ned-eh)*.
study the also downstairs

☐ **Portugal** *(por-too-gahl)* .... Portugal
  – **hvor de snakker portugisisk** *(por-too-gee-sisk)*
☐ **praktisk** *(prahk-tisk)* .... practical
☐ **en pris** *(prees)* .... price, cost
☐ **en prosent** *(proh-sent)* .... percent

p

Do not forget to remove the next group of stickers **og** label these things in your **hus** *(hoos)*. Okay, it is time to review. Here's a quick quiz to see what you remember.

men's (restroom)	**nede**
I understand	*(hair-air)* **herrer**
downstairs	*(tahk)* **takk**
thank you	**jeg forstår**
towels	*(bahd)* **bad**
upstairs	**rett frem**
bathroom	*(dah-mair)* **damer**
lavatory/restroom	*(hohn-klair-neh)* **håndklærne**
straight ahead	**ovenpå**
women's (restroom)	*(toh-ah-let-eh)* **toalettet**

❏ **en radio** *(rah-dee-oh)* . . . . radio
❏ **en resepsjon** *(ray-sep-shohn)* . . . . reception, lobby
❏ **en reservasjon** *(res-air-vah-shohn)* . . . . reservation, booking
❏ **ringer** *(ring-air)* . . . . ring, call up   **r**
❏ **romantisk** *(roh-mahn-tisk)* . . . . romantic

(nest-eh) *(kohn-tor-eh)* *(boor-eh)* *(skreev-eh-boor-eh)*
Neste stop – **kontoret,** specifically **bordet** eller **skrivebordet** på kontoret. **Hva er** på **bordet?**
next   table   desk   what   on

(ting-en-eh) *(fin-air)* *(skreev-eh-boor-eh)* *(hoos-uh)*
Let's identify **tingene** which one normally **finner på** **skrivebordet** or strewn about **i huset.**
                things the   finds

(fyairn-seen)
et fjernsyn
television

(blee-ahnt)
en blyant
pencil

(pen)
en penn
pen

(dah-tah)
en data
computer

(pah-peer)
et papir
paper

(pah-peer-koorv)
en papirkurv
wastebasket

(ah-vees)
ei avis
newspaper

(teed-skrift)
et tidsskrift
magazine

(bohk)
ei bok
book

(bril-air)
briller
eyeglasses

ei avis

❏ **romersk-katolsk** *(roh-mairshk-kah-tohlsk)* ..	Roman Catholic	
❏ **en ruin** *(roo-een)*	ruin	
❏ **rund** *(roon)*	round **r**	
❏ **rushtid** *(roosh-tee)*	rush hour	
❏ **en rute** *(roo-teh)*	route, schedule	

Don't forget these essentials!

(brave)
et brev
letter

(free-mair-keh)
et frimerke
stamp

(brave-koort)
et brevkort
postcard

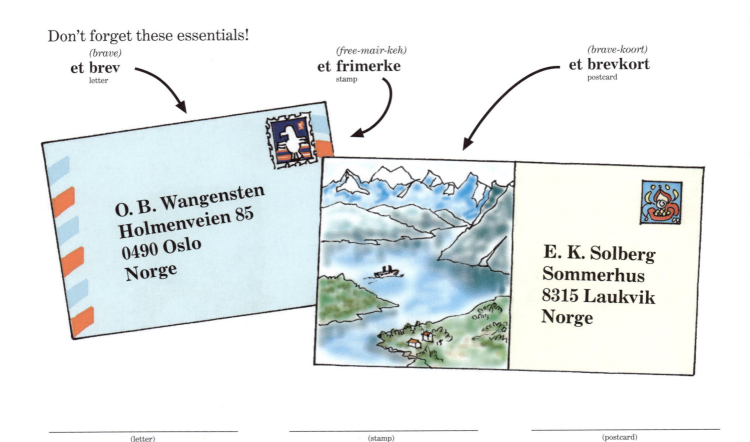

_____   _____   _____
(letter)   (stamp)   (postcard)

The words *(ick-eh)* "**ikke**," *(yah)* "**ja**" **og** *(yoh)* "**jo**" **er meget** useful **på norsk**.

(yay)
Jeg snakker bra norsk.
I   speak   well Norwegian

Jeg snakker ikke bra norsk.
I   don't speak

Vi finner hotellet.
we find

Vi finner ikke hotellet.
don't find

Du snakker dansk.
you speak   Danish

Du snakker ikke dansk.
don't speak

Han forstår engelsk.
he   understands

Han forstår ikke engelsk.

Both "*(yah)* **ja**" **og** "*(yoh)* **jo**" mean "yes" although "**ja**" *(ar)* **er** more common. "*(yoh)* **Jo**" **er** a fun **ord** which **er også** used to add emphasis when speaking. **Nordmenn** will say, "**Det** *(deh)* **var jo** *(yoh)* **fint!**" meaning "That was all right, *of course.*" **Nå,** do you know what this means? **Jeg snakker jo engelsk!** (I speak English *of course!*) **Du** do, don't **du**?

❐ **Russland** *(roos-lahn)* .... Russia
 – hvor de snakker russisk *(roos-isk)*
❐ **en ryggsekk** *(roog-sek)* .... rucksack   **r**
❐ **rå** *(roh)* .... raw, rare
❐ **råtten** *(roh-ten)* .... rotten, moldy

Simple, isn't it? **Nå,** after you fill in the blanks below, go back a second time and negate all these sentences by adding "**ikke**" after each **verb**. Don't get discouraged! Just look at how much **du har** already learned **og** think ahead to wonderful food, beautiful scenery **og** new adventures.

(oh) (say)
å se
to see

(oh) (sen-eh)
å sende
to send

(sohv-eh)
å sove
to sleep

(fin-eh)
å finne
to find

(oh) (say)
å se
to see

Jeg _ser/_ _____ *(torg-eh)* **torget.**
market the
Du _____ *(rohd-hoos-eh)* **Rådhuset.**
City Hall
Han / Hun / Det / Den _____ *(vee-king-sheep-moo-say-eh)* **Vikingskipmuseet.**
Viking Ship Museum
Vi _____ *(fyord-en)* **fjorden.**
De _____ **hotellet.**

(sen-eh)
å sende
to send

Jeg _____ et brev.
Du _sender/_ _____ et brevkort.
Han / Hun / Det / Den _____ *(bohk-uh)* **boka.**
Vi _____ tre brev.
De _____ to brevkort.

(sohv-eh)
å sove
to sleep

Jeg _____ *(hoh-tel-eh)* **på hotellet.**
Du _____ *(sohv-eh-rohm-eh)* **på soverommet.**
Han / Hun / Det / Den _____ *(brah)* **bra.**
well
Vi _sover/_ _____ *(meh)* *(dee-neh)* **med ei dyne.**
with comforter
De _____ *(oot-en)* *(poo-teh)* **uten ei pute.**
without pillow

(oh) (fin-eh)
å finne
to find

Jeg _____ *(rohd-hoos-eh)* **Rådhuset.**
Du _finner/_ _____ *(bril-air)* **briller.**
Han / Hun / Det / Den _____ *(ah-vees-uh)* **avisa.**
newspaper the
Vi _____ *(gaht-uh)* **gata.**
street the
De _____ *(moo-say-eh)* **museet.**
museum the

☐	**en sankt** *(sahngt)*	saint
☐	**en sardin** *(sar-deen)*	sardine
☐	**en saus** *(souse)*	sauce
☐	**en seiler** *(sail-air)*	yachtsman
☐	**en seilbåt** *(sail-boht)*	sailboat

S

Before **du** proceed **med** the **neste** step, **vær** *(vair)* **så** *(shoh)* **snill** *(snil)*, identify **tingene** **nedenfor** *(ned-en-for)*.
please below

(ah-vees)
ei avis

(pah-peer-koorv)
en papirkurv

et brevkort

ei bok

(free-mair-keh)
et frimerke

(pah-peer)
et papir

en penn

(blee-ahnt)
en blyant

et brev

briller

et tidsskrift

(fyairn-seen)
et fjernsyn

(dah-tah)
en data

☐ **et sentrum** *(sent-room)* .... city center
☐ **en sigar** *(see-gar)* .... cigar
☐ **en sigarett** *(see-gah-ret)* .... cigarette   **S**
☐ **en ski** *(shee)* .... ski
  – gå på ski *(goh)(poh)(shee)* .... to go skiing

16   *(post-en)* **Posten**
mail the

Du know **nå hvordan** *(how)* to count, **hvordan** *(how)* to ask **spørsmål** *(spursh-mohl)*, **hvordan** to use **verb med** the "plug-in" formula **og hvordan** to describe something, be it the location of **et hotell eller farger** *(farg-air)* of **et hus** *(hoos)*.
house

Let's take the basics that **du har** learned **og** expand them in special areas that will be most helpful in your travels. **Hva** *(vah)* does everyone do on a holiday? Send **brevkort**, postcards of course! Let's learn exactly **hvordan det** *(deh)* **norske postkontoret** *(post-kohn-tor-eh)* works.
the   post office the

(post-en) **posten**

(til) **til Italia**
to

(eng-lahn) **til England**

(dahn-mark) **til Danmark**

(ah-mair-ih-kuh) **til Amerika**

Postkontoret *(post-kohn-tor-eh)* **er hvor du kjøper frimerker** *(hyuhp-air) (free-mair-kair)*, **sender brev og brevkort. Postkontoret** *(post-kohn-tor-eh)* **har åpent** *(oh-pent)* **alle ukedager** *(ook-eh-dahg-air)* **fra klokka 8.00 til klokka 17.00. På lørdag** *(lur-dahg)* **har det åpent fra klokka**
open   weekdays   Saturday

8.00 til klokka 13.00.

- ❐ **sitte** *(sit-eh)* .... to sit
- ❐ **en sitteplass** *(sit-eh-plahs)* .... seat
- ❐ **sjøsyk** *(shuh-seek)* .... seasick   **S**
- ❐ **skandinavisk** *(skahn-dih-nah-visk)* .... Scandinavian
- ❐ **skarp** *(skarp)* .... sharp, strong

63

Her er the necessary **ordene for postkontoret.** Practice them aloud **og** write them in the blanks.

(brave)
et brev
a letter

(brave-koort)
et brevkort
postcard

_____   _____

(pahk-eh)
en pakke
package

(ay-post)
en e-post
email

_____   _____

(meh) *(flee-post)*
med flypost
by airmail

(fahks)
en fax

_____   _____

(free-mair-keh)
et frimerke
stamp

(tay-leh-fohn-hyohsk)
en telefonkiosk
telephone booth

_____   _____

(post-kah-seh)
en postkasse
mailbox

(tay-leh-fohn)
en telefon

_____   _____

❏ **et skip** *(sheep)* . . . . ship, boat   _____
❏ **en skole** *(skohl-eh)* . . . . school   _____
❏ **Spania** *(spah-nee-ah)* . . . . Spain   **S**   _____
   – hvor de snakker spansk *(spahnsk)*   _____
❏ **en sport** *(sport)* . . . . sport   _____

Next step — **du** ask **spørsmål** *(spursh-mohl)* like those **nedenfor** *(ned-en-for)*, depending on **hva du vil ha** *(would like)*. Repeat these sentences aloud many times. **På norsk når du** *(nor)* *(when)* "make a call" **du** actually "take a call" *(tar)*.

Hvor tar jeg en lokalsamtale? *(vor) (tar) (yay) (loh-kahl-sahm-tahl-eh)*
take I local call
_____

Hvor tar jeg en rikstelefon? *(reeks-tay-leh-fohn)*
long-distance call
_____

Hvor kjøper jeg frimerker? *(hyuhp-air) (free-mair-kair)*
buy
_____

Hvor kjøper jeg et brevkort?
_____

Hvor sender jeg en fax? *(sen-air) (fahks)*
send
_____

Hvor er postkassen? *(post-kah-sen)*
mailbox the
_____

Hvor sender jeg en pakke? *(pahk-eh)*
_____

Hvor mye koster det? *(mee-eh) (deh)*
_____

Nå quiz yourself. See if **du** can translate the following thoughts **på norsk**.

1. Where is a telephone booth? _____

2. Where do I make (take) a long-distance telephone call? _____

3. Where do I make (take) a local telephone call? _____

4. Where is the post office? _____

5. Where do I buy stamps? _____

6. How much is it? _____

7. Where do I send a package? _____

8. Where do I send a fax? _____

SVAR

1. Hvor er en telefonkiosk?
2. Hvor tar jeg en rikstelefon?
3. Hvor tar jeg en lokalsamtale?
4. Hvor er postkontoret?
5. Hvor kjøper jeg frimerker?
6. Hvor mye koster det?
7. Hvor sender jeg en pakke?
8. Hvor sender jeg en fax?

Her er fire flere verb.
(fear-eh) (flay-reh) — more

(oh) (yuhr-eh)
å gjøre _____
to make, do

(vees-eh)
å vise _____
to show

(skreev-eh)
å skrive _____
to write

(beh-tahl-eh)
å betale _____
to pay

Practice these verbs by not only filling in the blanks, but by saying them aloud many, many times until you are comfortable **med** the sounds **og ordene**.

(yuhr-eh)
å gjøre
to make, do

Jeg _____ mye. *(mee-eh) a lot*
Du _____ alt. *(ahlt) everything*
Han / Hun / Det / Den _____ ingenting. *(ing-en-ting) nothing*
Vi _gjør/_____ det.
De _____ litt. *(lit) a little*

(skreev-eh)
å skrive
to write

Jeg _____ fire brev. *(fear-eh)*
Du _skriver/_____ adressen. *(ah-dres-en) address the*
Han / Hun / Det / Den _____ et brevkort.
Vi _____ ikke mye. *(ick-eh) (mee-eh) not much*
De _____ ikke.

(vees-eh)
å vise
to show

Jeg _____ dem boka. *(dem) them book the*
Du _____ meg postkontoret. *(my) me*
Han / Hun / Det / Den _____ meg byen. *(bee-en) city the*
Vi _viser/_____ dem Rådhuset. *them*
De _____ meg museet. *(my) (moo-say-eh)*

(oh) (beh-tahl-eh)
å betale
to pay

Jeg _____ regningen. *(rine-ing-en) bill the*
Du _betaler/_____ ikke. *(ick-eh)*
Han / Hun / Det / Den _____ mye. *(mee-eh)*
Vi _____ prisen. *(prees-en) price the*
De _____ skatten. *(skaht-en) tax the*

❒	**en stasjon** (stah-shohn)	station, depot
❒	**en stat** (staht)	state
	– **De Forente Stater** (for-aint-eh)(staht-air) . .	United States **S**
❒	**en statue** (stah-too-eh)	statue
❒	**stille** (stil-eh)	still, quiet

17 Basic Traffic Signs and Conversions

Some of these signs you probably recognize, but take a couple of minutes to review them anyway.

(hyuhr) **Kjør** *(for-shik-tee)* **forsiktig!** *(go)* **God** *(toor)* **tur!**
drive carefully / have a good trip

(for-bewt) (ahl-eh) (beel-air)
forbudt for alle biler
road closed to vehicles

(tohl)
toll
customs

(in-hyuhr-sel) (for-bewt)
innkjørsel forbudt
no entrance

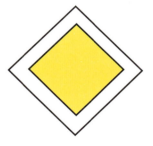
(for-hyuhrs-vay)
forkjørsvei
main road, you have the right of way

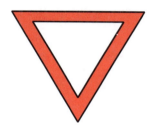
(vik-eh-plikt)
vikeplikt
yield

(farts-gren-seh)
fartsgrense
speed limit

(par-kair-ing) (for-bewt)
parkering forbudt
no parking

(for-bee-hyuhr-ing) (for-bewt)
forbikjøring forbudt
no passing

(stohp)
stopp
stop

(ohm-vay)
OMVEI
detour

What follows are approximate conversions, so when you order something by liters, kilograms or grams you will have an idea of what to expect and not find yourself being handed one piece of candy when you thought you ordered an entire bag.

To Convert		Do the Math	
liters (l) to gallons,	multiply by 0.26	4 liters x 0.26 =	1.04 gallons
gallons to liters,	multiply by 3.79	10 gal. x 3.79 =	37.9 liters
kilograms (kg) to pounds,	multiply by 2.2	2 kilograms x 2.2 =	4.4 pounds
pounds to kilos,	multiply by 0.46	10 pounds x 0.46 =	4.6 kg
grams (g) to ounces,	multiply by 0.035	100 grams x 0.035 =	3.5 oz.
ounces to grams,	multiply by 28.35	10 oz. x 28.35 =	283.5 g.
meters (m) to feet,	multiply by 3.28	2 meters x 3.28 =	6.56 feet
feet to meters,	multiply by 0.3	6 feet x 0.3 =	1.8 meters

For fun, take your weight in pounds and convert it into kilograms. It sounds better that way, doesn't it? How many kilometers is it from your home to school, to work, to the post office?

The Simple Versions		
one liter	=	approximately one US quart
four liters	=	approximately one US gallon
one kilo	=	approximately 2.2 pounds
100 grams	=	approximately 3.5 ounces
500 grams	=	slightly more than one pound
one meter	=	slightly more than three feet

Norge is approximately 1,600 miles long. How many kilometers would that be? It is 534 kilometers between **Oslo og Stockholm**. How many miles is that?

kilometers (km.) to miles,	multiply by 0.62	1000 km. x 0.62	=	620 miles
miles to kilometers,	multiply by 1.6	1000 miles x 1.6	=	1,600 km.

Inches	1	2	3	4	5	6	7

To convert centimeters into inches, multiply by 0.39   Example: 9 cm. x 0.39 = 3.51 in.
To convert inches into centimeters, multiply by 2.54   Example: 4 in. x 2.54 = 10.16 cm.

cm 1	2	3	4	5	6	7	8	9	10	11	12	13	14	15	16	17	18

18 Kvitteringen og Regningen
(kvit-air-ing-en) *(rine-ing-en)*
receipt the — bill the

Ja, det er bills to pay **i Norge også**. **Du har** just finished your evening meal **og du vil ha regningen**. **Hva gjør du? Du** call for the **kelner** (**Kelner!**) **eller** the **serveringsdame** (**Frøken!**). **Kelneren** will normally reel off **hva du har** eaten while writing rapidly. **Han** will then place **et papir på bordet, og** say, "**Det blir hundre og fem kroner, takk.**" **Du** will pay **kelneren eller** perhaps **du** will pay at **kassen.**

If your bill or the menu is marked "**service inkludert**," then your tip has **allerede** been included in your bill. If the service is not included in **regningen**, round the bill up **og** simply leave **hva du** consider an appropriate amount for your **kelner på bordet**. **Når du** dine out on your **reise, det er** always a good idea to make a reservation. It can be difficult to get into a popular **restaurant**. Nevertheless, the experience is well worth the trouble **du** might encounter to obtain a reservation. **Og** remember, **du** know enough **norsk** to make a reservation. Just speak slowly and clearly.

Jeg vil bestille et bord.

- ❐ **stopp!** *(stohp)* .... stop!
- ❐ **en storm** *(storm)* .... storm
- ❐ **Sverige** *(svair-ree-eh)* .... Sweden   **S**
    – hvor de snakker svensk *(svensk)*
- ❐ **en symfoni** *(soom-fohn-ee)* .... symphony

Remember these key **ordene når** dining out **i Norge**.

(kel-nair)
en kelner _____
waiter

(rine-ing)
en regning _____
bill

(spees-eh-kart) *(meh-nee)*
et spisekart / en meny _____
menu

(un-shool)
unnskyld _____
excuse me

(vair) (shoh) (snil)
vær så snill _____
please, be so kind

(sair-vair-ings-dahm-eh) *(fruhk-en)*
en serveringsdame / frøken _____
waitress

(drik-eh-peng-air)
drikkepenger _____
tip

(tahk)
takk _____
thank you

(mahng-eh) (tahk)
mange takk _____
many   thanks

(yee) (my)
gi meg . . . _____
give me

Her er a sample **samtale** involving paying **regningen** when leaving **et hotell**.
                                                     bill the

(gewd-ruhn)   *(rine-ing-en)*
Gudrun: **Unnskyld. Jeg vil betale regningen.**
                                    pay

Unnskyld. Jeg vil betale regningen.

(hoh-tel-vairt)   *(go)* *(vil-ket)*
Hotellvert: **Ja, vær så god. Hvilket rom var det?**
hotelkeeper   which   was

Gudrun: **Nummer tre hundre og ti.**

                         (uh-oy-eh-blik)
Hotellvert: **Takk. Ett øyeblikk, er du snill.**
                                 if you please

                    (rine-ing-en)
Hotellvert: **Her er regningen.**

(proh-blay-mair) *(num-ren-eh)*
If **du har** any **problemer med numrene,** just ask someone to write out **numrene**, so that **du**
                  problems
         (for-shtor)   *(rik-tee)*
can be sure **du forstår** everything **riktig,**
                                       correctly

             (shoh)   *(skreev)*   *(mahng-eh)*
"**Vær så snill og skriv numrene. Mange takk.**"
  please be so kind   write

Practice: _____
         (Please be so kind and write the numbers. Many thanks.)

❏ **sur** *(soor)* . . . . sour _____
❏ **en surmelk** *(soor-melk)* . . . . sour milk, buttermilk _____
❏ **Sveits** *(svites)* . . . . Switzerland _____
   – hvor de snakker tysk, fransk og italiensk   **S**
❏ **en sønn** *(suhn)* . . . . son _____

Nå, let's take a break from **regningene og** *(rine-ing-en-eh)* **penger og** learn some fun **nye** *(nee-eh)* **ord. Du** can always practice these **ord** by using your flash cards at the back of this **bok.** Carry these flash cards in your purse, pocket, briefcase **eller** knapsack **og** *use them!*

(oh-pent) **åpent** — open
(luhk-et) **lukket** — closed
(stor) **stor** — big
(lee-ten) **liten** — small
(frisk) **frisk** — healthy
(seek) **syk** — sick
(go) **god** — good
(dor-lee) **dårlig** — bad
(varm) **varm** — warm
(kahl) **kald** — cold

☐ **tennis** *(ten-is)* .... tennis
☐ **tinn** *(tin)* .... tin or pewter
☐ **et toalett** *(toh-ah-let)* .... toilet
☐ **et toalettpapir** *(toh-ah-let-pah-peer)* .... toilet paper
☐ **en tobakk** *(toh-bahk)* .... tobacco

t

(koort)
kort _____
short

(lahng)
lang _____
long

(lahng-sohm)
langsom _____
slow

(foort)
fort _____
fast

(huh-oy)
høy _____
tall, high

(koort) *(lahv)*
kort / lav _____
short   low

(gahm-el)
gammel _____
old

(uhng)
ung _____
young

(dewr)
dyr _____
expensive

(bil-ee)
billig _____
inexpensive

(reek)
rik _____
rich

(fah-tee)
fattig _____
poor

(mahng-eh)
mange _____
a lot

(lee-teh)
lite _____
a little

❑	**en topp** *(tohp)*	....	top, summit
❑	**trafikk** *(trah-feek)*	....	traffic
❑	**en tunnel** *(tuh-nel)*	....	tunnel
❑	**en tur** *(toor)*	....	trip, tour, ride, turn
	– God tur! *(go) (toor)*	....	Have a good trip!

t

Her er de nye verbene. They are all irregular but **meget** similar to **engelsk**.

(oh) (vil-eh) (vil)
å ville (vil) _____
to want to

(veet-eh) (vet)
å vite (vet) _____
to know (a fact)

(kuhn-eh) (kahn)
å kunne (kan) _____
to be able to, can

(moht-eh) (moh)
å måtte (må) _____
to have to, must

(ek-sem-plen-eh)   *(ohf-teh)*
Study **eksemplene nedenfor** closely, as **du** will use these **verbene ofte**.
      examples the   below   often

(vil-eh)
å ville
to want to

Jeg _vil/_ _____ lære norsk.
                          learn
Du _____ lære dansk.
                   (dahnsk)
Han / Hun / Det / Den _____ spise nå.
                              eat
Vi _vil/_ _____ forstå norsk.
                          understand
De _____ bli i Norge.
                   remain

(kuhn-eh)
å kunne   Jeg kan snakke norsk.
to be able to, can

Jeg _____ forstå norsk.
                    understand
Du _kan/_ _____ snakke norsk.
                          speak
Han / Hun / Det / Den _____ skrive et brevkort.
                              write
Vi _____ betale regningen.
De _kan/_ _____ gjøre alt.
                          do   everything

(veet-eh)
å vite
to know

Jeg _vet/_ _____ mye.
                           a lot
Du _____ bare litt.
                   only a little
Han / Hun / Det / Den _____ hvor hotellet er.
Vi _vet/_ _____ ikke.
De _____ noe.
                   something

(moht-eh)
å måtte
to have to, must

Jeg _må/_ _____ lære norsk.
Du _____ kjøpe billeter.
                   buy
Han / Hun / Det / Den _____ ta en drosje.
                              take taxi
Vi _må/_ _____ sende en pakke.
De _____ betale regningen.

☐ **en turist** *(toor-ist)* .... tourist
☐ **et turistbyrå** *(toor-ist-bew-roh)* .... travel agency
☐ **et turistkontor** *(toor-ist-kohn-tor)* .... tourist office   **t**
☐ **tykk** *(tewk)* .... thick, fat, big
☐ **Tyrkia** *(tewr-kee-ah)* .... Turkey

73

Did **du** notice that " **vil**," (vil) *want to* " **må**," (moh) *must* og **kan** (kahn) *can* can be combined with another verb just as in **engelsk**?

Jeg vil finne postkontoret. (post-kohn-tor-eh)
find

Jeg vil bestille et øl. (uhl)
order   beer

Vi kan bli i Norge. (vee) (blee)
stay

Vi kan sende et brevkort.

Han må sove nå. (hahn) (sohv-eh)
he   sleep

Hun må finne hotellet. (huhn)
she

Jeg vil snakke norsk. (snahk-eh)
I
Jeg kan snakke norsk. (kahn)
can
Jeg må snakke norsk. (moh)
must

(kahn)
Kan du translate the sentences **nedenfor på norsk? Svarene er nede.**
can

1. I can speak Norwegian. _____

2. They can pay the bill. _____

3. He has to (must) pay the bill. _____

4. We know the answers. ____Vi vet svarene. Vi vet svarene.____

5. She knows a lot. _____

6. We can understand Norwegian. _____

7. I can find the hotel. _____

8. We can understand Danish. _____

9. I want to stay in Bergen. _____

10. She must buy the newspaper. _____

SVAR

1. Jeg kan snakke norsk.
2. De kan betale regningen.
3. Han må betale regningen.
4. Vi vet svarene.
5. Hun vet mye.
6. Vi kan forstå norsk.
7. Jeg kan finne hotellet.
8. Vi kan forstå dansk.
9. Jeg vil bli i Bergen.
10. Hun må kjøpe avisen.

Nå, draw **linjer** *(lin-yair)* **mellom** *(mel-ohm)* the opposites **nedenfor.** Do **ikke** *(ick-eh)* forget to say them out loud. Say **disse** *(dis-eh)* **ordene** every **dag** to describe **tingene i huset, på skolen** *(skohl-en)* **eller på kontor.**

stor	**ovenpå**
venstre	*(oh-pent)* **åpent**
(uhng) **ung**	**kort**
(fah-tee) **fattig**	*(bil-ee)* **billig**
(seek) **syk**	*(lee-teh)* **lite**
(lahng) **lang**	**frisk**
(mahng-eh) (mee-eh) **mange / mye**	**fort**
(go) **god**	*(gahm-el)* **gammel**
(kahl) **kald**	*(lee-ten)* **liten**
nede	*(huh-oy-reh)* **høyre**
(lahng-sohm) **langsom**	*(dor-lee)* **dårlig**
(dewr) **dyr**	*(reek)* **rik**
(luhk-et) **lukket**	**varm**

- **ull** *(uhl)* .... wool
- **underklær** *(oon-air-klair)* .... underclothes
- **Ungarn** *(uhn-garn)* .... Hungary **u**
  – hvor de snakker **ungarsk** *(uhn-garshk)*
- **et universitet** *(oo-nih-vairsh-ih-tate)* .... university

19 En Reisende Reiser
(race-en-eh) *(race-air)*
traveler travels

(ee) (gor) (bairg-en) **I går Bergen!** yesterday

(dahg) (trohnd-haym) **I dag til Trondheim!** today

(mor-en) (trohm-suh) **I morgen til Tromsø!** tomorrow

If **du** know a few key **ord**, traveling *(kahn)* **kan** be **lett**, clean **og** efficient **i Norge**. **Norge er ikke stort.**
easy

Norge er only slightly larger than New Mexico, however, the country **er** over 1,600 miles long. **En reise** *(race-eh)* **fra Kirkenes** *(hyeer-ken-es)* **til Oslo** *(oh-shloh)* would be like traveling **fra** Boston **til** Atlanta. **Men det er** *(men) (deh)* but
trip from

meget scenic **å reise** *(race-eh)* **i Norge. Hvordan reiser** *(race-air)* **du i Norge?**
to travel how

(ahlf) (race-air) (beel)
Alf reiser med bil.
travels car

Randi reiser med båt. *(boht)*
boat

Ole reiser med motorsykkel. *(oh-leh) (moh-tor-seek-el)*

(race-air) (tohg)
Tordis reiser med tog.

Einar reiser med fly. *(eye-nar) (flee)*
airplane

Åge reiser med ferje. *(oh-geh) (fair-yeh)*
ferry

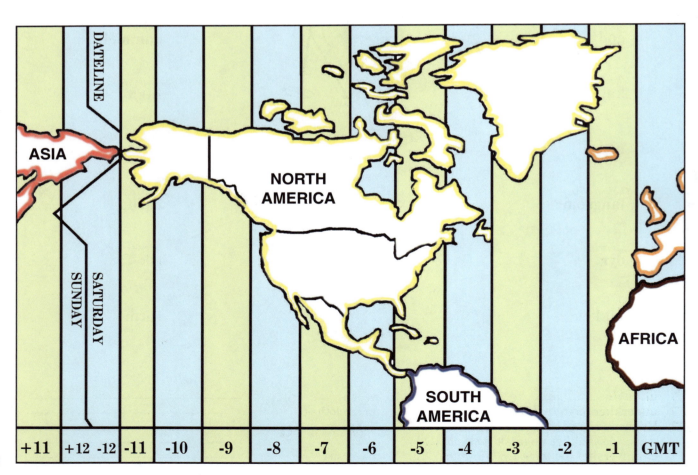

(nor)
Når du are traveling, **du** will want to tell others your nationality **og du** will meet people from all corners of the world. **Kan du** guess where people are from if they say one of the following? **Svarene** are in your glossary beginning **på side** 108.

(kohm-air) *(eng-lahn)*
Jeg kommer fra England. _____
 come   from

(roos-lahn)
Vi kommer fra Russland. _____
 we come

(kohm-air) *(ee-tahl-ee-ah)*
Jeg kommer fra Italia. _____
 come   from

(tewsk-lahn)
Vi kommer fra Tyskland. _____

(nay-dair-lahn)
Jeg kommer fra Nederland. _____

(ees-rah-el)
Vi kommer fra Israel. _____

(spah-nee-ah)
Jeg kommer fra Spania. _____

(svair-ree-eh)
Vi kommer fra Sverige. _____

(bel-gee-ah)
Jeg kommer fra Belgia. _____

(ees-lahn)
Han kommer fra Island. _____

(svites)
Jeg kommer fra Sveits. _____

(eer-lahn)
Han kommer fra Irland. _____

(dahn-mark)
Jeg kommer fra Danmark. _____

(pohl-en)
Hun kommer fra Polen. _____

(fin-lahn)
Jeg kommer fra Finland. _____

(sur-ah-frih-kuh)
Hun kommer fra Sør-Afrika. _____

(ust-air-reek-eh)
Jeg kommer fra Østerrike. _____

(kah-nah-dah)
Jeg kommer fra Kanada. _____

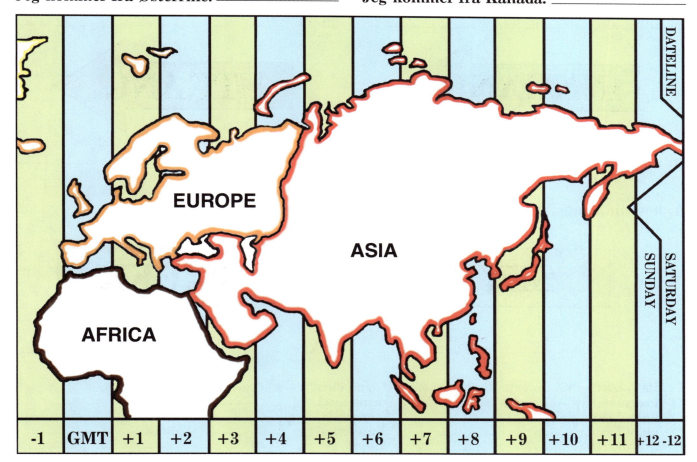

Ordet for "trip" is taken from **ordet "reise,"** *(race-eh)* which makes it easy: **en reise.** *(race-eh)* **Mange ord** revolve around the concept of travel which is exactly what **du vil gjøre.** *(yuhr-eh)* Practice the following **ord mange ganger.** *(gahng-air)* **Du** will see them **ofte.** *(ohf-teh)*

(oh) (race-eh)
å reise _____
to travel

(race-eh-bew-roh)
et reisebyrå _____
travel agency

(race-en-eh)
en reisende _____
traveler

(loo-keh) (race-en)
Lykke på reisen! _____
have a good trip

If **du** choose **å reise med bil, her er** a few key **ord.**
(race-eh) (beel)

(vay)
en vei _____
road

(beel-vairk-sted)
et bilverksted _____
car repair shop

(moh-tor-vay)
en motorvei _____
highway

(beel-oot-lay-eh)
en bilutleie _____
car-rental agency

(par-kair-eh)
parkere _____
to park

(ben-seen-stah-shohn)
en bensinstasjon _____
service station

Nedenfor er some basic signs which **du** should **lære** to recognize quickly. Most of **disse ordene** *(dis-eh)* these **kommer fra ordet "gang"** *(gahng)* aisle, hallway **og "gå."** *(goh)* to go, to walk

(goh) (in)
gå inn _____
to enter (go in)

(goh) (oot)
gå ut _____
to exit (go out)

INNGANG →

UTGANG →

(in-gahng)
en inngang _____
entrance

(oot-gahng)
en utgang _____
exit

(hoh-ved-in-gahng)
en hovedinngang _____
main

(nuhd-oot-gahng)
en nødutgang _____
emergency exit

SKYV

TREKK

(sheev-eh)
skyve _____
to push (doors)

(trek-eh)
trekke _____
to pull (doors)

På norsk the "**u**" is **ofte** the equivalent of "un-," "im-" **eller** "in-" **på engelsk.**
- ☐ **upersonlig** *(oo-pair-shohn-lee)* . . . . impersonal _____
- ☐ **upopulær** *(oo-poh-poo-lair)* . . . . unpopular   **u** _____
- ☐ **upraktisk** *(oo-prak-tisk)* . . . . impractical _____
- ☐ **uvel** *(oo-vel)* . . . . unwell, ill _____

Let's learn the basic travel **verb**. Take out a piece of paper **og** make up your own sentences **med** these **nye ordene**. Follow the same pattern **du har** in previous Steps.

(flee)
å fly _____
to fly

(kohm-eh) (til)
å komme til _____
to arrive at, arrive in

(goh) (frah)
å gå fra _____
to leave from, depart

(vent-eh) (poh)
å vente på _____
to wait for

(hyuhr-eh)
å kjøre _____
to drive

(lay-seh)
å lese _____
to read

(pahk-eh)
å pakke _____
to pack

(boot-eh) (tohg)
å bytte tog _____
to transfer (trains)

(hair) (noh-en) (nee-eh) (race-en)
Her er noen nye ord for reisen.
　　　　some　　trip

(flee-plahs)
en flyplass
airport

(spor)
et spor
(train) track

(roo-teh-plahn)
en ruteplan
timetable, schedule

Fra Bergen til Oslo		
Avreise	Tog Nr.	Ankomst
07:30	118	14:00
11:35	413	19:35
14:15	718	20:45
18:00	1132	00:30
God tur!		

(yairn-bahn-eh-stah-shohn)
en jernbanestasjon
train station

- **en vaffel** *(vah-fel)* . . . . waffle
- **en valnøtt** *(vahl-nuht)* . . . . walnut
- **vegetariansk** *(veg-et-ar-ee-ahnsk)* . . . . vegetarian　　**V**
- **velkommen** *(vel-kohm-en)* . . . . welcome
  – **velkommen til Norge** . . . . welcome to Norway

(meh) (dis-eh) (ar) (klar) (race-eh) (skoo-leh) (ick-eh) (proh-blay-mair)
Med disse verbene er du klar for any **reise**, anywhere. **Du skulle ikke ha problemer med**
   these   are ready   should

disse verbene, just remember the basic "plug-in" formula **du** have already learned. Use that

knowledge to translate the following thoughts **på norsk. Svarene er** below.
                                                into

1. I fly to Oslo. _____

2. I change trains in Kristiansand. _____

3. He departs from Trondheim. _____

4. We arrive in Gol tomorrow. _____

5. We pack today! _____

6. They travel to Kirkenes. _____

7. Where is the train to Lillehammer? _____

8. How can you fly to Norway? With Lufthansa or with SAS? _____
_____

(noh-en) (vik-tee-eh) (race-en-eh)
Her er noen viktige ord for den reisende.
         some   important   traveler the

Fra Oslo til Trondheim		
Avreise	Tog Nr.	Ankomst
07:00	175	13:48
10:30	450	17:18
14:30	768	21:03
19:45	982	02:23
God tur!		

(ohp-taht)
opptatt _____
occupied

(ahv-race-en)
avreisen _____
departure the

(lay-dee)
ledig _____
free

(ahn-kohmst-en)
ankomsten _____
arrival the

(vohgn)
ei vogn _____
compartment, wagon

(oot-en-lahns)
utenlands _____
foreign

(plahs)
en plass _____
seat

(in-en-lahns)
innenlands _____
domestic, internal (of the country)

SVAR

1. Jeg flyr til Oslo.
2. Jeg bytter tog i Kristiansand.
3. Han går fra Trondheim.
4. Vi kommer til Gol i morgen.
5. Vi pakker i dag!
6. De reiser til Kirkenes.
7. Hvor er toget til Lillehammer?
8. Hvordan flyr du til Norge? Med Lufthansa eller SAS?

Increase your **reiseord** *(race-eh-oor)* by writing out **ordene nedefor og** practicing the sample sentences out loud. Practice asking questions **med "hvor."** It will help you later.

travel words

(til)
til _____
to
              Hvor er toget til Bergen?

(spor-eh)
sporet _____
track the
              Hvor er spor sju?

(hit-eh-gohds-kohn-tor-eh)
hittegodskontoret _____
lost-and-found office the
              Hvor er hittegodskontoret?

(pair-ohng-en)
perrongen *Hvor er perrong to? Hvor er perrong to?*
platform the
              Hvor er perrong to?

(flee-toor-en)
flyturen _____
flight the
              Hvor er flyturen til Tromsø?

(race-eh-gohds)
reisegods _____
baggage office
              Hvor finner jeg reisegods?

(vek-shleh-kohn-tor-eh)
vekslekontoret _____
money-exchange office
              Hvor er vekslekontoret?

(bil-let-luhk-en)
billettluken _____
ticket counter / window
              Hvor er billetluken fire?

(vent-eh-rohm-eh)
venterommet _____
waiting room the
              Hvor er venterommet?

(spees-eh-vohgn-uh)
spisevogna _____
dining car the
              Hvor er spisevogna?

(sohv-eh-vohgn-uh)
sovevogna _____
sleeping car the
              Hvor er sovevogna?

(tah) (plahs)
Ta plass! _____
take place (all aboard)

_____(when)_____ _____(when)_____ *(gor) (tohg-eh)* **går toget?**

_____(what)_____ _____(what)_____ *(yuhr) (dee)* **gjør de?**
                  are they doing

❏ **Vesten** *(vest-en)* .... the West, Western world _____
 – **det Ville Vesten** .... the Wild West _____
❏ **en vin** *(veen)* .... wine   **V**
❏ **et vinglass** *(veen-glahs)* .... wine glass _____
❏ **et vinkart** *(veen-kart)* .... wine list _____

(kahn) *(lay-seh)*
Kan du lese the following?
　can　　read

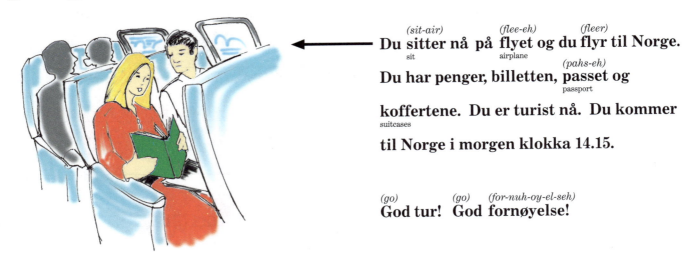

(sit-air) *(flee-eh)* *(fleer)*
Du sitter nå på flyet og du flyr til Norge.
　　sit　　　　airplane

(pahs-eh)
Du har penger, billetten, passet og
　　　　　　　　　　　　　passport

koffertene. Du er turist nå. Du kommer
　suitcases

til Norge i morgen klokka 14.15.

(go) *(go)* *(for-nuh-oy-el-seh)*
God tur! God fornøyelse!

(ek-spres-tohg) *(her-tee-tohg)*
I Norge there are many different types of trains – **ekspresstog (meget fort), hurtigtog (fort),**
　　　　　　　　　　　　　　　　　　　　　　　　　express train　　　　　　　　　fast train
(loh-kahl-tohg) *(for-shtahds-tohg)* *(spees-eh-vohgn)* *(sohv-eh-vohgn)*
lokaltog (meget langsomt) og forstadstog. Some **tog har spisevogn** og some **har sovevogn.**
local train　　　　　　　　suburban train　　　　　　　　　　　dining cars　　　　　　　　sleeping cars
　　　　　　　　　　　　　　　(roo-teh-plahn)　　　*(yairn-bahn-eh-stah-shohn-en)*
All this will be indicated on your **ruteplan.** Next step? **Jernbanestasjonen!** The Norwegian
　　　　　　　　　　　　　　　　　　schedule

State Railways (NSB) does not run north of Bodø except between Narvik and Sweden. If **du** are

looking for a spectacular, scenic train journey try either the route **fra Oslo til Bergen eller fra**

Dombås til Åndalsnes.

☐	**en vinkjeller** *(veen-hyel-air)*	wine cellar	
☐	**vinmonopol** *(veen-moh-noh-pohl)*	state liquor store	
☐	**vintersport** *(vint-air-sport)*	winter sport	**v**
☐	**voks** *(vox)*	wax (for skis)	
☐	**våt** *(voht)*	wet	

Knowing **disse reiseordene** *(race-eh-oor-en-eh)* will make your holiday twice as enjoyable **og** at least three times as easy. Review **disse nye ordene** *(nee-eh)* by doing the crossword puzzle below. Drill yourself on this Step by selecting other destinations **i Norge og** ask your own **spørsmål** *(spursh-mohl)* about **tog** *(tohg)*, **busser eller fly** *(boos-air)* *(flee)* that go there. Select more **nye ord** from your **ordbok** *(oor-bohk)* **og** ask your own questions beginning **med hvor, når og hva koster**. **Svarene** to the crossword puzzle are at the bottom of the next page.

ACROSS
1. busy, occupied
5. to sit
8. ticket
9. domestic
13. (it) costs
14. thank you
16. available
18. to come
21. arrival
22. foreign
24. at two o'clock
25. exit
26. to go, walk
27. schedule, timetable
28. forbidden, prohibited

DOWN
2. to
3. east
4. train station
6. (it) takes
7. money
10. Norwegian
11. airport
12. compartment
15. important
17. to order
19. excuse me
20. have a good trip
23. when

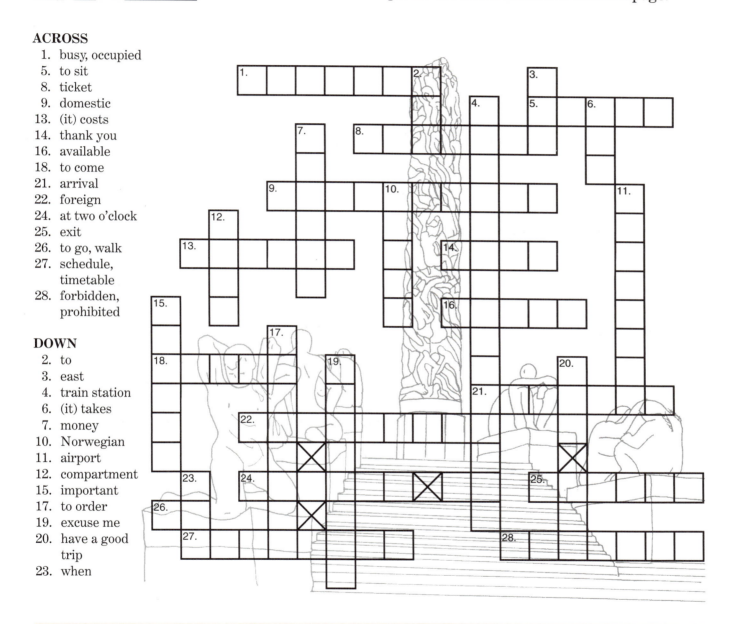

Vigelandsparken: The Monolith above was done by the Norwegian sculptor Gustav Vigeland (1869–1943) and can be found inside the Oslo park bearing his name. The Monolith symbolizes the struggle of life depicted by a mass of intertwined figures all attempting to get to the top.

Most "w" words are foreign additions to **norsk**.
- ❏ **et W.C.** *(vay-say)* . . . . toilet (water closet)
- ❏ **en weekend** *(veek-end)* . . . . weekend
- ❏ **en weekendtur** *(veek-end-toor)* . . . . weekend trip
- ❏ **en whisky** *(visk-ee)* . . . . whisky

W

83

What about inquiring about **prisen** *(prees-en)* of **billetter**? **Du kan også spørre** *(oh-soh)* *(spur-eh)* these questions.
price   tickets   can   ask

(kohst-air)   *(yuhr-vik)*
Hva koster en billett til Gjøvik? _____
what   costs

(ruh-rohs)
Hva koster en billett til Røros? _____

(ohn-dahls-nes)
Hva koster en billett til Åndalsnes? _____

(eng-kelt)
enkelt _____
one-way

(toor-ray-toor)
tur-retur _____
round-trip

What about **avgang og ankomst** *(ahv-gahng)* *(ahn-kohmst)* times? **Du kan også spørre om det.** *(spur-eh)* *(ohm)* *(deh)*
departure   arrival   ask   about   that

(nor) *(gor)* *(tohg-eh)* *(shee-en)*
Når går toget til Skien? _____
when   leaves   to

(flee-eh) *(hyuh-pen-hahvn)*
Når går flyet til Kjøbenhavn? _____
plane   Copenhagen

(fred-rik-stahd)
Når kommer toget fra Fredrikstad? _____
arrive

(mewr-dahl)
Når kommer toget fra Myrdal? _____

(kah-lih-for-nee-ah)
Når kommer flyet fra Kalifornia? _____

Du have just arrived **i Norge. Du er på jernbanestasjonen** *(yairn-bahn-eh-stah-shohn-en)* **nå. Hvor** would **du** like to go?
at

Well, tell that to **personen ved luken** *(pair-shohn-en)* *(veh)* *(luhk-en)* selling **billetter**!
person the   at   window the

(vil) *(race-eh)* *(nar-vik)*
Jeg vil reise til Narvik. _____

Når går toget til Narvik? _____

Hva koster en billett til Narvik? _____

SVAR TO KRYSSORD OPPGAVE

ACROSS				DOWN			
1. opptatt	14. takk	24. klokka to		2. til	10. norsk	19. unnskyld	
5. sitte	16. ledig	25. utgang		3. øst	11. flyplass	20. god tur	
8. billett	18. komme	26. gå		4. jernbanestasjon	12. vogn	23. når	
9. innenlands	21. ankomst	27. ruteplan		6. tar	15. viktig		
13. koster	22. utenlands	28. forbudt		7. penger	17. bestille		

Nå that **du vet** *(vet)* **ordene** essential for traveling **i Norge**, what are some specialty items **du** might go in search of?

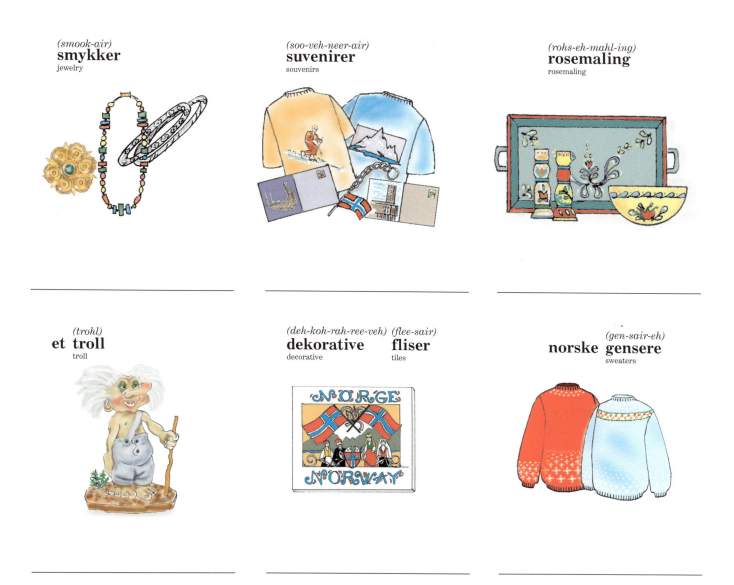

Consider using NORWEGIAN *a language map*® as well. NORWEGIAN *a language map*® is the perfect companion for your travels when **du** may not wish to take along this **bok**. Each section focuses on essentials for your trip. Your *Language Map*® is not meant to replace learning **norske**, but will help you in the event **du** forget something and need a little bit of help. For more information about the *Language Map*® Series please turn to page 132 or go to www.bbks.com.

❐	**en yacht** *(yoht)* . . . . yacht	**y**
❐	**en zoo** *(soh)* . . . . zoo	**z**
❐	**en zoologi** *(soh-oh-loh-gee)* . . . . zoology	
❐	**en zoologisk hage** *(soh-oh-loh-gisk)(hah-geh)* . . zoological garden	
❐	**ei zoomlinse** *(soom-lin-seh)* . . . . zoom lens	

20 Spisekartet eller Menyen
(spees-eh-kart-eh) *(meh-nee-en)*
menu the

Nå er du i Norge og du har hotellrom. Du er sulten *(suhl-ten)* (hungry)**. Hvor er en god** *(go)* **restaurant?** First of all, **det er** (there are) different types of places to eat. Let's learn them.

en restaurant *(res-tuh-rahng)* — exactly what it says with a variety of meals and prices

en grill *(gril)* — **en restaurant** specializing in grilled fish, meat **og** poultry

ei kaffestua *(ay) (kahf-eh-stoo-uh)* — reasonably priced, rural-style fare

et konditori *(et) (kohn-dih-tor-ee)* — pastry shop **med** a tearoom, especially popular for afternoon **kaffe og kake** (cake) **eller** pastry

ei kro *(ay) (kroh)* — reasonably priced tavern; menu is simple with an informal, cozy atmosphere

If **du** look around you **på restauranten, du** will see that some **norske** customs might be different from yours. **I Norge** it is common to have a choice of either warm dishes **eller** a lighter meal of **smørbrød** *(smur-bruh)* (open-faced sandwiches)**. I Norge** it is customary to say, "**Takk** *(tahk)* (thanks) **for maten** *(mah-ten)* (food the (meal))" after finishing your meal. Most individuals respond with "**Vel** *(vel)* **bekomme** *(beh-kohm-eh)*." (you're welcome) **Nå** your turn to practice!

_____ (thanks for the meal)

And at least one more time for practice!

_____ (thanks for the meal)

- ærdun *(air-doon)* .... eiderdown
- en økonomi *(uh-koh-noh-mee)* .... economy **æ**
- et øre *(ur-eh)* .... ear
- øst *(ust)* .... east **ø**
- øvre *(uhv-reh)* .... upper

Start imagining now all the new taste treats **du** will experience abroad. Try all of the different

types of eating establishments mentioned on the previous page. Experiment. If **du finner en restaurant** that **du vil** try, remember **du kan** call ahead to make **en bestilling**: *(beh-stil-ing)* reservation "**Jeg vil bestille** *(beh-stil-eh)* I reserve **et bord**." *(boor)* table If **du trenger et spisekart**, *(spees-eh-kart)* menu catch the attention of **kelneren**, saying,

"**Kan jeg se spisekartet?**"
(say) (spees-eh-kart-eh)

(Can I see the menu?)

Your **kelner** might say, "**Vær så god. Vil du** *(vair) (shoh) (go)* **også se på smørbrødlista?**"
(say) (smur-bruh-list-uh)
open-faced sandwich menu the

Most **restauranter** post **spisekartet** *(spees-eh-kart-eh)* **ute**. *(oot-eh)* outside Do not hesitate to ask to see **spisekartet** before being seated so **du vet** what type of **retter og priser** *(ret-air) (prees-air)* dishes prices **du** will encounter. Most **restauranter også** offer **dagens rett**. *(dahg-ens)* daily specials These are complete **måltider** *(mohl-tee-air)* meals at fair **priser**. *(prees-air)* prices

❏ **åpen** *(oh-pen)* .... open
❏ **et år** *(or)* .... year
❏ **ei årbok** *(or-bohk)* .... yearbook
❏ **årlig** *(or-lee)* .... yearly, annual
❏ **årsdag** *(orsh-dahg)* .... anniversary

å

I Norge er det tre main **måltider** *(mohl-tee-air)* to enjoy **hver dag** *(vair)*, plus perhaps **en kaffe og kake** *(kahk-eh)* for den
meals / *every* / *cake*

trette *(tret-eh)* **reisende** *(race-en-eh)*.
tired / *traveler*

frokost *(froh-kohst)* _____
breakfast

A substantial **kaldtbord** *(kahlt-boor)*, consisting of eggs, meats, cheeses, bread **og** coffee.
cold buffet
This meal can keep you going most of the day. Check serving times before **du** retire for the night or you might miss out!

lunsj *(luhnsh)* _____
lunch
generally served from 11.00 to 13.00; predominantly **smørbrød eller kaldtbord.**

middag *(mid-ahg)* _____
dinner
available either at the traditional time, 14.00 to 17.00 **eller** beginning around 19:00.

Nå for a preview of delights to come . . . At the back of this **bok, du** will find a sample **norsk**

spisekart *(spees-eh-kart)*. **Les** *(lace)* **spisekartet i dag og lær de nye ordene. Når du er klar** to leave on your
read / *today* / *learn* / *ready*

reise *(race-eh)*, cut out **spisekartet**, fold it, **og** carry it in your pocket, wallet **eller** purse. Before you go,

how do **du** say these **tre** phrases which are so very important for the hungry **reisende** *(race-en-eh)*?

Excuse me. I want to reserve a table. _____

Waiter! Can I see the menu? _____

Thanks for the food / meal! _____

_____ (who) _____ spiser fisken? *(fisk-en)* _____ (who) drikker teen? *(tay-en)*
eats / *fish the* / *drinks*

_____ (who) reiser *(race-air)* til Kjøbenhavn? *(hyuh-pen-hahvn)*

Learning the following should help you to identify **hva** kind of meat **du** have ordered **og hvordan** it will be prepared.
- ❏ **et oksekjøtt** *(ohk-seh-hyuht)* . . . . beef _____
- ❏ **et kalvekjøtt** *(kahl-veh-hyuht)* . . . . veal _____
- ❏ **et svinekjøtt** *(svee-neh-hyuht)* . . . . pork _____
- ❏ **et får** *(for)* . . . . mutton _____

(spees-eh-kart-eh)
Spisekartet below has the main categories **du** will find in most restaurants. Learn them **i dag** so that **du** will easily recognize them when you dine **i Norge**. Be sure to write the words in the blanks below.

- **høns** *(huns)* .... poultry
- **et lam** *(lahm)* .... lamb
- **et vilt** *(vilt)* .... wild game
- **stekt** *(stekt)* .... fried
- **ovenstekt** *(ohvn-stekt)* .... roasted

Du will **også** get **poteter** *(poh-tay-tair)* **med smør** *(smur)* **og** usually **grønnsaker med** *(gruhn-sahk-air)* your **måltid** *(mohl-tee)*. **En dag** at an open-air **marked** *(mar-ked)* will teach you **navnene** *(nahv-nen-eh)* for all the different kinds of **grønnsaker og frukt** *(gruhn-sahk-air)*, plus it will be a delightful experience for you. **Du kan** always consult your menu guide at the back of **denne boken** *(den-eh)* if **du** forget **de riktige navnene** *(rik-tee-eh)*. **Nå, du** are seated **og kelneren kommer**.

- potatoes, butter, vegetables, meal, one, market, names the, fruit, this, waiter the

Speech bubbles: **Spisekartet, takk.** — **Noe å drikke?** — **Et glass hvitvin, takk.**

Frokost *(froh-kohst)* **er litt** different **i Norge** because **det er** fairly standardized **og er** generally served buffet style **på hotellet.** At a **pensjon** *(pahng-shohn)*, **er frokost** served continental style **og** will be included **i prisen** *(prees-en)* of your **rom. Nedenfor er** a sample of what **du kan** expect to greet you **om morgenen** *(ohm)*.

- breakfast, a little, guest house, in

Drikkevarer

- kaffe
- te
- fruktsaft
- varm sjokolade
- melk, kald eller varm

Pålegg
sandwich fixings

- **ost: gulost, gammelost** (cheese, yellow, old)
- **kryddersild med rømme** (pickled herring, sour cream)

og . . .

- brød
- rundstykker (rolls)
- smør og syltetøy *(sool-teh-tuh-oy)* (jam)
- skinke (ham)
- ett egg
- egg og bacon
- eggeomelett
- speilegg (fried eggs)

- ❏ **kokt** *(kohkt)* .... cooked
- ❏ **bakt** *(bahkt)* .... baked
- ❏ **grillet** *(gril-et)* .... grilled
- ❏ **fylt** *(fewlt)* .... stuffed
- ❏ **røkt** *(ruhkt)* .... smoked

Nedenfor er an example of what **du** might select for your evening meal. Using your menu guide on pages 117 and 118, as well as what **du** have learned in this Step, fill in the blanks *in English* with what **du** believe your **kelner** will bring you. **Svarene er nede.**

Forretter
Røkt laks

Supper og Salater
Bergensk fiskesuppe

Fisk og Skalldyr
Hummer med erter og blomkål

Dessert
Is med sjokoladesaus

SVAR

Appetizer: Smoked salmon
Soups and Salads: Bergen fish soup
Fish and Seafood: Lobster with peas and cauliflower
Dessert: Ice cream with chocolate sauce

Nå er a good time for a quick review. Draw **linjer** *(lin-yair)* **mellom** *(mel-ohm)* the **norske ordene og** their English equivalents.
_{between}

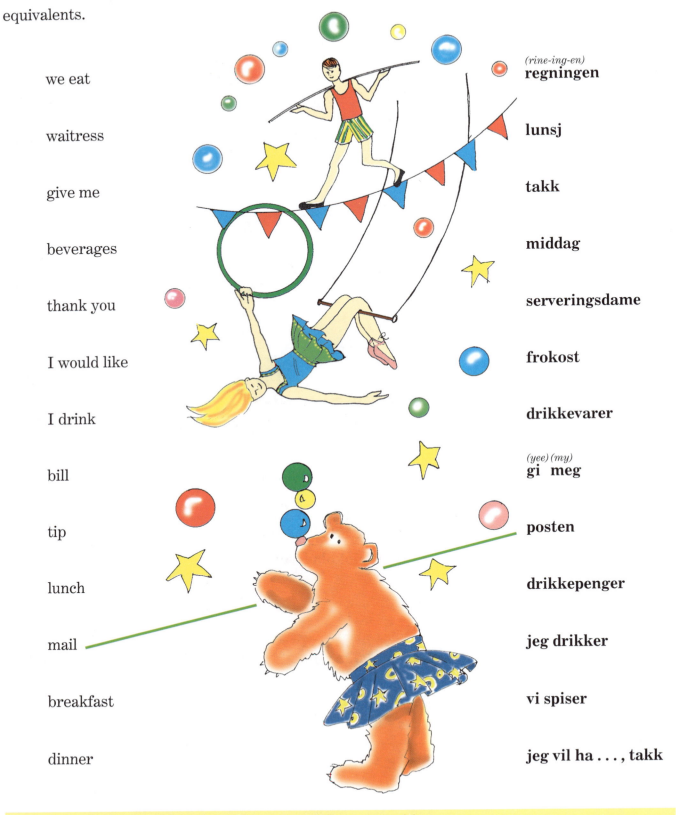

we eat — **regningen** *(rine-ing-en)*

waitress — **lunsj**

give me — **takk**

beverages — **middag**

thank you — **serveringsdame**

I would like — **frokost**

I drink — **drikkevarer**

bill — **gi meg** *(yee)(my)*

tip — **posten**

lunch — **drikkepenger**

mail — **jeg drikker**

breakfast — **vi spiser**

dinner — **jeg vil ha . . . , takk**

Her er a few holidays which you might experience during your visit.
- **Første nyttårsdag** *(fursht-eh)(neet-orsh-dahg)* . . . . New Year's Day (Jan. 1)
- **Første mai** *(fursht-eh)(my)* . . . . May Day (May 1)
- **Første juledag** *(fursht-eh)(yool-eh-dahg)* . . . . Christmas (Dec. 25)
- **Annen juledag** *(ahn-en)(yool-eh-dahg)* . . . . Second Day of Christmas (Dec. 26)

21 Telefonen
(tay-leh-fohn-en)
telephone the

Hva er different about **telefonen i Norge?** Well, **du** never notice such things until **du** want to use **dem.** **Telefoner** allow you to call friends, reserve **teaterbilletter og konsertbilletter,** make emergency calls, check on the hours of a **museum,** rent **en bil og** all those other things which **vi gjør** on a daily basis. It also gives you a certain amount of **frihet når du kan** make your own **telefonsamtaler.**

Telefoner can usually be found everywhere:

in **postkontoret, på gata,** in the **bar,** at **jernbanestasjonen** and in **lobbyen** of your **hotell.**

So, let's learn how to operate **telefonen.** The instructions can look complicated, but remember, **du** should be able to recognize some of these **ordene** already. Many public **telefoner** use **et telefonkort.** **Du kan** buy these **telefonkortene** at newsstands and in stores as well as in **postkontoret og jernbanestasjonen.**

Ready? Well, before you turn the page it would be a good idea to go back **og** review all your numbers one more time.

To dial from the United States to most other countries **du trenger** that country's international area code. Your **telefonkatalog** at home should have a listing of international area codes.

Her er some very useful words built around the word **"telefon."**
- ☐ **en telefonist** *(tay-leh-fohn-ist)* .... operator _____
- ☐ **en telefonkiosk** *(tay-leh-fohn-hyohsk)* .... telephone booth _____
- ☐ **en telefonkatalog** *(tay-leh-fohn-kah-tah-lohg)* ...... telephone book _____
- ☐ **en telefonsamtale** *(tay-leh-fohn-sahm-tahl-uh)* ..... telephone conversation _____

When **du** leave your contact numbers with friends, family **og** business colleagues, **du** should include your destination's country code **og** city code whenever possible. For example,

	Country Codes		Country Codes	
Norway	47	Finland	358
Denmark	45	Iceland	354
Sweden	46	Germany	49

To call from one city to another, **du** may need to go to **postkontoret eller** call **telefonisten** *(operator the)* in your **hotell**. Tell **telefonisten**, "**Jeg vil gjerne ringe til Seattle**," *(yairn-eh) (ring-eh)* **eller** "**Jeg vil gjerne ringe til Denver**." *(yairn-eh)*
gladly   ring / call

Now you try it: _____
(I want gladly to call / I would like to call . . .)

When answering **telefonen, du** pick up the receiver **og sier,** *(see-air)*

"**Hallo. Dette er** _____."
(hah-loh) (det-eh)
this   (your name)

When saying good-bye, **du sier,** *(see-air)* "**Ha det bra**," *(hah) (deh) (brah)* **eller** "**På gjensyn**." *(yen-soon)* Your turn —
so long / see you later

_____
(Hello. This is . . .)

_____ 　　　　　　_____
(good-bye) 　　　　　　　　　　　　　　(see you later)

Glem ikke that **du kan** ask . . .
(glem)
forget not

Hvor mye koster en rikstelefon til de Forente Stater? _____
(mee-eh) *(reeks-tay-leh-fohn)* *(for-aint-eh) (staht-air)*
　　　　long-distance call　　　　United   States

Hvor mye koster en rikstelefon til Kanada? _____

Her er some emergency telephone numbers in Oslo **eller** Bergen.
☐ **brann** *(brahn)* .... fire　　　 001 _____
☐ **politi** *(poh-lih-tee)* .... police　 002 _____
☐ **ambulanse** *(ahm-boo-lahns-eh)* ...... ambulance 003 _____
☐ **informasjon** *(in-for-mah-shohn)* ..... information 018 _____

Her er some sample sentences for **telefonen.** Write them in the blanks below.

Jeg vil gjerne ringe til New York. _____
(yairn-eh) gladly *(ring-eh)* call

Jeg vil gjerne ringe til SAS på flyplassen. _____
(yairn-eh) gladly *(ring-eh)* *(sahs)* Scandinavian Airlines *(flee-plahs-en)*

Jeg vil gjerne ringe til herr Nilsen. _____
(neel-sen) Mr.

Telefonnummeret mitt er 12 36 76. _____
(mit) my

Hva er telefonnummeret ditt? _____
(dit) your

Hva er telefonnummeret til hotellet? _____
of

Kirsten: **Hallo. Dette er fru Olsen. Jeg vil gjerne snakke med fru Farden.**
(froo) Mrs. *(yairn-eh)*

_____

Telefonist: **Et øyeblikk, takk. Dessverre er det opptatt.**
(uh-oy-eh-blik) one moment *(des-vair-eh)* unfortunately *(ohp-taht)* busy

_____

Kirsten: **Si det en gang til, takk. Snakk langsommere.**
(see) say *(gahng)* one time more *(lahng-sohm-air-eh)* more slowly

_____

Telefonist: **Dessverre er det opptatt.**

_____

Kirsten: **Ja vel. Takk. Ha det!**
(yah) okay *(deh)*

_____

Du er klar to use any **telefon i Norge.** Just take it **langsomt og snakk** clearly.
ready *(lahng-sohmt)* slowly *(snahk)*

Her er countries **du** may wish to call.
- ☐ **Østerrike** *(ust-air-reek-eh)* .... Austria _____
- ☐ **Belgia** *(bel-gee-ah)* .... Belgium _____
- ☐ **Kanada** *(kah-nah-dah)* .... Canada _____
- ☐ **Danmark** *(dahn-mark)* .... Denmark _____

22   T-bane, Trikk og Buss
(tay-bahn-eh) *(trik)* *(boos)*
subway   streetcar

An excellent means of transportation **i Oslo er T-banen.** *(tay-bahn-en)* subway the **Oslo og alle** *(ahl-eh)* all larger **norske byer** *(bee-air)* cities **har også trikk og buss** streetcars which are a more scenic way **å reise.** *(race-eh)* **Hvor det er** steep hills, such as **i Bergen, finner du ofte** *(ohf-teh)* often cable cars. **På reise** into the countryside, there is an extensive system of long-distance **busser heter** *(boos-air)* **rutebiler.** *(roo-teh-beel-air)* scheduled buses

(tay-bahn-en)
T-banen
subway the

(trik-en)
trikken
streetcar the

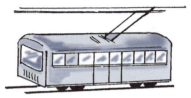

(tay-bahn-eh-stah-shohn-en)
T-banestasjonen
subway station the

(trik-eh-hold-eh-plahs-en)
trikkeholdeplassen
streetcar stop the

(boos-hold-eh-plahs-en)
bussholdeplassen
bus stop the

Maps displaying the various **linjer** *(lin-yair)* lines **er** generally posted outside every **inngang til** *(in-gahng)* entrance **T-banestasjonene** *(tay-bahn-eh-stah-shohn-en-eh)* subway stations **og** at **trikkeholdeplassene.** *(trik-eh-hold-eh-plahs-en-eh)* streetcar stops the **Et kart** map of **byen** *(bee-en)* city **har også** these transportation **ruter.** *(roo-tair)* routes **Linjer** *(lin-yair)* lines **er** color-coded to facilitate reading, just like your example on the next page. Remember, **du må kjøpe en billett** must before entering **T-banen eller trikken.**

☐ **Tyskland** *(tewsk-lahn)* . . . . Germany
☐ **England** *(eng-lahn)* . . . . England
☐ **Finland** *(fin-lahn)* . . . . Spain
☐ **Irland** *(eer-lahn)* . . . . Ireland
☐ **Italia** *(ee-tahl-ee-ah)* . . . . Italy

Other than having foreign **ord, norske T-baner er** just like **amerikanske eller engelske T-baner.**

Locate your destination, select the correct **linjen** on your practice **T-bane og** hop on board.

Say these questions aloud many times and don't forget you need **en billett** for **T-banen!**

(tay-bahn-eh-stah-shohn-en)
Hvor er T-banestasjonen?

(boos-hold-eh-plahs-en)
Hvor er bussholdeplassen?

(trik-eh-hold-eh-plahs-en)
Hvor er trikkeholdeplassen?

(droh-sheh-hold-eh-plahs-en)
Hvor er drosjeholdeplassen?
taxi stand the

❒	**Luxembourg** *(luke-sem-bewrg)*	Luxembourg
❒	**Nederland** *(nay-dair-lahn)*	Netherlands
❒	**Sverige** *(svair-ree-eh)*	Sweden
❒	**Sveits** *(svites)*	Switzerland
❒	**de Forente Stater** *(for-aint-eh)(staht-air)* . . .	the United States

Practice the following basic questions out loud **og** then write them in the blanks below.

1. Hvor ofte går *(gor)* T-banen til flyplassen *(flee-plahs-en)*? _____

   Hvor ofte går bussen til Holmenkollen *(hohl-men-kohl-en)*? _____

   Hvor ofte går trikken til Gamlebyen *(gahm-leh-bee-en)*? _____

2. Når *(nor)* går T-banen? _____
   when

   Når går bussen? _____*Når går bussen? Når går bussen?*_____

   Når går trikken? _____

3. Hva *(kohst-air)* koster en billett på T-banen? _____

   Hva koster en billett på bussen? _____

   Hva koster en billett på trikken? _____

4. Hvor er T-banestasjonen? _____

   Hvor er drosjeholdeplassen *(droh-sheh-hold-eh-plahs-en)*? _____

   Hvor er trikkeholdeplassen? _____

Let's change directions **og** learn **tre nye verb**. **Du vet** the basic "plug-in" formula, so write out
                                                    know
your own sentences using these new verbs.

å vaske *(oh)(vahsk-ah)* _____
to wash

å miste *(mist-eh)* _____
to lose

å ta *(tah)* _____
to take

Her er a few more greetings **på norsk**.
- **God jul** *(go)(yool)* .... Merry Christmas!
- **Godt nyttår** *(goht)(neet-or)* .... Happy New Year!
- **Gratulerer!** *(grah-tool-air-air)* .... Congratulations!
- **Gratulerer med dagen!** *(grah-tool-air-air)(meh)(dahg-en)* .... Happy Birthday!

23 Kjøpe og Selge
(hyuhp-eh) to buy *(sel-geh)* to sell

Shopping abroad is exciting. The simple everyday task of buying **en liter melk eller et eple** *(ep-leh)* (liter, milk, apple) becomes a challenge that **du skulle nå** *(skoo-leh)* (should) be able to meet quickly **og** easily. Of course, **du** will purchase **suvenirer, frimerker og brevkort,** *(soo-veh-neer-air)(free-mair-kair)* (souvenirs) **men glem ikke** (but forget not) those **mange** other things ranging **fra** shoelaces **til aspirin** *(ahs-peer-een)* that **du** might need unexpectedly. Locate your store, draw a line to it **og,** as always, write your new words in the blanks provided.

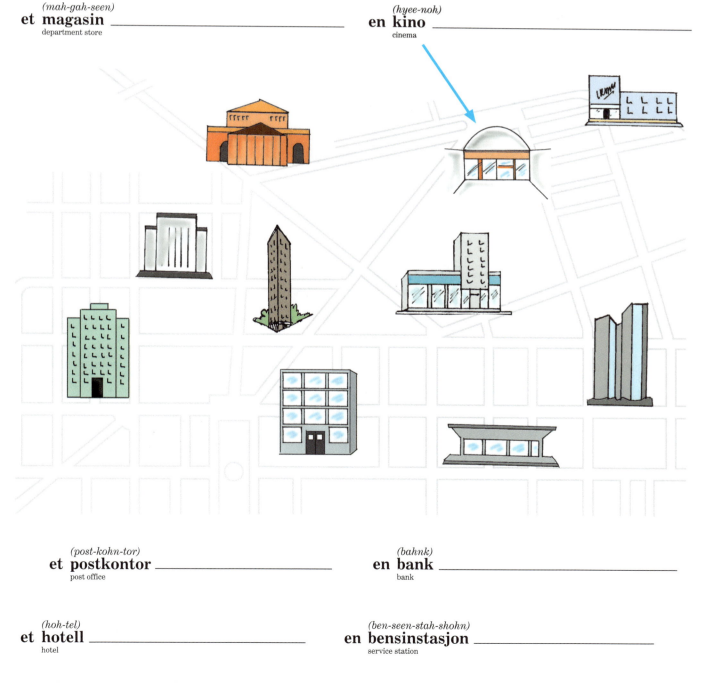

et magasin *(mah-gah-seen)* — department store

en kino *(hyee-noh)* — cinema

et postkontor *(post-kohn-tor)* — post office

en bank *(bahnk)* — bank

et hotell *(hoh-tel)* — hotel

en bensinstasjon *(ben-seen-stah-shohn)* — service station

(for-ret-ning-air) *(ook-eh-dahg-air)*
Forretninger are open **ukedager** **fra kl.**
stores   weekdays
9.00 til kl. 17.00 og lørdag til kl. 13.00. No
forretninger har åpent søndager!

(hyuht-for-ret-ning)
en kjøttforretning
meat market

(bohk-hahn-del)
en bokhandel
bookstore

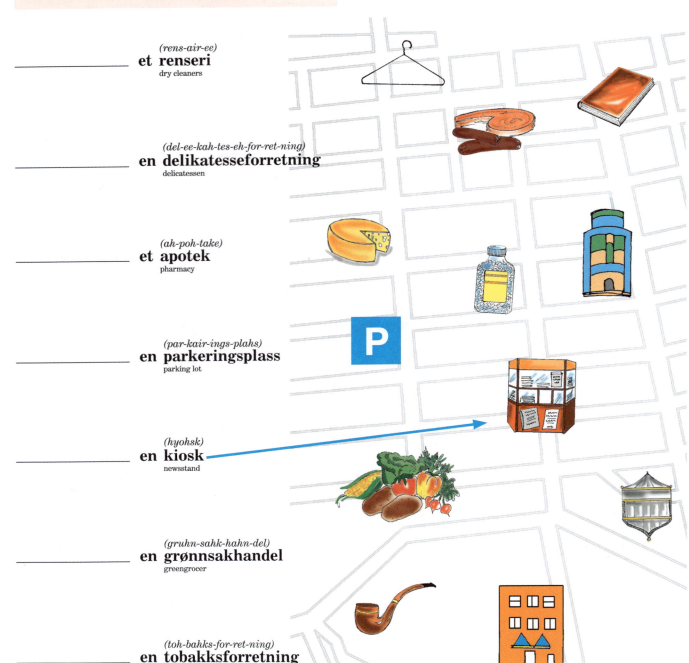

_____ *(rens-air-ee)* **et renseri** — dry cleaners

_____ *(del-ee-kah-tes-eh-for-ret-ning)* **en delikatesseforretning** — delicatessen

_____ *(ah-poh-take)* **et apotek** — pharmacy

_____ *(par-kair-ings-plahs)* **en parkeringsplass** — parking lot

_____ *(hyohsk)* **en kiosk** — newsstand

_____ *(gruhn-sahk-hahn-del)* **en grønnsakhandel** — greengrocer

_____ *(toh-bahks-for-ret-ning)* **en tobakksforretning** — tobacco store

(torg-eh) *(veh)* *(brew-gen)*
In coastal cities **torget er ofte ved bryggen**
               market the   at   wharf the
(fairshk-eh) *(ray-kair)* *(spees-eh)*
og du kan kjøpe ferske reker og spise
                        fresh   shrimp
dem on the spot.
them

(race-eh-bew-roh)
et reisebyrå
travel agency

(poh-lih-tee-stah-shohn)
en politistasjon
police station

(melk-eh-boo-teek)
en melkebutikk
dairy

(blohm-stair-for-ret-ning)
en blomsterforretning
florist

(fisk-eh-hahn-del)
en fiskehandel _____
fish shop

(frukt-hahn-lair)
en frukthandler _____
fruit vendor

(torg)
et torg _____
market

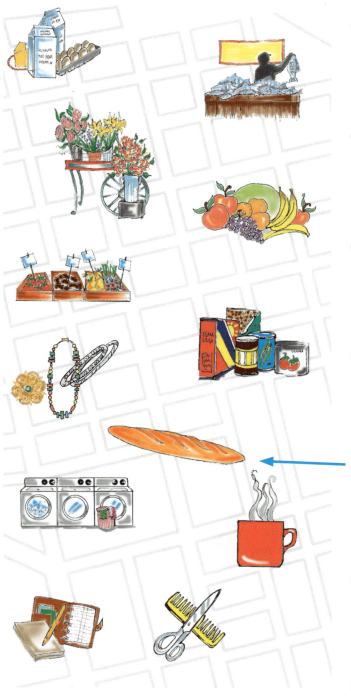

(koh-loh-nee-ahl-hahn-del)
en kolonialhandel _____
grocery store

(guhl-smeh)
en gullsmed _____
goldsmith / jeweler

(bah-kair-ee)
et bakeri _____*et bakeri*_____
bakery

(kohn-dih-tor-ee)
et konditori _____
coffee shop

(vahsk-air-ee)
et vaskeri _____
laundry

(pah-peer-hahn-del)
en papirhandel
stationery store

(free-sur)
en frisør
hairdresser

(hyel-air-eh-tah-sheh)
I Norge, the basement **heter "kjelleretasje."**

(eh-tah-shair)
The other **etasjer** **er** numbered as **i**
floors

Amerika.

24 Magasinet
(mah-gah-seen-eh)
department store the

At this point, **du skulle** just about be **klar til** your **tur til Norge**. **Du har** gone shopping **for** those last-minute odds 'n ends. Most likely, the store directory at your local **magasin** did **ikke** look like the one **nede**! **Du vet** that **"barn"** er det norske ordet for "child" so if **du trenger** something **for et barn, du** would probably look on the **annen eller tredje etasje, ikke sant?**

4. ETASJE	husholdningsartikler krystall møbler lamper	bestikk kjøkkentøy tepper speil	lås keramikk porselen bilder
3. ETASJE	bøker fjernsyn barnemøbler leketøy	radioer musikkinstrumenter papirvarer plater	tobakksvarer restaurant aviser tidsskrifter
2. ETASJE	barnetøy dameklær damehatter babyartikler	herreklær fotografi senger sengetøy	klokker antikviteter norske kofter
1. ETASJE	bilavdeling undertøy lommetørklær	badeartikler damesko herresko	verktøy sportsartikler bakeri
K	paraplyer kart herrehatter smykker	hansker lærtøy strømper kafeteria	toalettsaker parfyme sjokolade delikatesser

Let's start a checklist **for** your **tur**. Besides **klær, hva trenger du?** As you learn these **ord**, assemble these items **i et hjørne** of your **hus**. Check **og** make sure that **de er rene og klare for** your **reise**. Be sure to do the same **med resten** of **tingene** that **du pakker**. On the next pages, match each item to its picture, draw a line to it and write out the word many times. As **du** organize these things, check them off on this list. Do **ikke** forget to take the next group of sticky labels and label these **ting i dag!**

(pahs)
et pass
passport

(bil-let)
en billett
ticket

(kohf-airt)
en koffert   _en koffert, en koffert_ ✓
suitcase

(hohnd-vesk-eh)
ei håndveske
handbag

(lohm-eh-bohk)
ei lommebok
wallet

(peng-air)
penger
money

(kray-deet-koort-en-eh)
kreditkortene
credit cards the

(race-eh-shek-en-eh)
reisesjekkene
travelers checks the

(foh-toh-grah-fee-ah-pah-raht)
et fotografiapparat
camera

(film)
en film
film

(bahd-eh-drahkt)
ei badedrakt
swimsuit, swimming trunks

(bahd-eh-drahkt)
ei badedrakt
swimsuit, swimming trunks

(sahn-dahl-air)
sandaler
sandals

(sohl-bril-air)
solbriller
sunglasses

(tahn-bursh-teh)
en tannbørste
toothbrush

(tahn-krame)
en tannkrem
toothpaste

(sohp-eh)
såpe
soap

(bar-bair-huh-vel)
en barberhøvel
razor

(day-oh-doh-rahnt)
en deodorant
deodorant

103

(kahm) **en kam** — comb	en kam, en kam, en kam ✓
(rine-frahk) **en regnfrakk** — raincoat	
(pah-rah-plee) **en paraply** — umbrella	
(kohp-eh) **en kåpe** — overcoat	
(hahn-skair) **hansker** — gloves	
(loo-eh) **ei lue** — ski hat	
(haht) **en hatt** — hat	
(stuv-lair) **støvler** — boots	
(skoh) **sko** — shoes	
(ten-is-skoh) **tennissko** — tennis shoes	
(dres) **en dress** — suit	
(shlips) **et slips** — tie	
(short-eh) **en skjorte** — shirt	
(lohm-eh-tur-klay) **et lommetørkle** — handkerchief	
(yahk-eh) **ei jakke** — jacket, blazer	
(buhx-air) **bukser** — trousers	
(jeans) **jeans** — jeans	
(shorts) **shorts** — shorts	
(tay-short-eh) **en T-skjorte** — T-shirt	

(oon-air-buhx-air)
underbukser
underpants

(oon-air-short-eh)
en underskjorte
undershirt

(hyoh-leh)
en kjole
dress

(bloos-eh)
en bluse
blouse

(shirt)
et skjørt — et skjort, et skjort ✓
skirt

(gen-sair)
en genser
sweater

(oon-air-hyoh-leh)
en underkjole
slip

(bay) (hoh)
en B. H.
bra

(troos-air)
truser
underpants

(sohk-air)
sokker
socks

(strump-air)
strømper
pantyhose, tights

(pee-shah-mahs)
en pyjamas
pajamas

(naht-short-eh)
en nattskjorte
nightshirt

(bahd-eh-kohp-eh)
en badekåpe
bathrobe

(tuf-lair)
tøfler
slippers

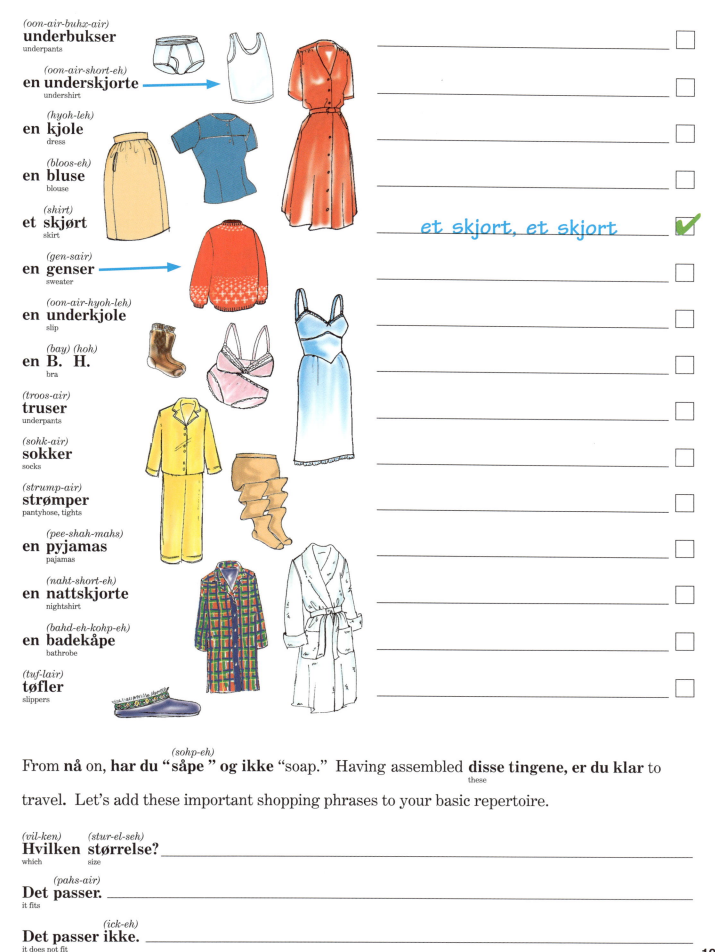

From **nå** on, **har du "såpe"** *(sohp-eh)* **og ikke** "soap." Having assembled **disse tingene, er du klar** to travel. Let's add these important shopping phrases to your basic repertoire.

(vil-ken) (stur-el-seh)
Hvilken størrelse? _____
which   size

(pahs-air)
Det passer. _____
it fits

(ick-eh)
Det passer ikke. _____
it does not fit

105

Treat yourself to a final review. **Du vet navnene** *(nahv-nen-eh)* of the different **butikker** *(boo-teek-air)* **og forretninger,** *(for-ret-ning-air)* so
know names the   shops   stores
let's practice shopping. Just remember your key question **ord** that you learned in Step 2.
Whether **du** need to buy **en hatt** *(haht)* **eller ei bok** *(bohk)* the necessary **ordene** are the same.

1. First step — **Hvor?**

Hvor er melkebutikken? *(melk-eh-boo-teek-en)*   **Hvor er banken?**   **Hvor er kinoen?**

_____
(Where is the department store?)

_____
(Where is the grocery store?)

_____
(Where is the market?)

2. Second step — tell them **hva du** are looking for, **trenger eller vil ha!**

Jeg trenger . . .   **Jeg vil gjerne ha . . .** *(yairn-eh)*   **Har du . . . ?**
I   need   I   would like (gladly)   do you have

_____
(Do you have postcards?)

_____
(I want four stamps.)

_____
(I need toothpaste.)

_____
(I want to buy film.)

_____
(Do you have coffee?)

Go through the glossary at the end of **denne boka og** select **tjue** (hyoo-eh) **ord**. Drill the above patterns
this
med disse tjue ordene. Don't cheat. Drill them **i dag. Nå, ta tjue ord til fra** your glossary,
these *take* *more*
eller ordbok, og do the same.

3. Third step — find out **hvor** (mee-eh) **mye** (deh) **det** (kohst-air) **koster.**

| **Hva koster det?** | **Hvor mye koster det?** | **Hva koster et frimerke?** (free-mair-keh) |

_____
(How much does the toothpaste cost?)

_____
(How much does the soap cost?)

_____
(How much does a cup of tea cost?)

4. Fourth step — success! I found it!

Once **du finner hva du vil ha, du sier,** (see-air)
say

Jeg vil ha det, takk. _____

or

Jeg tar det, takk.   *Jeg tar det, takk.   Jeg tar det, takk.*
take

Eller if **du** would not like it, **du sier,**

Jeg vil ikke ha det, takk. _____

or

Jeg tar det ikke, takk. _____
do not take

Congratulations! You have finished. By now you should have stuck your labels, flashed your cards, cut out your menu guide and packed your suitcases. You should be very pleased with your accomplishment. You have learned what it sometimes takes others years to achieve and you hopefully had fun doing it. **God tur! Lykke til!**

Glossary

This glossary contains words used in this book only. It is not meant to be a dictionary. Consider purchasing a dictionary which best suits your needs - small for traveling, large for reference, or specialized for specific vocabulary needs. Don't forget that the Norwegian letters "ø," "å" and "æ" come at the end of the alphabet.

Each word is followed by the pronunciation guide used in this book. In addition, after each noun you will see the suffix (-et, -en, -n, -t, etc.) which indicates the definite (or "the") form of the word, i.e.

adresse -n ⟶ adressen
address   address the

A

-a *(uh)* .... the
absolutt *(ahp-soh-loot)* .... absolutely
adresse -n *(ah-dres-eh)* .... address
aerogram -met *(air-oh-grahm)* .... aerogram
akkurat *(ah-koo-raht)* .... accurate
alkohol -en *(ahl-koh-hohl)* .... alcohol
alle *(ahl-eh)* .... all
allerede *(ahl-eh-red-eh)* .... already
alt *(ahlt)* .... everything
ambassadør -en *(ahm-bah-sah-dur)* ..... ambassador
ambulanse -n *(ahm-boo-lahns-eh)* ...... ambulance
Amerika *(ah-mair-ih-kuh)* .... America
amerikaner -en *(ah-mair-ih-kahn-air)* ... American
ankomst -en *(ahn-kohmst)* .... arrival
annen *(ahn-en)* .... second
apotek -et *(ah-poh-take)* .... pharmacy
appetitt -en *(ah-peh-teet)* .... appetite
aprikos -en *(ah-pree-kohs)* .... apricot
april *(ah-preel)* .... April
arm -en *(arm)* .... arm
aspirin -en *(ahs-peer-een)* .... aspirin
atten *(ah-ten)* .... eighteen
august *(ow-goost)* .... August
automat -en *(ow-toh-maht)* .... vending machine
avgang -en *(ahv-gahng)* .... departure
avis -a *(ah-vees)* .... newspaper
avreise -n *(ahv-race-eh)* .... departure

B

bad -et *(bahd)* .... bathroom
badedrakt -a *(bahd-eh-drahkt)* ... swimsuit, swimming trunks
badekåpe -a *(bahd-eh-kohp-eh)* .... bathrobe
bagasje -n *(bah-gah-sheh)* .... baggage, luggage
bak *(bahk)* .... behind, in back of
bakeri -et *(bah-kair-ee)* .... bakery
bakt *(bahkt)* .... baked
bakverk -et *(bahk-vairk)* .... pastry
balkong -en *(bahl-kohng)* .... balcony
banan -en *(bah-nahn)* .... banana
bank -en *(bahnk)* .... bank
bar -en *(bar)* .... bar
barberhøvel -en *(bar-bair-huh-vel)* ...... razor
bare *(bar-eh)* .... just, only
barn -et *(barn)* .... child
bedre *(bed-reh)* .... better
Belgia *(bel-gee-ah)* .... Belgium
benk -en *(benk)* .... bench
bensinstasjon -en *(ben-seen-stah-shohn)* ..... gas station
best *(best)* .... best
bestefar -en *(best-eh-far)* .... grandfather
bestemor -a *(best-eh-mor)* .... grandmother
bestille *(beh-stil-eh)* .... to order, reserve
bestilling -en *(beh-stil-ing)* .... reservation
bestilt *(beh-stilt)* .... reserved, ordered
betale *(beh-tahl-eh)* .... to pay
B. H. -en *(bay)(hoh)* .... bra
biff -en *(bif)* .... beef, steak
bil -en *(beel)* .... car
bilde -t *(bild-eh)* .... picture
billett -en *(bil-let)* .... ticket
billettluke -a *(bil-let-luhk-eh)* .. ticket window, ticket counter
billig *(bil-ee)* .... inexpensive
biluteie -en *(beel-oot-lay-eh)* .... car rental
bilverksted -et *(beel-vairk-sted)* .... car repair
bli *(blee)* .... to remain, stay, come to (bill)
blomst -en *(blohmst)* .... flower
blomstene *(blohm-sten-eh)* .... flowers
blomsterforretning -en *(blohm-stair-for-ret-ning)* . florist
bluse -n *(bloos-eh)* .... blouse
blyant -en *(blee-ahnt)* .... pencil
blå *(bloh)* .... blue
blåse *(bloh-seh)* .... to blow (wind)
bok -a *(bohk)* .... book
bokhandel -en *(bohk-hahn-del)* .... bookstore
bo *(boh)* .... to live, reside
bord -et *(boor)* .... table
bra *(brah)* .... well
brann -en *(brahn)* .... fire
brev -et *(brave)* .... letter
brevkort -et *(brave-koort)* .... postcard
briller *(bril-air)* .... glasses
british *(brih-tisk)* .... British
bror -en *(bror)* .... brother
brun *(broon)* .... brown, tanned
brygge -a *(brew-geh)* .... wharf
brød -et *(bruh)* .... bread
bukser *(buhx-air)* .... trousers, pants
buss -en *(boos)* .... bus
bussholdeplass -en *(boos-hold-eh-plahs)* .... bus stop
butikk -en *(boo-teek)* .... shop
by -en *(bee)* .... city
bytte *(boot-eh)* .... to change, swap
bytte tog *(boot-eh)(tohg)* .... to change trains
båt -en *(boht)* .... boat

C

campingplass -en *(kam-ping-plahs)* .... campground
CD-plate -n *(say-day-plaht-eh)* .... CD
CD-spiller -en *(say-day-spil-air)* .... CD player
Celsius *(sel-see-oos)* .... Centigrade
centigram -met *(sen-tih-grahm)* .... centigram
champagne -n *(shahm-pahn-yeh)* .... champagne
chanse -n *(shang-seh)* .... chance
choke -n *(shohk)* .... choke (in a car)
clutch -en *(kluhtsh)* .... clutch (in a car)
cocktail -en *(kohk-tail)* .... cocktail

D

dag -en *(dahg)*	day
dame -n *(dah-meh)*	lady
Danmark *(dahn-mark)*	Denmark
dans -en *(dahnsk)*	dance
dansk *(dahnsk)*	Danish
data -en *(dah-tah)*	computer
datter -a *(dah-tair)*	daughter
de *(dee)*	the, they
De *(dee)*	you (formal)
dekorativ *(deh-koh-rah-teev)*	decorative
delikatesseforretning -en *(del-ee-kah-tes-eh-for-ret-ning)*	delicatessen
dem *(dem)*	them
den *(den)*	the, it
denne *(den-eh)*	this
deodorant -en *(day-oh-doh-rahnt)*	deodorant
der *(dair)*	there
desember *(des-em-bair)*	December
dessert -en *(des-air)*	dessert
dessverre *(des-vair-eh)*	unfortunately
det *(deh)*	the, it, that
dette *(det-eh)*	this
disse *(dis-eh)*	these
ditt *(dit)*	your
dobbeltrom -met *(dohb-elt-rohm)*	double room
dress -en *(dres)*	suit
drikk -en *(drik)*	drink
drikke *(drik-eh)*	to drink
drikkepenger *(drik-eh-peng-air)*	tip
drikkevare -n *(drik-eh-var-eh)*	beverage
drosje -n *(droh-sheh)*	taxi
drosjeholdeplass -en *(droh-sheh-hold-eh-plahs)*	taxi stand
du *(doo)*	you
dum *(doom)*	dumb
dusj -en *(doosh)*	shower
dyne -a *(dee-neh)*	comforter
dyp *(dewp)*	deep
dyr *(dewr)*	expensive
dør -a *(dur)*	door
dårlig *(dor-lee)*	bad, badly

E

egg -et *(egg)*	egg
ei *(ay)*	a, an
eksempel -et *(ek-sem-pel)*	example
eksport -en *(ek-sport)*	export
ekspresstog -et *(ek-spres-tohg)*	express train
ekstra *(ek-strah)*	extra
elektrisk *(el-ek-trisk)*	electric
eller *(el-air)*	or
elleve *(elv-eh)*	eleven
en *(en)*	a, an, one
-en *(en)*	the
en gang til *(en)(gahng)(til)*	once again, one more time
-ene *(en-eh)*	the
engelsk *(eng-elsk)*	English
England *(eng-lahn)*	England
enkelt *(eng-kelt)*	single, one-way, simple
enkeltrom -met *(eng-kelt-rohm)*	single room
eple -t *(ep-leh)*	apple
e-post, en *(ay-post)*	email
er *(ar)*	is, are
er du snill *(ar)(doo)(snil)*	be so kind, if you please
et *(et)*	a, an
-et *(et)*	the
etasje -n *(eh-tah-sheh)*	floor
ett *(et)*	one
ettermiddag -en *(et-tair-mid-ahg)*	afternoon
Europa *(oy-roh-puh)*	Europe
europeisk *(oy-roh-pay-isk)*	European

F

Fahrenheit *(far-en-hite)*	Fahrenheit
familie -n *(fah-meel-yeh)*	family
fantastisk *(fahn-tahs-tisk)*	fantastic
far -en *(far)*	father
farge -n *(farg-eh)*	color
fasong -en *(fah-sohng)*	fashion, clothes style
fattig *(fah-tee)*	poor
fax -en *(fahks)*	fax
feber -en *(fay-bair)*	fever
februar *(fay-broo-ar)*	February
fem *(fem)*	five
femten *(fem-ten)*	fifteen
femti *(fem-tee)*	fifty
ferje -a *(fair-yeh)*	ferry
fersk *(fairshk)*	fresh
fest -en *(fest)*	festival, party
fet *(fet)*	fat
film -en *(film)*	film
fin *(feen)*	fine
finger -en *(fing-air)*	finger
Finland *(fin-lahn)*	Finland
finne *(fin-eh)*	to find
fire *(fear-eh)*	four
fisk -en *(fisk)*	fish
fiskehandel -en *(fisk-eh-hahn-del)*	fish store
fjernsyn -et *(fyairn-seen)*	television
fjord -en *(fyord)*	fjord
fjorten *(fyor-ten)*	fourteen
flere *(flay-reh)*	more
flerfarget *(flair-farg-et)*	multi-colored
flis -en *(flees)*	tile
fly -et *(flee)*	airplane
fly *(flee)*	to fly
flyplass -en *(flee-plahs)*	airport
flypost -en *(flee-post)*	airmail
flyr *(fleer)*	fly/flies
flytur -en *(flee-toor)*	flight
folkemuseum -et *(folk-eh-moo-say-oom)*	folk art museum
for *(for)*	because, for
foran *(for-ahn)*	before, in front of
forbudt *(for-bewt)*	prohibited, forbidden
foreldre *(for-el-dreh)*	parents
Forente Stater, de *(for-aint-eh)(staht-air)*	United States
forlenge *(for-leng-eh)*	to prolong
forretning -en *(for-ret-ning)*	store, business
forrett -en *(for-ret)*	appetizer
forsiktig *(for-shik-tee)*	careful
forstadstog -et *(for-shtahds-tohg)*	suburban train
forstå *(for-shtoh)*	to understand
fort *(foort)*	fast, quick
foto -et *(foh-toh)*	photo
fotografiapparat -et *(foh-toh-grah-fee-ah-pah-raht)*	camera
fottur -en *(foh-toor)*	hike, "foot tour"
fra *(frah)*	from
Frankrike *(frahnk-reek-eh)*	France
fransk *(frahnsk)*	French
fredag *(fray-dahg)*	Friday
fri *(free)*	free
frihet -en *(free-het)*	freedom
frimerke -t *(free-mair-keh)*	stamp
frisk *(frisk)*	healthy

Norwegian	Pronunciation	English
frisør -en	(free-sur)	hairdresser
frokost -en	(froh-kohst)	breakfast
fru	(froo)	Mrs.
frukt -en	(frukt)	fruit
frukthandler -en	(frukt-hahn-lair)	fruit vendor
frøken	(fruhk-en)	Miss
fugl -en	(fuel)	fowl
fylt	(fewlt)	stuffed
førti	(fur-tee)	forty
får -et	(for)	mutton

G

gaffel -en	(gah-fel)	fork
galt	(gahlt)	wrong
gamleby -en	(gahlm-leh-bee)	old town
gammel	(gahm-el)	old
gang -en	(gahng)	aisle, hallway
garasje -n	(gah-rah-sheh)	garage
gardin -et	(gar-deen)	curtain
gate -n	(gaht-eh)	street
genser -en	(gen-sair)	sweater
gi	(yee)	to give
gin	(jin)	gin
gjerne	(yairn-eh)	gladly
gjest -en	(yest)	guest
gjøre	(yuhr-eh)	to do, make
glad	(glah)	glad, happy
glass -et	(glahs)	glass
glemme	(glem-eh)	to forget
god	(go)	good
god fornøyelse	(go)(for-nuh-oy-el-seh)	have fun
god tur	(go)(toor)	have a good trip
godt	(goht)	good
grad -en	(grahd)	degree
gram -met	(grahm)	gram
grapefrukt -en	(grep-frukt)	grapefruit
gresk	(gresk)	Greek
grill -en	(gril)	grill, restaurant
grillet	(gril-et)	grilled
grønn	(gruhn)	green
grønnsaker	(gruhn-sahk-air)	vegetables
grønnsakshandel -en	(gruhn-sahk-hahn-del)	greengrocer
grå	(groh)	gray
gud -en	(gewd)	God
gul	(guhl)	yellow
gull	(guhl)	gold
gullsmed -en	(guhl-smeh)	jeweler, goldsmith
gutt -en	(guht)	boy
gå	(goh)	to go, walk
gå fra	(goh)(frah)	to leave from, depart
gå inn	(goh)(in)	to enter, go in
gå ut	(goh)(oot)	to exit, go out
gås -ei	(gaws)	goose

H

Norwegian	Pronunciation	English
ha	(hah)	to have
ha det	(hah)(deh)	good-bye
ha det bra	(hah)(deh)(brah)	good-bye
hage -n	(hah-geh)	garden
halv	(hahl)	half
han	(hahn)	he
handlebag -en	(hahn-leh-bayg)	shopping bag
hanske -n	(hahn-skeh)	glove
har	(har)	have/has
hard	(har)	hard
hardkokt	(har-kohkt)	hard-boiled
hatt -en	(haht)	hat
hei	(hay)	hi, hello
helligdag -en	(hel-ee-dahg)	holiday
her	(hair)	here
herberge -t	(hair-bairg-eh)	hostel
herr	(hair)	Mr.
herre -n	(hair-eh)	gentleman
hete	(het-eh)	to be called, named
heter	(het-air)	is/are called
hittegodskontor -et	(hit-eh-gohds-kohn-tor)	lost-and-found
hjelp!	(yelp)	help!
hjem -met	(yem)	home
hjørne -t	(yurn-eh)	corner
holdeplass -en	(hold-uh-plahs)	stop
Holmenkollen	(hohl-men-kohl-en)	ski jump in Oslo
hotell -et	(hoh-tel)	hotel
hotellrom -met	(hoh-tel-rohm)	hotel room
hotellvert -en	(hot-tel-vairt)	hotelkeeper
hovedinngang -en	(hoh-ved-in-gahng)	main entrance
hun	(huhn)	she
hund -en	(hoon)	dog
hundre	(huhn-dreh)	hundred
hurtigtog -et	(her-tee-tohg)	fast train
hus -et	(hoos)	house
hva	(vah)	what
hvem	(vem)	who
hver	(vair)	each, every
hvilke	(vil-keh)	which
hvit	(veet)	white
hvitvin -en	(veet-veen)	white wine
hvor	(vor)	where
hvor mange	(vor)(mahng-eh)	how many
hvor mye	(vor)(mee-eh)	how much
hvordan	(vor-dahn)	how
hvorfor	(vor-for)	why
hydrofoilbåt -en	(hee-droh-foil-boht)	hydrofoil
hytte -n	(hew-teh)	cabin
høns	(huns)	poultry
høst -en	(hust)	autumn
høy	(huh-oy)	high, tall
høyre	(huh-oy-reh)	right
hånd -en	(hohn)	hand
håndbagasje	(hohn-bah-gah-sheh)	hand baggage
håndkle -et	(hohn-klay)	towel
håndklærne	(hohn-klair-neh)	towels
håndverk -et	(hohn-vairk)	handwork, handicraft
håndveske -a	(hohn-vesk-eh)	purse
hår -et	(hor)	hair

I

Norwegian	Pronunciation	English
i	(ee)	in, for, at
i dag	(ee)(dahg)	today
i går	(ee)(gor)	yesterday
i morgen	(ee)(mor-en)	tomorrow
ide -en	(ee-day)	idea
ikke	(ick-eh)	no, not
ikke sant	(ick-eh)(sahnt)	not true, sure enough
immigrant -en	(im-ih-grahnt)	immigrant
immun	(ih-moon)	immune
import -en	(im-port)	import
informasjon -en	(in-for-mah-shohn)	information
ingen	(ing-en)	none, no one
ingenting	(ing-en-ting)	nothing
inn i	(in)(ee)	into
inne i	(in-eh)(ee)	in, inside
innenlands	(in-en-lahns)	domestic, internal (of a country)
inngang -en	(in-gahng)	entrance
Irland	(eer-lahn)	Ireland

Norwegian	Pronunciation	English
Island	(ees-lahn)	Iceland
Israel	(ees-rah-el)	Israel
Italia	(ee-tahl-ee-ah)	Italy
italiensk	(ee-tahl-ee-ensk)	Italian

J

Norwegian	Pronunciation	English
ja	(yah)	yes
ja vel	(yah)(vel)	okay
jakke -a	(yahk-eh)	jacket
januar	(yah-noo-ar)	January
Japan	(yah-pahn)	Japan
japansk	(yah-pahnsk)	Japanese
jazz -en	(jahss)	jazz
jeans	(jeans)	jeans
jeg	(yay)	I
jente -a	(yen-teh)	girl
jernbanestasjon -en	(yairn-bahn-eh-stah-shohn)	train station
jo	(yoh)	yes, okay, all right
job -en	(yohb)	job
journalist -en	(shuhr-nah-list)	journalist
juli	(yoo-lee)	July
juni	(yoo-nee)	June
jødisk	(yuh-disk)	Jewish

K

Norwegian	Pronunciation	English
kafé -n	(kah-fay)	café
kaffe -n	(kahf-eh)	coffee
kakao -en	(kah-kah-oh)	cocoa
kake -a	(kahk-eh)	cake
kald	(kahl)	cold
kaldtbord -et	(kahlt-boor)	cold buffet, smørgåsbord
kalender -en	(kah-len-dair)	calendar
kalvekjøtt -et	(kahl-veh-hyuht)	veal
kam -men	(kahm)	comb
kan	(kahn)	can/am able to
Kanada	(kah-nah-dah)	Canada
kanadier	(kah-nah-dyair)	Canadian
kart -et	(kart)	map
kasse -n	(kahs-uh)	cash register
katedral -en	(kah-tay-drahl)	cathedral
katolsk	(kah-tohlsk)	Catholic
katt -en	(kaht)	cat
kelner -en	(kel-nair)	waiter
kilo -en	(hyee-loh)	kilo
kilometer -en	(hyee-loh-may-tair)	kilometer
Kina	(hyee-nah)	China
kinesisk	(hyee-nay-sisk)	Chinese
kino -en	(hyee-noh)	movie theater
kiosk -en	(hyohsk)	newsstand
kirke -n	(hyeer-keh)	church
kjeller -en	(hyel-air)	basement
kjelleretasje -n	(hyel-air-eh-tah-sheh)	basement floor
kjole -n	(hyoh-leh)	dress
Kjøbenhavn	(hyuh-pen-hahvn)	Copenhagen
kjøkken -et	(hyuh-ken)	kitchen
kjøleskap -et	(hyul-eh-skahp)	refrigerator
kjøpe	(hyuhp-eh)	to buy
kjøre	(hyuhr-eh)	to drive
kjøtt -et	(hyuht)	meat
kjøttforretning -en	(hyuht-for-ret-ning)	meat market
klar	(klar)	clear, ready
klasse -en	(klahs-eh)	class
klesskap -et	(kles-skahp)	wardrobe
klokke -a	(klohk-eh)	clock
klubb -en	(klub)	club
klær	(klair)	clothing
kne -et	(knay)	knee
kniv -en	(kneev)	knife
koffert -en	(kohf-airt)	suitcase
kofte -t	(kohf-teh)	sweater in a colorful pattern
kokt	(kohkt)	cooked
kolonialhandel -en	(koh-loh-nee-ahl-hahn-del)	grocery store
komfyr -en	(kohm-fewr)	stove
komme	(kohm-eh)	to come
komme til	(kohm-eh)(til)	to arrive at, arrive in
kompass -et	(kohm-pahs)	compass
konditori -et	(kohn-dih-tor-ee)	pastry shop with a tea room
konge -n	(kohng-eh)	king
konsert -en	(kohn-sairt)	concert
konsertbillett -en	(kohn-sairt-bil-let)	concert ticket
konsulat -et	(kohn-sue-laht)	consulate
kontaktlinser	(kohn-tahkt-lin-sair)	contact lenses
kontor -et	(kohn-tor)	study, office
kopp -en	(kohp)	cup
korrekt	(koh-rekt)	correct
kort	(koort)	short
koste	(kohst-eh)	to cost
koster	(kohst-air)	cost/costs
krabbe -n	(krahb-eh)	crab
kredittkortene	(kray-deet-koort-en-eh)	credit cards
kro -a	(kroh)	tavern
krone -a	(krohn-eh)	krone (currency)
kryddersild -a	(krew-dair-sil)	pickled herring
kryssord oppgave -a	(krees-oor)(ohp-gah-veh)	crossword puzzle
krystall	(krew-stahl)	crystal
kultur -en	(kool-toor)	culture
kunne	(kuhn-eh)	to be able to, can
kvarter -et	(kvart-air)	quarter hour
kvart over	(kvart)(oh-vair)	quarter after
kvart på	(kvart)(poh)	quarter to
kveld -en	(kvel)	evening
kvittering -en	(kvit-air-ing)	receipt
kåpe -a	(kohp-eh)	overcoat

L

Norwegian	Pronunciation	English
lam -met	(lahm)	lamb
lampe -a	(lahm-peh)	lamp
land -et	(lahn)	land, country
lang	(lahng)	long
langsom	(lahng-sohm)	slow
langsommere	(lahng-sohm-air-eh)	more slowly
latter -en	(laht-air)	laughter
lav	(lahv)	low
ledig	(lay-dee)	available, free
lege -n	(lay-geh)	doctor
legitimasjon -en	(lay-gih-tih-mah-shohn)	legitimation, ID
lenge	(leng-eh)	for a long time, long
lese	(lay-seh)	to read
lett	(let)	easy
lik	(leek)	alike, equal
like	(leek-eh)	to like
linje -n	(lin-yeh)	line
liste -a	(list-eh)	list
lite	(lee-teh)	little
liten	(lee-ten)	small, little
liter -en	(leet-air)	liter
litt	(lit)	a little, some
litteratur -en	(lit-air-ah-toor)	literature
liv -et	(leev)	life
lobby -en	(loh-bee)	lobby
logisk	(loh-gisk)	logical
lokal	(loh-kahl)	local
lokalsamtale -n	(loh-kahl-sahm-tahl-eh)	local call

lokaltog -et (loh-kahl-tohg)	local train
lommebok -a (lohm-eh-bohk)	wallet
lommetørkle -et (lohm-eh-tur-klay)	handkerchief
losji -et (loh-shee)	lodging
lue -a (loo-eh)	ski hat
luke -a (luhk-eh)	counter, window (bank)
lukket (luhk-et)	closed
luksus -en (luke-soos)	luxury
lunsj -en (luhnsh)	lunch
lykke på reisen (loo-keh)(poh)(race-en)	bon voyage, have a good trip
lykke til (loo-keh)(til)	good luck
lyserød (lew-seh-ruh)	pink (light red)
lære (lair-eh)	to learn
lørdag (lur-dahg)	Saturday

M

magasin -et (mah-gah-seen)	department store
mai (my)	May
makrell -en (mah-krel)	mackerel
mandag (mahn-dahg)	Monday
mange (mahng-eh)	a lot, many
mange takk (mahng-eh)(tahk)	thank you very much
mann -en (mahn)	man
margarin -en (mar-gah-reen)	margarine
marked -et (mar-ked)	market
marmelade -n (mar-mel-ah-deh)	marmalade
mars (marsh)	March
maskin -en (mah-sheen)	machine
mat -en (maht)	food
med (meh)	with
medisin -en (med-ih-seen)	medicine
meg (my)	me
meget (may-get)	very
melk -a (melk)	milk
melkebutikk -en (melk-eh-boo-teek)	dairy
mellom (mel-ohm)	between
men (men)	but
menneske -t (men-es-keh)	person
meny -en (meh-nee)	menu
mer (mayr)	more
mest (mest)	most
meter -en (may-tair)	meter
middag -en (mid-ahg)	dinner, noon
midnatt -a (mid-naht)	midnight
midtsommer -en (mid-sohm-air)	Midsummer (day)
mild (mil)	mild
million -en (mil-yohn)	million
minutt -et (min-oot)	minute
miste (mist-eh)	to lose
mitt (mit)	my
moderne (moh-dair-neh)	modern
mor -a (mor)	mother
morgen (mor-en)	morning
motorsykkel -en (moh-tor-seek-el)	motorcycle
motorvei -en (moh-tor-vay)	highway
museum -et (moo-say-oom)	museum
musikk -en (moo-seek)	music
mye (mee-eh)	much, a lot
mynt -en (mewnt)	coin
må (moh)	must, have to
måltid -et (mohl-tee)	meal
måned -en (moh-ned)	month
måtte (moht-eh)	to have to, must

N

naken (nah-ken)	naked
nasjon -en (nah-shohn)	nation
nasjonal (nah-shohn-ahl)	national
natt -a (naht)	night
nattskjorte -n (naht-short-eh)	nightshirt
natur -en (nah-toor)	nature
navn -et (nahvn)	name
nede (ned-eh)	below, downstairs
nedenfor (ned-en-for)	below
Nederland (nay-dair-lahn)	the Netherlands
nei (nay)	no
neste (nest-eh)	next
nevø -en (nev-uh)	nephew
ni (nee)	nine
niese -en (nee-ay-seh)	niece
nitten (neet-ten)	nineteen
nitti (neet-tee)	ninety
noe, noen (noh-eh)(noh-en)	some, something
nord (noor)	North
Nord-Amerika (noor-ah-mair-ih-kuh)	North America
nordmenn (noor-men)	Norwegians
Nordpolen (noor-pohl-en)	the North Pole
Nordsjøen (noor-shuh-en)	the North Sea
Norge (nor-geh)	Norway
norsk (norshk)	Norwegian
november (noh-vem-bair)	November
null (nool)	zero
nummer (num-air)	number
numrene (num-ren-eh)	numbers
ny (nee)	new
nær (nair)	near
nødutgang -en (nuhd-oot-gahng)	emergency exit
nå (noh)	now
når (nor)	when, at what time

O

ofte (ohf-teh)	often
og (oh)	and
også (oh-soh)	also
oksekjøtt -et (ohk-seh-hyuht)	beef
oktober (ohk-toh-bair)	October
om (ohm)	in, about
onkel -en (ohnk-el)	uncle
onsdag (ohns-dahg)	Wednesday
opera -en (oh-pair-uh)	opera
operasjon -en (oh-pair-ah-shohn)	operation
opp (ohp)	up
opptatt (ohp-taht)	busy, occupied
optiker -en (ohp-tik-air)	optician
oransje (oh-rahn-sheh)	orange (color)
ord -et (oor)	word
ordbok -a (oor-bohk)	dictionary
organisasjon -en (or-gahn-ih-sah-shohn)	organization
orkester -et (or-kest-air)	orchestra
ost -en (ohst)	cheese
ovenpå (oh-ven-poh)	above, upstairs
over (oh-vair)	over, after
ovnstekt (ohvn-stekt)	roasted

P

pakke -n (pahk-eh)	package
pakke (pahk-eh)	to pack
papir -et (pah-peer)	paper
papirhandel -en (pah-peer-hahn-del)	stationery store
papirkurv -en (pah-peer-koorv)	wastebasket
paraply -en (pah-rah-plee)	umbrella
parfyme -n (par-few-meh)	perfume
park -en (park)	park

parkere (par-kair-eh)	to park
parkeringsplass -en (par-kair-ings-plahs)	parking lot
pass -et (pahs)	passport
passasjer -en (pah-sah-share)	passenger
passe (pahs-eh)	to fit
pen (pen)	nice
penger (peng-air)	money
penn-en (pen)	pen
pensjon -en (pahng-shohn)	guest house, pension
pepper -en (pep-air)	pepper
perfekt (pair-fekt)	perfect
perrong -en (pair-ohng)	platform
person -en (pair-shohn)	person
personlig (pair-shohn-lee)	personally, personal
pipe -en (pee-peh)	pipe
plass -en (plahs)	place, seat; plaza
polarsirkel -en (pohl-ar-seer-kel)	polar circle
Polen (pohl-en)	Poland
politi -et (poh-lih-tee)	police
politistasjon -en (poh-lih-tee-stah-shohn)	police station
polsk (pohlsk)	Polish
Portugal (por-too-gahl)	Portugal
portugisisk (por-too-gee-sisk)	Portuguese
post -en (post)	mail
postkasse -n (post-kah-seh)	mailbox
postkontor -et (post-kohn-tor)	post office
potet -en (poh-tate)	potato
praktisk (prahk-tisk)	practical
pris -en (prees)	price, cost
problem -et (proh-blame)	problem
prosent -en (proh-sent)	percent
protestantisk (proh-tes-tahn-tisk)	Protestant
purpur (puhr-puhr)	purple
pute -a (poo-teh)	pillow
pyjamas -en (pee-shah-mahs)	pyjamas
på (poh)	in, at, on, before
på gjensyn (poh)(yen-soon)	so long, see you later
pålegg -et (poh-leg)	sandwich fixings

R

radio -en (rah-dee-oh)	radio
regne (rine-eh)	to rain
regnfrakk -en (rine-frahk)	raincoat
regning -en (rine-ing)	bill
reise -n (race-eh)	journey, trip
reise (race-eh)	to travel
reisebyrå -et (race-eh-bew-roh)	travel agency
reisegods -et (race-eh-gohds)	baggage office
reisende -n (race-en-eh)	traveler
reisesjekk -en (race-eh-shek)	travelers check
reker (ray-kair)	shrimp
religion -en (reh-lih-gee-ohn)	religion
rene (ray-neh)	clean
renseri -et (rens-air-ee)	dry cleaners
resepsjon -en (ray-sep-shohn)	reception, lobby
reservasjon -en (res-air-vah-shohn)	reservation, booking
rest -en (rest)	rest
restaurant -en (res-tuh-rahng)	restaurant
rett -en (ret)	food, dish
rett frem (ret)(frem)	straight ahead
rik (reek)	rich
rikstelefon –en (reeks-tay-leh-fohn)	long-distance call
riktig (rik-tee)	correct, right
ringe (ring-eh)	to ring, call up, telephone
rom –met (rohm)	room
romantisk (roh-mahn-tisk)	romantic
romersk-katolsk (roh-mairshk-kah-tohlsk)	Roman Catholic
rosemaling (rohs-eh-mahl-ing)	rosemaling
ruin -en (roo-een)	ruin
rund (roon)	round
rundstykke -t (roon-stewk-eh)	hard roll (bread)
rushtid (roosh-tee)	rush-hour
russisk (roos-isk)	Russian
Russland (roos-lahn)	Russia
rute -n (roo-teh)	route, schedule
rutebil -en (roo-teh-beel)	long-distance bus
ruteplan -en (ro-teh-plahn)	timetable, schedule
ryggsekk -en (roog-sek)	rucksack
rød (ruh)	red
røkt (ruhkt)	smoked
rømme -n (ruhm-eh)	sour cream
rå (roh)	raw, rare
Rådhus -et (rohd-hoos)	City Hall
råtten (roh-ten)	rotten, moldy

S

salat -en (sah-laht)	salad
salt –et (sahlt)	salt
samtale -n (sahm-tahl-eh)	conversation
sandal -en (sahn-dahl)	sandal
sankt -en (sahngt)	saint
sardin -en (sar-deen)	sardine
saus -en (souse)	sauce
se (say)	to see, look at
seddel -en (sed-el)	bill (currency)
seilbåt -en (sail-boht)	sailboat
seiler -en (sail-air)	yachtsman
seks (sex)	six
seksten (sigh-ten)	sixteen
seksti (sex-tee)	sixty
sekund -et (sek-oond)	second (time)
selge (sel-geh)	to sell
sende (sen-eh)	to send
seng -a (seng)	bed
sentrum -et (sent-rum)	city center, downtown
september (sep-tem-bair)	September
serveringsdame -n (sair-vair-ings-dahm-eh)	waitress
service inkludert (sair-vees)(in-kloo-dairt)	service included
serviett -en (sair-vee-et)	napkin
shorts -en (shorts)	shorts
si (see)	to say
si ... en gang til (see)(en)(gahng)(til)	to say again/repeat
side -a (seed-eh)	page
sigar -en (see-gar)	cigar
sigarett -en (see-gah-ret)	cigarette
sitte (sit-eh)	to sit
sitteplass -en (sit-eh-plahs)	seat
sjokolade -n (shoh-koh-lahd-eh)	chocolate
sju (shoe)	seven
sjøsyk (shuh-seek)	seasick
skalldyr -et (skahl-dewr)	shellfish
skandinavisk (skahn-dih-nah-visk)	Scandinavian
skap -et (skahp)	cupboard
skarp (skarp)	sharp, strong
skatt -en (skaht)	tax
ski -en (shee)	ski
gå på ski (goh)(poh)(shee)	to go skiing
skinke -a (shink-eh)	ham
skip -et (sheep)	ship, boat
skje -en (shay)	spoon
skjorte -n (short-eh)	shirt
skjørte -et (shirt-eh)	skirt
sko (skoh)	shoe, shoes
skole -n (skohl-eh)	school

Norwegian	Pronunciation	English
skrive	(skreev-eh)	to write
skrivebord -et	(skreev-eh-boor)	desk
skulle	(skoo-leh)	should
skyve	(sheev-eh)	to push
slektning -en	(shlekt-ning)	relative (family)
slips -et	(shlips)	tie
smykker	(smook-air)	jewelry
smør -et	(smur)	butter
smørbrød -et	(smur-bruh)	open-faced sandwich
småpenger	(smoh-peng-air)	small change (money)
snakke	(snahk-eh)	to speak
snakker	(snahk-air)	speak/speaks
snø	(snuh)	to snow
sofa -en	(soh-fah)	sofa
sokk -en	(sohk)	sock
solbriller	(sohl-bril-air)	sunglasses
sommer -en	(sohm-air)	summer
sort	(sort)	black
sov godt	(sohv)(goht)	sleep well
sove	(sohv-eh)	to sleep
soverom -met	(sohv-eh-rohm)	bedroom
sovevogn -a	(sohv-eh-vohgn)	sleeping car
Spania	(spah-nee-ah)	Spain
spansk	(spahnsk)	Spanish
speil -et	(spail)	mirror
speilegg -et	(spail-egg)	fried egg
spesialrett -en	(spes-ee-ahl-ret)	speciality
spise	(spees-eh)	to eat
spisekart -et	(spees-eh-kart)	menu
spisestue -a	(spees-eh-stoo-eh)	dining room
spisevogn -a	(spees-eh-vohgn)	dining car
spor -et	(spor)	track (train)
sport -en	(sport)	sport
spørre	(spur-eh)	to ask
spørsmål -et	(spursh-mohl)	question
stasjon -en	(stah-shohn)	station
stat -en	(staht)	state
statue -n	(stah-too-eh)	statue
stavkirke -n	(stahv-hyeer-keh)	stave church
stekt	(stekt)	fried
stengt	(stengt)	closed
stille	(stil-eh)	still, quiet
stol -en	(stohl)	chair
stopp -en	(stohp)	stop
stor	(stor)	big
storm -en	(storm)	storm
strømper	(strump-air)	pantyhose, tights
stue -a	(stoo-eh)	living room
stykke -t	(stewk-eh)	coin, piece
størrelse -n	(stur-el-seh)	size
støvler	(stuv-lair)	boots
sulten	(suhl-ten)	hungry
suppe -n	(suhp-eh)	soup
sur	(soor)	sour
surmelk -en	(soor-melk)	sour milk, buttermilk
suvenir -en	(soo-veh-neer)	souvenir
svar -et	(svar)	answer
Sveits	(svites)	Switzerland
Sverige	(svair-ree-eh)	Sweden
svinekjøtt -et	(svee-neh-hyuht)	pork
syk	(seek)	sick
sykehus -et	(seek-eh-hoos)	hospital
sykkel -en	(seek-el)	bicycle
syltetøy -et	(sool-teh-tuh-oy)	jam
symfoni -en	(soom-fohn-ee)	symphony
sytten	(suh-ten)	seventeen
sytti	(soo-tee)	seventy
søndag	(suhn-dahg)	Sunday
sønn -en	(suhn)	son
sør	(sur)	South
Sør-Afrika	(sur-ah-frih-kuh)	South Africa
Sør-Amerika	(sur-ah-mair-ih-kuh)	South America
Sørpolen	(sur-pohl-en)	South Pole
søster -a	(suhs-tair)	sister
så	(soh)	then, so
såpe -a	(sohp-eh)	soap

T

ta	(tah)	to take
ta plass!	(tah)(plahns)	all aboard
takk	(tahk)	thank you
takk for maten	(tahk)(for)(mah-ten)	thanks for the meal
tallerken -en	(tahl-air-ken)	plate
tannbørste -n	(tahn-bursh-teh)	toothbrush
tannkrem -en	(tahn-krame)	toothpaste
tante -a	(tahnt-eh)	aunt
taxi -en	(tahx-ee)	taxi
T-bane -n	(tay-bahn-eh)	subway
T-banestasjon -en	(tay-bahn-eh-stah-shohn)	subway station
T-skjorte -n	(tay-short-eh)	T-shirt
te -en	(tay)	tea
teaterbillett -en	(tay-ah-tair-bil-let)	theater ticket
telefon -en	(tay-leh-fohn)	telephone
telefonist -en	(tay-leh-fohn-ist)	operator
telefonkatalog -en	(tay-leh-fohn-kah-tah-lohg)	telephone book
telefonkiosk -en	(tay-leh-fohn-hyohsk)	telephone booth
telefonkort -et	(tay-leh-fohn-kort)	telephone card
telefonnummer -et	(tay-leh-fohn-num-air)	telephone number
telefonsamtale -en	(tay-leh-fohn-sahm-tahl-eh)	telephone conversation, call
telegram -met	(tay-leh-grahm)	telegram
temperatur -en	(temp-air-ah-toor)	temperature
tennis -en	(ten-is)	tennis
tennissko	(ten-is-skoh)	tennis shoes
teppe -t	(tep-eh)	carpet
ti	(tee)	ten
tid -en	(tee)	time
tidsskrift -et	(tee-skrift)	magazine
til	(til)	to, more, for
time -n	(teem-eh)	hour
ting -en	(ting)	thing
tinn	(tin)	tin, pewter
tirsdag	(teersh-dahg)	Tuesday
tjue	(hyoo-eh)	twenty
to	(too)	two
toalett -et	(toh-ah-let)	toilet
toalettpapir -et	(toh-ah-let-pah-peer)	toilet paper
tobakk -en	(toh-bahk)	tobacco
tobakksforretning -en	(toh-bahks-for-ret-ning)	tobacco store
tog -et	(tohg)	train
toll -en	(tohl)	customs
tolv	(tohl)	twelve
topp -en	(tohp)	top, summit
torg -et	(torg)	market
torsdag	(torsh-dahg)	Thursday
trafikk -en	(trah-feek)	traffic
tre	(tray)	three
tredje	(tred-yeh)	third
trekke	(trek-eh)	to pull
trenge	(treng-eh)	to need
trette	(tret-eh)	tired
tretten	(tret-ten)	thirteen

tretti *(tret-tee)* . . . . thirty
trikk -en *(trik)* . . . . streetcar
trikkeholdeplass -en *(trik-eh-hold-eh-plahs)* . . . streetcar stop
troll -et *(trohl)* . . . . trolls
truse -n *(troos-eh)* . . . . underpants
tunnel -en *(tuh-nel)* . . . . tunnel
tur -en *(toor)* . . . . trip, tour, ride, turn
tur-retur *(toor-ray-toor)* . . . . round-trip
turist -en *(toor-ist)* . . . . tourist
turistbyrå -et *(toor-ist-bew-roh)* . . . . travel agency
turistkontor -et *(toor-ist-kohn-tor)* . . . . . . tourist office
tusen *(too-sen)* . . . . thousand
tykk *(tewk)* . . . . thick
typiske *(too-pisk-eh)* . . . . typical
Tyrkia *(tewr-kee-ah)* . . . . Turkey
tysk *(tewsk)* . . . . German
Tyskland *(tewsk-lahn)* . . . . Germany
tøfler *(tuf-lair)* . . . . slippers
tørst *(tursht)* . . . . thirsty

U

uke -n *(ook-eh)* . . . . week
ukedager *(ook-eh-dahg-air)* . . . . weekdays
ull -a *(uhl)* . . . . wool
under *(oon-air)* . . . . under
underbukse -a *(oon-air-buhx-eh)* . . . . underpants
underkjole -n *(oon-air-hyoh-leh)* . . . . slip
underklær *(oon-air-klair)* . . . . underclothes
underskjorte -n *(oon-air-short-eh)* . . . . undershirt
ung *(uhng)* . . . . young
Ungarn *(uhn-garn)* . . . . Hungary
ungarsk *(uhn-garshk)* . . . . Hungarian
universitet -et *(oo-nih-vairsh-ih-tate)* . . . . university
unnskyld *(un-shool)* . . . . excuse me
upersonlig *(oo-pair-shohn-lee)* . . . . impersonal
upopulær *(oo-poh-poo-lair)* . . . . unpopular
upraktisk *(oo-prak-tisk)* . . . . impractical
U. S. A. *(oo-es-ah)* . . . . United States
ut av *(oot)(ahv)* . . . . out of, from
ute *(oot-eh)* . . . . outside
uten *(oot-en)* . . . . without
utenlands *(oot-en-lahns)* . . . . foreign
utgang -en *(oot-gahng)* . . . . exit
uvel *(oo-vel)* . . . . unwell, ill

V

vaffel -en *(vah-fel)* . . . . waffle
valnøtt -en *(vahl-nuht)* . . . . walnut
vann -et *(vahn)* . . . . water
var *(var)* . . . . was
varm *(varm)* . . . . warm
vask -en *(vahsk)* . . . . washbasin, sink
vaske *(vahsk-eh)* . . . . to wash
vaskeri -et *(vahsk-air-ee)* . . . . laundry
ved *(veh)* . . . . at
ved siden av *(vay)(seed-en)(ahv)* . . . . next to
vegetariansk *(veg-et-ar-ee-ahnsk)* . . . . vegetarian
vei -en *(vay)* . . . . road, way
vekkerklokke -a *(vek-kair-klohk-eh)* . . . . alarm clock
vekslekontor -et *(vek-shleh-kohn-tor)* . . . money-exchange office
vel bekomme *(vel)(beh-kohm-eh)* . . . . you're welcome
velkommen *(vel-kohm-en)* . . . . welcome
venstre *(ven-streh)* . . . . left
vente på *(vent-eh)(poh)* . . . . to wait for
venterom -met *(vent-eh-rohm)* . . . . waiting room
verb -et *(vairb)* . . . . verb
vest *(vest)* . . . . west
Vesten *(vest-en)* . . . . the West, Western world
Vestindia *(vest-in-dee-ah)* . . . . West Indies
vet *(vet)* . . . . know/knows
vi *(vee)* . . . . we
videre *(vee-dair-eh)* . . . . further
viktig *(vik-tee)* . . . . important
vil ha *(vil)(hah)* . . . . would like
ville *(vil-eh)* . . . . to want to
viltretter *(vilt-ret-air)* . . . . game
vin -en *(veen)* . . . . wine
vindu -et *(vin-doo)* . . . . window
vinglass -et *(veen-glahs)* . . . . wine glass
vinkart -et *(veen-kart)* . . . . wine list
vinkjeller -en *(veen-hyel-air)* . . . . wine cellar
vinmonopol -et *(veen-moh-noh-pohl)* . . . . . state liquor store
vinter -en *(vint-air)* . . . . winter
vintersport -en *(vint-air-sport)* . . . . winter sport
vise *(vees-eh)* . . . . to show
vite *(veet-eh)* . . . . to know (a fact)
vogn -a *(vohgn)* . . . . compartment, wagon
voks -et *(vox)* . . . . wax (for skis)
vær -et *(vair)* . . . . weather
vær så snill *(vair)(shoh)(snil)* . . . . please, be so kind
vær så god *(vair)(shoh)(go)* . . . . please, here you are/you're welcome
vår -en *(vor)* . . . . spring
våt *(voht)* . . . . wet

W

W. C. -et *(vay-say)* . . . . toilet (water closet)
weekend -en *(veek-end)* . . . . weekend
weekendtur -en *(veek-end-toor)* . . . . weekend trip
whisky -en *(visk-ee)* . . . . whisky

Y

yacht -en *(yoht)* . . . . yacht

Z

zoo -en *(soh)* . . . . zoo
zoologi -en *(soh-oh-loh-gee)* . . . . zoology
zoologisk hage -n *(soh-oh-loh-gisk)(hah-geh)* . . . . zoo
zoomlinse -ei *(soom-lin-seh)* . . . . zoom lens

Æ

ærdun *(air-doon)* . . . . eiderdown

Ø

økonomi -en *(uh-koh-noh-mee)* . . . . economy
øl -et *(uhl)* . . . . beer
øre -n *(ur-eh)* . . . . ore (Norwegian coin)
øre -t *(ur-eh)* . . . . ear
øst *(ust)* . . . . East
Østerrike *(ust-air-reek-eh)* . . . . Austria
Østersjøen *(ust-air-shuh-en)* . . . . the Baltic Sea
øvre *(uhv-reh)* . . . . upper
øyeblikk -et *(uh-oy-eh-blik)* . . . . moment

Å

å *(oh)* . . . . to (with infinitive)
åpen, åpent, åpne *(oh-pen)(oh-pent)(ohp-neh)* . . . . open
år -et *(or)* . . . . year
årbok -ei *(or-bohk)* . . . . yearbook
årlig *(or-lee)* . . . . yearly, annual
årsdag -en *(orsh-dahg)* . . . . anniversary
åtte *(oh-teh)* . . . . eight
åtti *(oh-tee)* . . . . eighty

25 Beverage and Menu Guides

This beverage guide is intended to explain the variety of beverages available to you while **i Norge.** It is by no means complete. Some of the experimenting has been left up to you, but this should get you started.

VARME DRIKKER (hot drinks)

en kopp kaffe	a cup of coffee
med fløte	with cream
med sukker	with sugar
med en sukkerbit	with a sugar cube
en espresso	espresso coffee
en kaffedoktor	coffee and brandy
en kopp te	a cup of tea
med melk	with milk
med sitron	with lemon
kamillete	camomile tea
peppermyntete	peppermint tea
nypete	rosehip tea
kakao/varm sjokolade	hot chocolate
varm melk	warm milk
gløgg	hot, mulled wine with brandy, raisins, almonds and sugar
rødvinstoddy	hot, mulled red wine with sugar

ALKOHOLFRIE DRIKKER (non-alcoholic drinks)

melk	milk
surmelk	buttermilk
kefir	a yogurt-like drink
vann	water
mineralvann	mineral water
sodavann	soda water
brus	soda pop/soda
sitronbrus	lemon pop/soda
bringebærbrus	raspberry pop
saft	juice
eplesaft	apple juice
ananassaft	pineapple juice
tomatsaft	tomato juice
grapefruktsaft	grapefruit juice
solbærsaft	black currant juice
vørterøl	non-alcoholic beer

VIN (wine)
May be available by the **glass** (glass), **karaffel** (carafe), **halv flaske** (half bottle) or **flaske** (bottle).

rødvin	red wine
hvitvin	white wine
rosévin	rosé wine
musserende/sprudlende vin	sparkling wine
champagne	champagne
søt	sweet
tørr	dry
meget tørr	extra dry

ØL (beer)
Alcoholic content varies and is indicated on the bottle cap with the number 1-4, from the weakest to the strongest. Øl is ordered by the bottle or in a large half-liter glass.

Brigg/zero	almost non-alcoholic
lettøl	low-alcohol beer
pils	light lager
export	stronger light lager
bayer	dark beer
bokk	strong, dark beer
juleøl	"Christmas beer," brewed for release just before Christmas.

AKEVITT (aquavit)
Aquavit can be called the national drink **i Norge.** Distilled from barley or potatoes and generally flavored with caraway, aquavit is very strong. It is usually enjoyed ice-cold and straight, with a beer chaser. Be sure to drink aquavit only as an accompaniment to **koldtbord** or a main dish, but not as an aperitif. (**Det er meget sterkt!**) The most famous brand is **Linjeakevitt,** which is stored in casks in the holds of ships that travel around the world. The flavor is said to be enhanced by the motion of the ship.

Spisekartet
menu

Frukt (fruit)

ananas	pineapple
appelsin	orange
aprikos	apricot
banan	banana
druer	grapes
eple	apple
fersken	peach
grapefrukt	grapefruit
korinter	currants
nype	rosehip
plomme	plum
pære	pear
rabarbra	rhubarb
rosiner	raisins
sitron	lemon
svisker	prunes

Bær (berries)

blåbær	blueberry
bjørnebær	blackberry
bringebær	raspberry
jordbær	strawberry
kirsebær	cherry
morell	bing cherry
rips	red currant
solbær	black currant

Ost (cheese)

ekte geitost	real goat cheese
gammelost	"old" cheese; aged, yellow-brown, strong-smelling
gulost	yellow cheese
hvitost	white cheese
mysost	mild brown cheese
nøkkelost	cheese spiced with cloves
pultost	soft, sharp cheese

Tilberedning (preparation)

dampet	steamed
kokt	boiled
stekt	fried, braised
ovnstekt	roasted
bakt	baked
grillet	grilled
saltet/lagret/speket	cured
forlorent	poached
krydret	spiced
ristet	toasted
fersk	fresh
rå	raw
medium	medium
godt stekt	well-done
grateng	au gratin
panert	breaded

Annet (others)

marmelade	marmalade, preserves
syltetøy	jelly, jam
honning	honey
surmelk	buttermilk
fløte	cream
rømme	sour cream
krem	whipping cream
pisket krem	whipped cream
is	ice cream
fromasj	custard
riskrem	rice pudding
risengrynsgrøt	rice pudding
rømmegrøt	rich cream pudding
sukker	sugar
eddik	vinegar

Fisk og skalldyr (fish and shellfish)

sei	pollack
sild	herring
sjøørret	sea trout
torsk	cod
tunfisk	tuna
ørret	trout
østers	oyster

Egg (eggs)

hardkokte egg	hard-boiled eggs
bløtkokte egg	soft-boiled eggs
eggerøre	scrambled eggs
forlorent egg	poached eggs
speilegg	fried eggs

Grønnsaker (vegetables)

agurk	cucumber
asparges	asparagus
blomkål	cauliflower
bønner	beans
erter	peas
gresskar	squash, pumpkin
gulrøtter	carrots
hvitløk	garlic
kål	cabbage
kålrabi	kohlrabi, rutabaga
linser	lentils
løk	onion
nepe	turnip
nesle	nettle
paprika	red pepper
persille	parsley
potet	potato
purre	leek
rosenkål	brussels sprouts
rødkål	red cabbage
salat	lettuce
selleri	celery
sellerirot	celery root
sopp	mushrooms
spinat	spinach

Takk for maten!
thanks for the meal

Annet (other)

olje	oil
sennep	mustard
majones	mayonnaise
mandler	almonds
valnøtter	walnuts
hasselnøtter	hazelnuts
smørbrød	open-faced sandwich
pålegg	sandwich fixings

Brød og Bakst (bread and baked goods)

hvetebrød	wheat bread
grovbrød	whole-grain bread
loff	white bread
rundstykker	rolls
boller	sweet buns
lefse	soft, flat bread
lompe	soft, flat potato bread
kavring	rusk
kake	cake
fyrstekake	Prince's cake
vørterkake	spice cake
fløtekake/bløtkake	layer cake with whipped cream
kringle	pretzel-shaped almond pastry
wienerbrød	Danish pastry
vafler	waffles
julekake	Christmas bread
krumkake	crisp, cone-shaped cookie
småkaker	cookies
kjeks	cookies, biscuits (cakes)
smultringer	doughnuts
pai	pie
terte	torte

Supper (soups)

aspargessuppe	asparagus soup
betasuppe	meat, marrow and vegetable
blomkålsuppe	cauliflower soup
buljong	consommé
dagens suppe	soup of the day
grønnsaksuppe	vegetable soup
gul ertesuppe	yellow pea soup
hønsesuppe	chicken soup
løksuppe	onion soup
oksehalesuppe	oxtail soup
potetsuppe	potato soup

Kjøtt (meat)

hjerte	heart
kjøttboller	meatballs
lapskaus	hash
lever	liver
leverpostei	liver pate
nyrer	kidneys
pølser	sausages
ribbe	ribs
spekekjøtt	cured, dried meat
sylte	spiced, pressed pork roll
tunge	tongue

Svinekjøtt (pork)

skinke	ham
spekeskinke	cured ham
svinekam	saddle of pork
svinekotelett	pork chop
svinesteik	pork roast
ribbe	roasted spareribs

Lammekjøtt og Fårekjøtt (lamb and mutton)

lammesteik	lamb roast
lammekotelett	lamb chop
fårekotelett	mutton fricassee
fårelår	leg of mutton

Oksekjøtt (beef)

bankebiff	beef slices in gravy
steik	beef roast
okserull	rolled beef roast
oksebryst	brisket of beef
oksekotelett	beef cutlet
biff	steak

Kalvekjøtt (veal)

kalvesteik	roast veal
kalvedans	jellied veal
kalvefilet	filet of veal

Viltretter (game)

dyresteik	venison
elg	moose
fasan	pheasant
hare	hare
kanin	rabbit
rapphøne	partridge
reinsdyrsteik	reindeer roast
vaktel	quail

Høns (poultry)

kylling	chicken
kyllingbryst	chicken breast
hønsefrikasse	chicken fricassee
and	duck
gås	goose
kalkun	turkey

Fisk og skalldyr (fish and shellfish)

ansjos	anchovies
ål	eel
blåskjell	mussel
fiskegrateng	fish au gratin
fiskekaker	fish cakes
fiskepudding	fish mousse
flyndre	flounder
hummer	lobster
karpe	carp
krabbe	crab
kveite	halibut
laks	salmon
lutefisk	cod treated with lye
lysing	hake
makrell	mackerel
reker	shrimp
rogn	roe
sardin	sardine

(yay)
jeg

(vee)
vi

(hahn)
han

(doo)
du

(huhn)
hun

(dee)
de

(deh)
det

(den)
den

(oh) *(snahk-eh)*
å snakke
(yay) *(snahk-air)*
jeg snakker

(oh) *(kohm-eh)*
å komme
(yay) *(kohm-air)*
jeg kommer

(oh) *(lair-eh)*
å lære
(yay) *(lair-air)*
jeg lærer

(oh) *(beh-stil-eh)*
å bestille
(yay) *(beh-stil-air)*
jeg bestiller

we	I
you	he
they	she
it	it
to come	to speak
I come	I speak
to order / reserve	to learn
I order / reserve	I learn

(oh) *(hyuhp-eh)* **å kjøpe** *(yay)* *(hyuhp-air)* **jeg kjøper**	*(oh)* *(het-eh)* **å hete** *(yay)* *(het-air)* **jeg heter**
(oh) *(goh)* **å gå** *(yay)* *(gor)* **jeg går**	*(oh)* *(hah)* **å ha** *(yay)* *(har)* **jeg har**
(oh) *(leek-eh)* **å like** *(yay)* *(leek-air)* **jeg liker**	*(oh)* *(treng-eh)* **å trenge** *(yay)* *(treng-air)* **jeg trenger**
(oh) *(boh)* **å bo** *(yay)* *(bor)* **jeg bor**	*(oh)* *(blee)* **å bli** *(yay)* *(bleer)* **jeg blir**
(oh) *(spees-eh)* **å spise** *(yay)* *(spees-air)* **jeg spiser**	*(oh)* *(drik-eh)* **å drikke** *(yay)* *(drik-air)* **jeg drikker**
(oh) *(see)* **å si** *(yay)* *(see-air)* **jeg sier**	*(oh)* *(for-shtoh)* **å forstå** *(yay)* *(for-shtor)* **jeg forstår**

to be called	to buy
I am called	I buy
to have	to go
I have	I go
to need	to like
I need	I like
to remain / stay	to live / reside
I remain / stay	I live / reside
to drink	to eat
I drink	I eat
to understand	to say
I understand	I say

(oh) *(sel-geh)* **å selge** *(yay)* *(sel-gair)* **jeg selger**	*(oh)* *(see)* *(en)* *(gahng)* *(til)* **å si ... en gang til** *(yay)* *(see-air)* *(gahng)* **jeg sier ... en gang til**
(oh) *(say)* **å se** *(yay)* *(sair)* **jeg ser**	*(oh)* *(sen-eh)* **å sende** *(yay)* *(sen-air)* **jeg sender**
(oh) *(sohv-eh)* **å sove** *(yay)* *(sohv-air)* **jeg sover**	*(oh)* *(fin-eh)* **å finne** *(yay)* *(fin-air)* **jeg finner**
(oh) *(yuhr-eh)* **å gjøre** *(yay)* *(yuhr)* **jeg gjør**	*(oh)* *(skreev-eh)* **å skrive** *(yay)* *(skreev-air)* **jeg skriver**
(oh) *(vees-eh)* **å vise** *(yay)* *(vees-air)* **jeg viser**	*(oh)* *(beh-tahl-eh)* **å betale** *(yay)* *(beh-tahl-air)* **jeg betaler**
(oh) *(vil-eh)* **å ville** *(yay)* *(vil)* **jeg vil**	*(oh)* *(kuhn-eh)* **å kunne** *(yay)* *(kahn)* **jeg kan**

to repeat	to sell
I repeat	I sell
to send	to see
I send	I see
to find	to sleep
I find	I sleep
to write	to make / do
I write	I make / do
to pay	to show
I pay	I show
to be able to / can	to want to
I am able to / can	I want to

(oh) *(veet-eh)* **å vite** *(yay)* *(vet)* **jeg vet**	*(oh)* *(moht-eh)* **å måtte** *(yay)* *(moh)* **jeg må**
(oh) *(flee)* **å fly** *(yay)* *(fleer)* **jeg flyr**	*(oh)* *(hyuhr-eh)* **å kjøre** *(yay)* *(hyuhr-air)* **jeg kjører**
(oh) *(kohm-eh)* *(til)* **å komme til** *(yay)* *(kohm-air)* *(til)* **jeg kommer til**	*(oh)* *(lay-seh)* **å lese** *(yay)* *(lay-sair)* **jeg leser**
(oh) *(goh)* *(frah)* **å gå fra** *(yay)* *(gor)* *(frah)* **jeg går fra**	*(oh)* *(pahk-eh)* **å pakke** *(yay)* *(pahk-air)* **jeg pakker**
(oh) *(vent-eh)* *(poh)* **å vente på** *(yay)* *(vent-air)* *(poh)* **jeg venter på**	*(oh)* *(boot-eh)* *(tohg)* **å bytte tog** *(yay)* *(boot-air)* *(tohg)* **jeg bytter tog**
(oh) *(race-eh)* **å reise** *(yay)* *(race-air)* **jeg reiser**	*(yee)* *(my)* **gi meg...**

to have to / must	to know (a fact)
I have to / must	I know
to drive	to fly
I drive	I fly
to read	to arrive
I read	I arrive
to pack	to depart / leave from
I pack	I depart / leave from
to change trains	to wait for
I change trains	I wait for
give me . . .	to travel
	I travel

(vair) *(shoh)* *(snil)* **vær så snill**	*(vair)* *(shoh)* *(go)* **vær så god**
(ee) *(gor)* **i går**	*(ee)* *(dahg)* **i dag**
(ee) *(mor-en)* **i morgen**	*(tahk)* **takk**
(un-shool) **unnskyld**	*(vor-dahn)* *(har)* **Hvordan har** *(doo)* *(deh)* **du det?**
(gahm-el) *(nee)* **gammel - ny**	*(vor)* *(mee-eh)* **Hvor mye** *(kohst-air)* *(deh)* **koster det?**
(stor) *(lee-ten)* **stor - liten**	*(oh-pent)* *(luhk-et)* **åpent - lukket**

you're welcome / please, here you are / please, go ahead	please, be so kind
today	yesterday
thank you	tomorrow
How are you? / How's it going?	excuse me
How much does this cost?	old - new
open - closed	big - small

(frisk) (seek)	(go) (dor-lee)
frisk - syk	**god - dårlig**

(varm) (kahl)	(koort) (lahng)
varm - kald	**kort - lang**

(huh-oy) (lahv)	(oh-ven-poh) (ned-eh)
høy - lav	**ovenpå - nede**

(ven-streh) (huh-oy-reh)	(lahng-sohm) (foort)
venstre - høyre	**langsom - fort**

(gahm-el) (uhng)	(dewr) (bil-ee)
gammel - ung	**dyr - billig**

(fah-tee) (reek)	(mahng-eh) (lee-teh)
fattig - rik	**mange - lite**

good - bad	healthy - sick
short - long	hot - cold
upstairs - downstairs	high - low
slow - fast	left - right
expensive - inexpensive	old - young
a lot - a little	poor - rich

Now that you've finished…

You've done it!

You've completed all the Steps, stuck your labels, flashed your cards, cut out your beverage and menu guides and practiced your new language. Do you realize how far you've come and how much you've learned? You've accomplished what it could take years to achieve in a traditional language class.

You can now confidently

- ask questions,
- understand directions,
- make reservations,
- order food and
- shop for anything.

And you can do it all in a foreign language! Go anywhere with confidence — from a large cosmopolitan restaurant to a small, out-of-the-way village where no one speaks English. Your experiences will be much more enjoyable and worry-free now that you speak the language.

As you've seen, learning a foreign language can be fun. Why limit yourself to just one? Now you're ready to learn another language with the *10 minutes a day*® Series!

Kristine Kershul

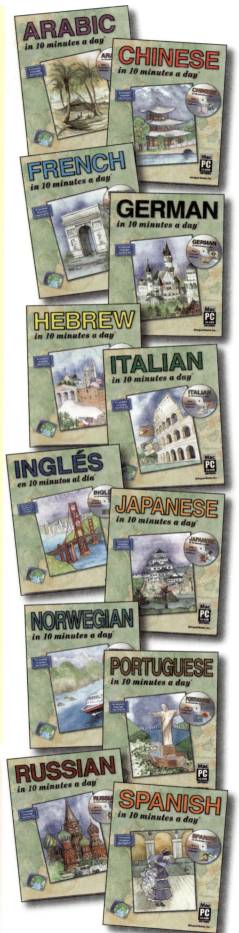

To place an order –

- Visit us at **www.bbks.com**, day or night.
- Call us at (800) 488-5068 or (206) 284-4211 between 8:00 a.m. and 5:00 p.m. Pacific Time, Monday - Friday.
- If you have questions about ordering, please call us. You may also fax us at (206) 284-3660 or email us at customer.service@bbks.com.

Also available at www.bbks.com!

Language Map® Series

These handy *Language Maps®* provide hundreds of words and phrases to cover the basics for any trip.

- Don't leave home without one! It's an absolute must-have for anyone traveling abroad.

- Snap-open-and-fold design allows for quick reference.

- Take it everywhere! Laminated to resist damage even under the toughest travel conditions.

- See why it's the favorite of world travelers everywhere! Watch the video at www.bbks.com/languagemap.aspx.

10 minutes a day® AUDIO CD Series

The *10 minutes a day® AUDIO CD Series* is based on the ever-popular *10 minutes a day® Series*. Millions of people have used this program with great success!

- Demand the best! Excellent for the classroom, homeschoolers, business professionals and travelers.

- An entertaining program with eight hours of personal instruction on six CDs.

- Practice along with native speakers.

- Use the CDs with the companion book and maximize your progress!

 Bilingual Books, Inc.

 @BilingualBooks1

 Bilingual Books, Inc.

Visit us at www.bbks.com for more information.